WITTGENSTEI
INVE.

M000304574

In this new introduction to a classic philosophical text, David Stern examines Wittgenstein's *Philosophical Investigations.* He gives particular attention to both the arguments of the *Investigations* and the way in which the work is written, and especially to the role of dialogue in the book. While he concentrates on helping the reader to arrive at his or her own interpretation of the primary text, he also provides guidance to the unusually wide range of existing interpretations, and to the reasons why the *Investigations* have inspired such a diversity of readings. Following closely the text of the *Investigations* and meant to be read alongside it, this survey is accessible to readers with no previous background in philosophy. It is well suited to university-level courses on Wittgenstein, but can also be read with profit by students in other disciplines.

DAVID G. STERN is Professor of Philosophy at the University of Iowa. He is the author of *Wittgenstein on Mind and Language* (1995), editor of *The Cambridge Companion to Wittgenstein* (1996) and co-editor, with Béla Szabados, of *Wittgenstein Reads Weininger: A Reassessment* (2004).

CAMBRIDGE INTRODUCTIONS TO KEY
PHILOSOPHICAL TEXTS

This new series offers introductory textbooks on what are considered to
be the most important texts of Western philosophy. Each book guides the
reader through the main themes and arguments of the work in question,
while also paying attention to its historical context and its philosophical
legacy. No philosophical background knowledge is assumed, and the books
will be well suited to introductory university-level courses.

Titles published in the series:

DESCARTES'S *MEDITATIONS* by Catherine Wilson

WITTGENSTEIN'S *PHILOSOPHICAL INVESTIGATIONS* by
David G. Stern

WITTGENSTEIN'S
PHILOSOPHICAL
INVESTIGATIONS

An Introduction

DAVID G. STERN

University of Iowa

CAMBRIDGE UNIVERSITY PRESS
Cambridge, New York, Melbourne, Madrid, Cape Town, Singapore,
São Paulo, Delhi, Dubai, Tokyo

Cambridge University Press
The Edinburgh Building, Cambridge CB2 8RU, UK

Published in the United States of America by Cambridge University Press, New York

www.cambridge.org
Information on this title: www.cambridge.org/9780521814423

First published 2004
Reprinted 2006

A catalogue record for this publication is available from the British Library

Library of Congress Cataloguing in Publication data
Stern, David G.
Wittgenstein's Philosophical investigations : an introduction / David G. Stern.
p.   cm. – (Cambridge introductions to key philosophical texts)
Includes bibliographical references and index.
ISBN 0 521 81442 1 (hardback); 0 521 89132 9 (paperback)
1. Wittgenstein, Ludwig, 1889–1951. Philosophische Untersuchungen.   2. Philosophy.
3. Language and languages – Philosophy.   4. Semantics (Philosophy)   I. Title.   II. Series.
B3376.W563P532   2004
192–dc22   2004045823

ISBN 978-0-521-81442-3 Hardback
ISBN 978-0-521-89132-5 Paperback

Transferred to digital printing 2010

For Cheryl

Contents

Acknowledgements

Parts of this book are based on work written while I was an Alexander von Humboldt Fellow at the University of Bielefeld, Germany during 1998–9, but most of it was written while I was a Faculty Scholar at the University of Iowa during 1999–2002. I would like to thank the Alexander von Humboldt Foundation and the University of Iowa Faculty Scholar Program for providing the time away from other responsibilities which enabled me to write this book, and the Departments of Philosophy at the University of Iowa and the University of Bielefeld for their generous support. Eike von Savigny, Joachim Schulte, and Hans-Johann Glock continually provoked me to think afresh about Wittgenstein while I was in Bielefeld; students in my Wittgenstein classes at the University of Iowa in 1999, 2001, and 2003 provided the first audience for many of the ideas presented in this book. I am particularly grateful to Marianne Constable, James Duerlinger, Hilary Gaskin, Cheryl Herr, Joachim Schulte, Hans Sluga, George Wrisley, and an anonymous reader for Cambridge University Press for their very helpful comments on preliminary drafts of the book. Thomas Williams was an invaluable guide to the intricacies of Augustine's Latin. I also want to thank my copy-editor, Angela Blackburn, and my proof-readers, George Wrisley and Amber Griffioen, for their very careful and thorough work on the text. While I am indebted to all of the above in one way or another, none is responsible for the views presented in this book. That responsibility is mine alone.

What follows is based, in part, on the following publications. The permission of the editors to make use of this material is hereby gratefully acknowledged.

'The Central Arguments of the *Philosophical Investigations*: An Elementary Exposition'. Forthcoming in the *Journal of Foreign Philosophy* 17 (1) (2004). Forthcoming (in French) in the proceedings of the international symposium on 'Wittgenstein Aujourd'hui', Nice, France. An edited version of this paper was presented at the seminar on 'Reading Wittgenstein's *Philosophical Investigations* Fifty Years Later', Bertinoro, Italy, October 2003. Source for 1.1–1.3.

'The Methods of the *Tractatus*: Beyond Positivism and Metaphysics?' In *Logical Empiricism: Historical and Contemporary Perspectives*, a volume in the Pittsburgh-Konstanz Studies in the Philosophy and History of Science series, edited by Paolo Parrini, Wes Salmon, and Merrilee Salmon, 125–56. Pittsburgh, Pittsburgh University Press, 2003. Source for the part of chapter 2 on the interpretation of the *Tractatus*.

'How to Read the *Philosophical Investigations*.' Forthcoming (in French) in a special issue of *Philosophie*, accompanying translations of the first reviews of the *Philosophical Investigations*, 2004. Source for 2.1, 4.3, and 5.2.

'Nestroy, Augustine, and the Opening of the *Philosophical Investigations*.' In *Wittgenstein and the Future of Philosophy: A Reassessment after 50 Years*, pp. 429–49. Proceedings of the 24th International Wittgenstein Symposium, edited by Rudolf Haller and Klaus Puhl. Vienna: Hölder-Pichler-Tempsky, 2002. Source for 3.1, 3.2, and 4.1.

'Sociology of Science, Rule Following and Forms of Life.' In *History of Philosophy of Science: New Trends and Perspectives*, pp. 347–67, edited by Michael Heidelberger and Friedrich Stadler. Dordrecht: Kluwer, 2002. A source for the discussion of Winch and Kripke in chapter 6.

'The Practical Turn.' In *The Blackwell Guidebook to the Philosophy of the Social Sciences*, pp. 185–206, edited by Stephen P. Turner and Paul Roth. Oxford: Blackwell, 2003. A source for the discussion of Winch and Kripke in chapter 6.

Note on the text

During his lifetime, Wittgenstein published only one philosophical
book, *Tractatus Logico-Philosophicus*, written while he was a soldier in
the First World War and published shortly afterwards. After publishing a short conference contribution in 1929, which he had repudiated
by the time he was due to read it, none of his subsequent work satisfied
him enough that he was willing to give it to the printer. In his will, he
left his unpublished papers, usually referred to as his *Nachlass*, consisting of approximately twelve thousand pages of manuscript and
eight thousand pages of typescript, to G. E. M. Anscombe, Rush
Rhees, and G. H. von Wright. Shortly after Wittgenstein's death,
Anscombe and Rhees edited, and Anscombe translated, *Philosophical
Investigations*, the book Wittgenstein had worked on from 1929 to
1949.

All references to the *Philosophical Investigations* are in parentheses
in the body of the text. Material from the numbered sections in Part I
is referred to by section number. For more fine-grained references, I
follow these conventions: §1a refers to the first paragraph of section 1,
§1b3 to the third sentence of the second paragraph. A reference to the
remainder of the text provides two page numbers: the first is the
one for all English and bilingual texts published prior to 2001;
the second is to the revised third edition, published in 2001. For
instance, 'PI II.xi, 194/166' is a reference to a passage within section xi
of Part II of the *Philosophical Investigations*, to be found on page
166 of the edition published in 2001, and on page 194 of any earlier

Parts of this note are based on my paper 'The Availability of Wittgenstein's Philosophy' (Stern
1996a), which provides a more detailed discussion of the relationship between Wittgenstein's
published and unpublished writings.

edition. The author/date reference system is used for all other published sources. References to Wittgenstein's *Nachlass* typescripts (TS)
and manuscripts (MS) use the numbering system in von Wright's
catalogue of the Wittgenstein papers, except for TS 213, a lengthy
rearrangement and reworking of material dating from the first half
of the 1930s, where I use the name by which it is commonly known,
the Big Typescript.[1] The *Nachlass* is available in a CD-ROM edition,
produced by the Wittgenstein Archives at the University of Bergen
(Wittgenstein 2000), which permits the accompanying software to
display the text in a number of formats. For instance, when studying
a heavily revised typescript, one can move between a colour photo-
graph of each page, a 'normalized' text which shows the text as finally
revised, and a 'diplomatic' text which shows all revisions, deletions,
and variant wordings. As this electronic edition is organized on the
basis of the von Wright catalogue, it can be used to look up any
reference to the source typescripts and manuscripts.

   Translations from the *Philosophical Investigations* are based on
Anscombe's revised translation, in the 2001 edition of the text; where
I have modified them, this is indicated by an asterisk after the parenthetical reference. For most English-speaking readers, Anscombe's
translation has a status comparable to the King James Bible's in its
heyday. However, it is, in certain respects, a highly unreliable guide to
Wittgenstein's German. First, the translation of a number of important terms obscures Wittgenstein's choice of words. For instance,
'define' is always used to translate *definieren*, to define, and sometimes
for *erklären*, to explain. Thus §43a, often glossed as Wittgenstein's
definition of meaning as use, does not say anything about *defining*
meaning as use. Roughly speaking, it says that in many cases we can
explain the meaning of a word by looking at how it is used. Second,
there are many places where Anscombe does not follow Wittgenstein's
grammar as closely as possible. Finally, much of Wittgenstein's style,
his care in his choice of phrasing, and his conversational informal-
ity and intimacy is lost in Anscombe's English. (See 5.1 on use and
explanation; Stern 1996b on the translation.)

---

[1] Von Wright's catalogue was first published in the *Philosophical Review* in 1969; an updated
version can be found in Wittgenstein 1993, 480–510. The Big Typescript will be published,
with an English translation, in November 2004 (Wittgenstein 2004).

In reading Wittgenstein, it is essential to keep in mind that his characteristic unit of writing was not the essay or the book, but the 'remark' (*Bemerkung*). A remark is a unit of text that can be as short as a single sentence or as long as a sequence of paragraphs spanning several pages. The beginning and end of a remark in his own writing – and in most of the published texts – is usually indicated by an extra blank line between paragraphs. The numbering of the remarks in Part I of *Philosophical Investigations* is Wittgenstein's; however, in most of the other published texts, including Part II, the numbering is the editors'. Throughout his life, his writing took the form of a large number of these relatively small units which he repeatedly revised and rearranged. In the preface to the *Philosophical Investigations*, Wittgenstein describes his writing as composed of 'remarks, short paragraphs, of which there is sometimes a fairly long chain about the same subject, while I sometimes make a sudden change, jumping from one topic to another' (PI, vii/ix). During the 1930s Wittgenstein experimented with a number of ways of organizing the material into a single coherent piece of writing, in which 'the thoughts should proceed from one subject to another in a natural order and without breaks' (PI, vii/ix), none of which entirely satisfied him. Eventually, he realized that he would never succeed, that 'the best I could write would never be more than philosophical remarks' (PI, vii/ix).

The way of writing and thinking that Wittgenstein describes in his Preface led him to continually rewrite and rearrange his work, with the result that it can be extremely difficult to separate one piece of writing from another. Much of the groundwork for tracing the relations between Wittgenstein's drafts and revisions was carried out by von Wright and two of his colleagues at the University of Helsinki, Heikki Nyman and André Maury. After he published the catalogue of the Wittgenstein papers in 1969, von Wright continued his research into the process of revision that led to the production of the *Tractatus* and *Philosophical Investigations*. The results of this research are summarized in his highly informative studies of the origins of those books, reprinted in his *Wittgenstein* (von Wright 1982). The meticulously edited 'Helsinki edition' of the principal sources of the *Philosophical Investigations* reconstructed several successive stages in the construction of the *Investigations*. It showed not just the result of Wittgenstein's revisions to the typescript or manuscript, but also where revisions were inserted, variant readings, deletions, and the like, and every significant difference between their text and the 'final' text, thus providing an invaluable overview of some of the principal stages in the composition of the *Philosophical Investigations*. The Helsinki edition formed the basis for Joachim Schulte's 'critical-genetic edition' of the *Philosophical Investigations* (Wittgenstein 2001), which identifies five distinct stages or 'versions' of the text of Part I. For our purposes, three of them, the Early, Intermediate, and Late Investigations are particularly significant. These were put together ca. 1936–9, 1942–4, and 1945–6, respectively. The Early Investigations is divided into two parts: the first, which was typed up in 1937, is closely related to §§1–188 of Part I of the *Philosophical Investigations*, although it contains a number of remarks that were either substantially changed or dropped from later versions of the book. Part II of the early version of the *Investigations* is the basis for the published Part I of the *Remarks on the Foundations of Mathematics*. The Intermediate Investigations consists of a slight revision and rearrangement of the material in the first part of the Early Investigations, followed by roughly half of the material in §§189–425 of the *Philosophical Investigations*. The Late Investigations, consisting of two heavily revised copies of the typescript that was used in printing Part I (the printer's copy of the typescript has been lost), was constructed ca. 1945, primarily by adding remarks from *Bemerkungen I* (TS 228), a typescript containing a large number of remarks selected from his previous work. The manuscript of what we now know as Part II was composed in 1946–8 and probably reached its final form in 1949; the printer's copy of the typescript used in publishing the book has also been lost. The critical-genetic edition of these versions of the *Philosophical Investigations* consists of the full text of each version, accompanied by an editorial apparatus which gives variant readings, and the closest typescript and manuscript sources of the remarks. This apparatus, together with a copy of the relevant parts of the *Nachlass*, makes it possible to explore some of the succesive formulations and rearrangements of Wittgenstein's remarks in the *Investigations*, although it does not attempt to trace the full genealogy of each remark.

In an editorial note to the *Investigations*, Anscombe and Rhees said that if 'Wittgenstein had published his work himself, he would have suppressed a good deal of what is in the last thirty pages or so of Part I

[§§525–693] and worked what is in Part II, with further material, into its place' (PI, vi/vii). Von Wright has suggested that Wittgenstein may have planned to use the remarks published as *Zettel* as a way of '"bridging the gap" between the present Part I and Part II of the *Investigations*'.[2] Wittgenstein's final Preface, dated January 1945, was, in any case, written before Part II was even drafted, and nothing he wrote provides any support for the view that he regarded what we know as 'Part II' as the second part of the *Investigations*. Unfortunately, the typescripts used to print the *Investigations* were lost shortly afterward, and there is no surviving typescript of Part II. There are, however, two surviving typescripts of the Preface and what we now know as Part I, both of which Wittgenstein had revised extensively. Although neither corresponds precisely to the published text, the book almost always follows one typescript or the other; the published text is apparently the result of collating the revisions from the two typescripts. However, there is no indication, either in Wittgenstein's hand or anyone else's, that the main text, which begins on the same page as the Preface ends, is to be printed as 'Part I'. While the editors' inclusion of Part II is presumably based on Wittgenstein's verbal request, the fact remains that it is only the last of a number of arrangements that he had settled on for the time being. But because he never carried out the revisions that he envisaged, 'Part II' is a collection of material he might have used in revising Part I, not a sequel.

[2] Von Wright 1982, 136.

Introduction

In the half century since the *Philosophical Investigations* was published, and the eighty years since the first review of the *Tractatus*, Wittgenstein's writing not only inspired two of the principal philosophical movements of the twentieth century – the Vienna Circle and Oxford ordinary language philosophy – but also had a far-reaching influence on an extraordinarily wide range of philosophers and researchers in almost every field of the humanities and social sciences. While the other leading figures of logical empiricism and ordinary language philosophy have receded into the historical background, Wittgenstein is one of a small group of twentieth-century philosophers who have become canonical figures, both within and beyond the world of professional philosophy. In an end-of-the-century poll, professional philosophers in the USA and Canada were asked to name the five most important books in philosophy in the twentieth century. The *Philosophical Investigations* came first, and the *Tractatus* fourth. The *Philosophical Investigations* was 'cited far more frequently than any other book and was listed first on more ballots . . . the one crossover masterpiece in twentieth-century philosophy, appealing across diverse specializations and philosophical orientations'.[1] Wittgenstein has also become an iconic figure: he is the only philosopher to appear on *Time's* turn-of-the-millennium list of the 100 'most important people of the century'[2] and has been the subject of biographies, novels, poetry, films, and artworks.

[1] Lackey 1999, 331–2.
[2] http://www.time.com/time/time100/scientist/ Several others on the *Time* list, such as Einstein, Freud, Gödel, and Turing, have certainly had an impact on twentieth-century philosophy, but in each case, their principal contribution was to other fields.

However, there is almost no agreement on even the most basic questions about how to understand Wittgenstein's contribution to philosophy. Books have been written connecting him with almost every field of thought. Frequently, these different currents of interpretation have taken on a life of their own, with the result that readers have been confronted with a bewildering variety of introductions, each claiming to offer authoritative advice.

One reason for this is the fact that Wittgenstein published so little during his lifetime: apart from the *Tractatus*, first published in 1922, the only other book he saw to the press was a spelling dictionary for schoolchildren, produced while he was a village schoolteacher not far from Vienna during the first half of the 1920s. While he worked on the *Philosophical Investigations* for most of the 1930s and 1940s, and on several occasions came close to publishing earlier versions of what we now know as Part 1, it remained unpublished when he died. As a result, the *Philosophical Investigations*, like all of the other books published under Wittgenstein's name after his death, is the product of an editorial decision by a committee of literary trustees which he set up in his will. After the final typescript of Part 1 was produced in the mid-1940s, Wittgenstein continued to work on related topics, and it is likely that if his life had not been cut short in 1951 by prostate cancer he would have worked some of that material into the end of that typescript. As a result, his trustees decided to include a rearrangement of the most polished work from the second half of the 1940s in the *Philosophical Investigations*, and to call it 'Part II'. However, what we now have as 'Part I' is the final version of the book that Wittgenstein worked on during the second half of his philosophical career. For that reason, this introduction to the *Philosophical Investigations* is about Part I, which has a very different status from the rest of his posthumous publications.[3]

For the last twenty years, the most influential and widely discussed interpretation of the *Philosophical Investigations* has been Saul Kripke's *Wittgenstein on Rules and Private Language*. Kripke identifies the central argument of the book as a far-reaching and novel scepticism concerning rules. On Kripke's reading, Wittgenstein's principal philosophical contribution in the *Philosophical Investigations* was

---

[3] For further discussion of Wittgenstein's writing and its publication see pp. xi–xv and my 1996a; for an introduction to the relationship between Wittgenstein's life and work, see Hans Sluga's introduction to Sluga and Stern 1996, and the biographical books listed on pp. 189–90.

to make a powerful case for a new, and radical, scepticism about following a rule. Specifically, Kripke reads Wittgenstein as arguing that when we apply any rule, even one as familiar and seemingly unproblematic as addition, in a new circumstance, such as adding two numbers one has not added before, it is impossible to prove that one has followed the rule correctly. The focal point of Kripke's discussion can be summed up in the following paradox: we take it for granted that we are justified in following the everyday rules of our language, or arithmetic, as we do, yet we are unable to give a satisfactory reply to the sceptical problem that Kripke's Wittgenstein poses. While Kripke was not the first person to read Wittgenstein in this way, his short, provocative, and clearly written book marked a decisive step forward in the literature on the *Philosophical Investigations*. While very few people accepted the particular interpretation of Wittgenstein that Kripke advocated, he did succeed in redirecting attention to the central role of Wittgenstein's discussion of rule-following and sceptical doubts about rule-following.

One leading theme of this book, then, is the issue that Kripke placed in the philosophical spotlight: the place of scepticism about rule-following in the overall argument of the *Philosophical Investigations*. However, like much previous (and subsequent) writing on the *Philosophical Investigations*, Kripke's interpretation and the discussion of the specific views he attributed to Wittgenstein remained, for the most part, at a considerable distance from the text under discussion. As Kripke put it, his method was to 'present the argument as it struck me, as it presented a problem for me, rather than to concentrate on the exegesis of specific passages . . . almost like an attorney presenting a major philosophical argument'.[4]

Like Kripke, Wittgenstein's interpreters rarely pay much attention to the character of the dialogues in which the particular position and arguments they extract from the text are debated. It is commonly taken for granted that the conversational exchanges that make up the *Philosophical Investigations* take the form of a debate between two voices. One of them, usually identified as 'Wittgenstein', supposedly sets out the author's views, while the other voice, usually identified as 'the interlocutor', plays the role of the naive stooge or fall guy. On this approach, the debate between the two voices is 'simply

---

[4] Kripke 1982, viii–ix; see also 5 and 69–70.

a stylistic and literary preference',[5] a superficial feature of the text. One of Wittgenstein's characteristic strategies is to present us with what appears to be a dilemma, a choice between two unattractive but apparently exclusive alternatives. Many of the dialogues between the narrator and the interlocutor in the *Philosophical Investigations* are exchanges between proponents of such opposing views. How are we to understand Wittgenstein's use of such dialogical argumentation? Like Kripke, most readers identify the author's own views with the ones they attribute to his narrator. Certainly, the narrator almost always gets the better of the other voice, or voices, in those exchanges. For these readers, the principal task of the interpreter is to extract 'Wittgenstein's' train of argument and his solutions to familiar philosophical problems from his unusual way of writing, and present them in an accessible and clear-cut way.

However, if one reads the *Philosophical Investigations* in this way, it then becomes very hard to explain why 'Wittgenstein' is also so dismissive of philosophical problems, and why he proposes a way of doing philosophy that is very different from the problem-solving approach Kripke takes for granted. For the book also insists, in a voice that is clearly not the interlocutor's, that traditional philosophical problems are more like a disease than a question in need of an answer, and that the author's own approach to philosophy aims, not to solve those problems, but to dissolve or undo them – to get us to see that they are nonsense:

Philosophical problems arise when language *idles*. (§38*)

A philosophical problem has the form: 'I don't know my way about.' (§123)

The results of philosophy are the uncovering of one or another piece of plain nonsense. (§119)

What we are destroying are nothing but cloud-castles, and we are clearing up the ground of language on which they stand. (§118*)

There is not *a* philosophical method, though there are indeed methods, like different therapies. (§133)

The philosopher treats a question; like an illness. (§255*)

---

[5] Kripke 1982, 5.

Interpreters who share Kripke's argument-centred approach, and who read the *Philosophical Investigations* as providing answers to philosophical problems, have usually done their best to steer around the pitfall that these passages about Wittgenstein's methods present for their reading. They first draw a sharp distinction between Wittgenstein's philosophical practice, on the one hand – which, they insist, is full of argumentative solutions to philosophical problems – and his statements about the nature of philosophy, on the other. Having drawn such a distinction, they then go on to praise the arguments they attribute to Wittgenstein, while playing down the significance of his way of writing and his remarks about method. For instance, Kripke proposes that Wittgenstein's 'inability to write a work with conventionally organized arguments and conclusions' was not simply stylistic, but at least in part due to the need to avoid the contradiction between his insistence that he was not formulating philosophical theses and the sceptical theses Kripke's interpretation attributes to Wittgenstein.[6]

Rather than attributing such a fundamental inconsistency to the author of the *Philosophical Investigations*, this book proposes that we distinguish between two different voices, voices that are usually lumped together as 'Wittgenstein's'. On the one hand we have the voice of Wittgenstein's narrator – who does argue for positive philosophical theses – and on the other hand we have Wittgenstein's commentator, the speaker of the lines quoted above, who dismisses philosophical problems and compares his way of doing philosophy to therapy. Readers who focus only on what Wittgenstein's narrator has to say usually give a Kripke-style reconstruction of the *Philosophical Investigations* in terms of traditional philosophical argumentation, as consisting of reasoned argument that aims to solve philosophical problems. Readers who focus only on what Wittgenstein's commentator has to say often regard the argument as no more than a means to an end: the dissolution of philosophical problems and the end of traditional philosophy. One aim of this book is to do justice to both sides of the *Philosophical Investigations*, and so help the reader see how its argumentative aspect and its therapeutic aspect are actually complementary and interwoven.

[6] See Kripke 1982, 69.

This, then, is the other leading theme of this introduction to the *Philosophical Investigations*: the problems raised by the multiplicity of voices and perspectives it contains, the question of how best to understand the relationship between those voices and the author's intentions, and the related question of what conclusions the reader should draw from his or her examination of this tangle of trains of thought. In other words: where does Wittgenstein's argument lead us? What, ultimately, are we are to make of the trains of argument that we find in the *Philosophical Investigations*?

These two leading themes – the argumentative structure of the book, and the significance of the place of dialogue in the book – are set out in more detail in chapter 1. The first two sections provide an elementary exposition of the argumentative structure of the *Philosophical Investigations*. That structure is both small-scale – here the whole argument is usually begun and concluded within a remark, or a short series of remarks at most – and large-scale – for these smaller units also form part of larger trains of argument. In particular, I identify two small-scale patterns of argument that are repeatedly used throughout the book, the 'method of §2' and the 'method of paradox', and discuss how they are interwoven in the argument of the book as a whole. As a result, the book has considerably more structure than one might expect from its 693 numbered sections, without any chapter headings or a table of contents. The final section of chapter 1 proposes that the point of those argumentative strategies only emerges once we see that the *Philosophical Investigations* has more in common with a Socratic dialogue, or an Augustinian confession, than a conventional philosophical treatise.

While the first chapter discusses the argument and style of the book as a whole, chapters 2 to 7 take successive parts of the book as their point of departure. Each chapter focuses on a limited number of issues raised by that part of the primary text, and draws connections between the central themes in key passages within that text and the rest of the book. In other words, I do not aim to provide another summary of the *Philosophical Investigations* that might substitute for actually reading the book, but rather aim to provide advice and guidance that will help readers arrive at their own judgements. Chapters 2, 3 and 4 each take as their text different ways of beginning to read the *Philosophical Investigations*: chapter 2 discusses the preface to the

Philosophical Investigations, and its relationship to the preface to the *Tractatus*; chapter 3 discusses the motto, and what guidance it provides the reader; and chapter 4 concerns the opening sections of the text of the *Philosophical Investigations*. Chapters 4 to 7 provide guidance to reading the main units of the book, units that are introduced in chapter 1.[7] Chapter 4 covers §§1–64; chapter 5 is about §§65–133, and draws connections with §§428–36; chapter 6 discusses §§134–242; chapter 7 concerns §§243–68. They are followed by a brief conclusion and suggestions about further reading, including scholarly resources as well as some of the best books about the *Philosophical Investigations*.

The second chapter turns to a discussion of the issues raised by the advice to the reader in the prefaces to the *Tractatus* and *Philosophical Investigations*. This leads to a brief review of the principal approaches to Wittgenstein interpretation in the secondary literature. One aim of the brief outline of the main currents of Wittgenstein interpretation in the second chapter is to orient first-time readers, so that they will be able to make better sense of the kaleidoscopically different approaches to be found in the list of recommended further reading. However, this overview of the secondary literature also amounts to a preliminary presentation of my approach to reading the *Philosophical Investigations*. To understand the particular attraction of that book, and the fact that philosophers and theorists of almost every stripe have found support for their own views there, we need to see that the way the book is written invites each of us to find what one might call 'my Wittgenstein' there.[8] Because the book takes the form of a dialogue, a dialogue without clearly identified voices or boundaries, each reader has to work out for him- or herself what positions are being attacked and defended, and in so doing, will inevitably find his or her concerns addressed there.

The third chapter concerns the motto of the *Philosophical Investigations*, 'Anyway, the thing about progress is that it looks much

[7] See 1.2, esp. pp. 16–19.

[8] Terry Eagleton's 'My Wittgenstein' (1994), the title of his piece on writing the screenplay for Jarman's film, *Wittgenstein*, is my source for this expression. Eagleton's Wittgenstein tried to prove the primacy of the everyday over the philosophical, but did so in such an inaccessible way that hardly anyone understood him. Eagleton's Wittgenstein is an odd, but recognizable, reading of the narrator of the *Philosophical Investigations*, but does not begin to do justice to the voice of the commentator – or the fact that the narrator is as plainspoken and conversational as Socrates.

greater than it really is.'[9] Few of Wittgenstein's readers have paid any attention to the motto. Most of those who do have taken its significance to be unambiguous and straightforward. Reviewing the previous interpretations of the motto, I argue that while there is some truth to each of them, the very fact that each of them has something to offer is an indication that none of them can be the whole truth, and that even the motto is ambiguous and far from straightforward. Indeed, my positive proposal is that the principal point of the motto lies in the fact that it opens up a number of very different ways of understanding those words, and in so doing provides an exemplary model of the importance of context, perspective, and background for a full appreciation of the argument of the *Philosophical Investigations*.

My exposition of the central arguments of the *Philosophical Investigations* often turns on a detailed discussion of others' interpretations of specific passages in the primary text, as examples of some of the leading ways in which readers, both experts and beginners, have understood – and misunderstood – these arguments. Readers who pick up this introduction to the *Philosophical Investigations* expecting a summary of Stern's interpretation of that book may think this an unnecessarily roundabout approach to the primary text. I take this approach for two related reasons. First, the alternate interpretations I discuss and criticize from the secondary literature are ones that are often taken for granted, by both students and teachers. The very 'facts' about the *Philosophical Investigations* that are routinely repeated in reference works and popular expositions of Wittgenstein's work – for instance, that the *Philosophical Investigations* and *Tractatus* are diametrically opposed, or that the *Philosophical Investigations* and *Tractatus* are in fundamental agreement[10] – are actually one of the main obstacles standing in the way of new readers of the *Philosophical Investigations*. Second, the interpretations I discuss are chosen not only as examples of common misreadings, but also because they serve as exemplary statements of just the sort of views that we must confront if we are to understand the *Philosophical Investigations*. For the *Philosophical Investigations* takes the form, not of a treatise, but of a dialogue, an informal discussion among a number of different voices, voices that

---

[9] My translation, based on Wittgenstein 2001, 741. See 3.1 on the translation, 3.2 on its interpretation.

[10] For further discussion of the relationship between the two books, see chapter 2.

are rarely clearly identified. Instead of simply stating the author's reasoned defence of his conclusions, the book leaves its readers with the task of working out what conclusions to draw from the philosophical exchanges it contains. The views that it criticizes are not treated as worthless errors, but rather as an integral part of the process of searching for the truth. Wittgenstein's philosophy arises out of an extended interrogation of the views he rejects: 'In a certain sense one cannot take too much care in handling philosophical mistakes, they contain so much truth.'[11] As a result, one of the best ways of appreciating what the *Philosophical Investigations* has to offer is to critically examine competing interpretations.

However, my principal aim in this book is to help readers interpret the dialogues of the *Philosophical Investigations* for themselves. Whether or not readers agree with my particular interpretation of Wittgenstein's intentions, once they are aware of the range of possible approaches to these questions about the author's intentions they will be much better equipped to make up their own minds as they read the *Philosophical Investigations* for themselves. Wittgenstein says in the preface that he would not like his writing 'to spare other people the trouble of thinking. But, if possible, to stimulate someone to thoughts of his own.' The aim of this introduction to that book is not to spare other people the trouble of thinking about the *Philosophical Investigations*, but rather to provide readers with an orientation that will enable them to read that book in ways that will stimulate thoughts of their own.

---

[11] *Zettel*, §460.

CHAPTER I

Philosophical Investigations §§1–693: *an elementary exposition*

1.1 THE 'METHOD OF §2'

In the *Philosophical Investigations*, topics are repeatedly introduced in the following way.

Stage 1. A brief statement of a philosophical position that Wittgenstein opposes, which usually emerges out of an exchange with another voice. Thus, in §1, we are presented with a conception of meaning that arises out of Wittgenstein's reading of a passage from Augustine's *Confessions*:

Every word has a meaning. This meaning is correlated with the word. It is the object for which the word stands. (§1b)

Stage 2. The description of a quite specific set of circumstances in which that position is appropriate:

That philosophical concept of meaning has its place in a primitive idea of the way language functions. But one can also say that it is the idea of a language more primitive than ours.

Let us imagine a language for which the description given by Augustine is right. (§2)

In §2 of the *Philosophical Investigations*, the passage just quoted leads in to the famous story of 'Wittgenstein's builders', a tribe who only have four words, each of which is used by a builder to instruct his assistant to bring one of four kinds of building blocks.

Stage 3. The deflationary observation that the circumstances in question are quite limited, and that once we move beyond them, the position becomes inappropriate:

Augustine, we might say, does describe a system of communication; only not everything that we call language is this system. And one has to say this in many cases where the question arises: 'Is this an appropriate description or not?' The answer is: 'Yes, it is appropriate, but only for this narrowly circumscribed region, not for the whole of what you were claiming to describe.' (§3a)

To drive the point home, Wittgenstein later adds other uses of signs that don't fit Augustine's description: §8 describes an expansion of the language in §2 to include numerals, demonstratives, and colour samples, and §15 adds names for particular objects.

This three-stage argument scheme suggests a more general recipe for unsettling philosophical preconceptions. First, describe a case the preconception fits as well as possible, 'a language-game for which this account is really valid' (§48), then change just enough about the case in question, either by adding or removing some aspect, or by changing the context or our point of view, so that we run up against the limitations of the preconception. This 'method of §2', as Wittgenstein calls it in §48, is used repeatedly in the remarks that follow.

It is also characteristic of Wittgenstein's use of this argument scheme that all three stages follow each other so quickly. In §§1–3 and §§46–8, each stage of the argument is presented quite explicitly; in many other cases the argument is only sketched, and Stage 3 may be left as an exercise for the reader. Because he aims, not to solve philosophical problems, but to undo or 'dissolve' them, Wittgenstein frequently presents the materials for a Stage 3 reply immediately before setting out Stage 2. The aim of the reply in Stage 3 is not to articulate a philosophical answer to the proto-philosophical question with which we began, but to get us to give up the question. The story of the grocer and his different ways of using words in §1d plays this role in the argument of §§1–3.[1] Similarly, the multiplication of examples in §47 of alternative conceptions of complexity comes between Socrates' Stage 1 discussion of simples, the 'primary elements' out of which the world is made in §46, and the use of the 'method of §2' in §48 to attack the very idea of a 'primary element'.

---

[1] For further discussion of §1d, see 4.1, final pages.

Wittgenstein frequently uses a complementary method: attend more closely to the 'best cases' we come up with in Stage 2, to get us to see that they themselves unravel when one pushes them a little; that ultimately we cannot even make sense of what at first sight seem like the most straightforward applications of a given account. In the three-stage argument above, we are expected to take it as a matter of course that words stand for objects, or that the story of the builders in §2b, like the grocer in §1d, makes perfect sense. The complementary strategy is to approach these matters of course in a way that defamiliarizes them, and so makes us see how much we took for granted when we took them at face value. This is already anticipated in the final words of §2, separated from the story of the builders by a double dash, usually an indication of a change of voice: '——Conceive this as a complete primitive language.' For despite the repeated insistence that we 'could imagine that the language of §2 was the *whole* language of A and B; even the whole language of a tribe' (§6), it is far from clear that we can. Of course, we can speak the words, and imagine many ways of performing or filming the scenario Wittgenstein describes. But can we fill out such a story: can we make sense of a tribe whose linguistic abilities were exhausted by the routines described in §2? Only, it seems, at the price of turning them into creatures without a life all that much like our own.[2]

One might reply, in defence of the first moves towards philosophical theorizing Wittgenstein is criticizing, and the theories they give rise to, that the approach to philosophy he opposes aims at a 'view from nowhere', a position that is correct for all possible circumstances and contexts, not just a position that fits a few carefully selected cases. In defence of Wittgenstein's 'method of §2', one can say that if we grant, for the sake of argument, that such philosophical accounts do any work, they must applicable to specific cases, and ultimately these must include not only the 'best cases', but the problem cases, too. Furthermore, Wittgenstein will suggest, the 'view from nowhere' is a distinctively philosophical fiction, a fiction that always starts out from a quite specific somewhere, and begins its theorizing with particular examples of familiar objects and activities. The philosophy Wittgenstein takes as his target begins, in other words, with our

---

[2] For further discussion of this question, see *Zettel*, §99.

taking familiar matters out of context, and taking them as the model for a universal account, true everywhere and at any time, of how things must be. The relationship between everyday life, science, and philosophy is a central concern throughout the course of Wittgenstein's writing. He regarded philosophy, properly conducted, as an autonomous activity, a matter of clarifying our understanding of language. Wittgenstein thought philosophy should state the obvious as a way of disabusing us of the belief that we can formulate philosophical theories of meaning, knowledge, language, or science, and was deeply opposed to the naturalist view that philosophy is a form of science.

Confronted with §2-type examples, the Socratic philosopher dismisses the concrete cases as irrelevant, insisting that what matters is to get clear about the rules that determine which cases the term really applies to, and what they have in common. In 1944, when Wittgenstein was putting the first part of the *Philosophical Investigations* into its final form, he told a friend that he was reading Plato's *Theaetetus*, and that 'Plato in this dialogue is occupied with the same problems that I am writing about.'[3] Wittgenstein owned a five-volume German translation of Plato by Preisendanz, and refers to passages in Plato quite frequently in his writings. The philosophical discussion in the *Theaetetus* begins with Socrates' asking Theaetetus 'what is knowledge?' His first answer is as follows:

Th.: I think the things Theodorus teaches are knowledge – I mean geometry and the subjects you enumerated just now. Then again there are the crafts such as cobbling, whether you take them together or separately. They must be knowledge, surely.

Soc.: That is certainly a frank and indeed a generous answer, my dear lad. I ask you for one thing and you have given me many; I wanted something simple, and I have got a variety. . . . You were not asked to say what one may have knowledge of, or how many branches of knowledge there are. It was not with any idea of counting these up that the question was asked; we wanted to know what knowledge itself is. – Or am I talking nonsense?[4]

We can see much of Wittgenstein's later philosophy as an extended defence of Theaetetus' initial answer – the best we can do in answering questions about the essence of a word such as 'knowledge' is to give

---

[3] Drury 1984, 149.   [4] Plato 1997, 162–3; *Theaetetus* 146c–e.

examples, with the aim of showing that Socrates *is* talking nonsense, and so 'bring words back from their metaphysical to their everyday use' (§116).[5] In the *Blue Book*, Wittgenstein explicitly opposes his approach to Socrates':

> When Socrates asks the question, 'what is knowledge?' he does not even regard it as a *preliminary* answer to enumerate cases of knowledge . . . the discussion begins with the pupil giving an example of an exact definition, and then analogous to this a definition of the word 'knowledge' is asked for.[6] As the problem is put, it seems that there is something wrong with the ordinary use of the word 'knowledge'. It appears we don't know what it means, and that therefore, perhaps, we have no right to use it. We should reply: 'There is no one exact usage of the word "knowledge"; but we can make up several such usages, which will more or less agree with the ways the word is actually used.' (*Blue Book*, 20, 27)

On the other hand, there are also deep affinities between Wittgenstein's and Plato's dialogues: each of the definitions of knowledge Socrates proposes in the *Theaetetus* proves unsuccessful.

In the early 1930s, Wittgenstein emphatically rejected systematic approaches to understanding language and knowledge. His answer to the Socratic question about the nature of knowledge is that it has no nature, no essence, and so it is a mistake to think one can give a single systematic answer:

> If I was asked what knowledge is, I would list items of knowledge and add 'and suchlike'. There is no common element to be found in all of them, because there isn't one.[7]

In the *Philosophical Investigations*, one of the principal reasons for Wittgenstein's opposition to systematic philosophical theorizing is that our use of language, our grasp of its meaning, depends on a background of common behaviour and shared practices – not on agreement in opinions but in 'form of life' (§241).[8] But to say this so quickly is potentially misleading, for a great deal turns on how one understands this 'agreement'. Most readers take it to be a gesture towards a positive theory of practice or the place of community in

---

[5] For further discussion of §116, see 5.2, pp. 125–9.   [6] See *Theaetetus* 146ff.
[7] Wittgenstein, TS 302, 'Diktat für Schlick', 1931–3. For further discussion of the *Theaetetus*, see 4.4. See also Stern 1991 or 1995, 6.1 on Wittgenstein's use of Heraclitus' and Plato's river imagery.
[8] See 6.2 for further discussion of §241.

a theory of meaning. I shall be proposing that we take Wittgenstein at his word when he tells us that the work of the philosopher 'consists in assembling reminders for a particular purpose' (§127) – that the remarks about common behaviour, shared practices, and agreement in opinions are intended as reminders of what we ordinarily do, reminders assembled for the purpose of helping his readers see the shortcomings of certain theories of knowledge, meaning, and the like.

1.2 THE CENTRAL ARGUMENTS OF THE *PHILOSOPHICAL INVESTIGATIONS*

There is a sense in which the argument of §2 is over almost before it has begun, for the limitations of the language proposed in §2 are anticipated in §1d and set out quite explicitly in §3 and the sections immediately following. On the other hand, the further discussion of the language-game of §2 connects many of the remaining sections of Part I in a number of far-reaching ways.

There are a large number of explicit cross-references between sections in the first 186 sections of Part I, and almost all of these links ultimately lead back to the language-game of §2.[9] This cat's-cradle of cross-references, which ultimately extend as far as §185, not only gives this part of the book a strongly interlinked and hypertextual character; it also draws our attention to many of the crucial turning points in the overall argument of the first 242 sections of the book.[10]

---

[9] Thus there are explicit references to §2 in §§6–8, §§18–19, §27, §37, §48, and §86, and one can find language-games that extend or draw on the example of §2 throughout the book. However, §8, §15, §48, and §86 play a particularly prominent role, for each of these three variations on §2 generates its own sequence of subsequent cross-references. Section 8, §15, and §86 each introduce language-games by making additions to the game described in §2: numerals, colours, 'this', and 'there' in §8, names in §15, and a table of instructions in §86. There are references to §8 in §13, §§16–18, §27, §38, and §41; references to §15 in §41 and §60; and a reference to §86 in §163. The language-game described in §48 is not an extension of §2, but it is said to 'apply the method of §2'; there are references to §48 in §§50–1, §53, and §64.

[10] The first 188 remarks were the first part of the book to be written. The 'early' pre-war version, which for the most part closely corresponds to §§1–188, was written out in a manuscript dating from November and December 1936, and typed up in 1937. In 1939 Wittgenstein considered publishing this version; Rush Rhees drafted a translation of the first 100 or so remarks, and Wittgenstein made extensive corrections to Rhees' translation. This would have been in connection with Wittgenstein's application for a chair in philosophy in 1939. The next draft, the 'intermediate' version, dates from around 1944, and is numbered up

While there are no chapter or section headings, and no table of contents, the text of the *Philosophical Investigations* does contain many passages that clearly and explicitly indicate the topics under discussion, some of the principal links between them, and where they begin and end. Thus, just as §1b identifies one of the principal topics of §§1–38, §39 identifies the point of departure for §§39–64: '*a name ought really to signify a simple*'. The language-games of §2 and §8, repeatedly cited and discussed throughout much of §§1–38, provide a point of reference that connects the various threads of this discussion. The language-game of §48, itself modelled on the 'method of §2', plays a very similar role in §§48–64. A further trail of explicit cross-references leads from §2, via §86, to §143, §151, §§162–4, §179, §183, and §185.

The argument of Part 1 of the book can be divided into five main chapters, of which the first three focus on language, and the last two on the philosophy of mind. The central theme of the first chapter, §§1–64, is a critique of the idea that our words get their meaning by standing for something independent of language. The next two chapters concern what might seem like the natural alternative to the view that words get their meaning by standing for something independent of language, that we must look within language for a theory of meaning. Thus, chapters 2 and 3, §§65–242, are a critique of the idea that linguistic or logical rules are the basis of the meaning of words and sentences. Chapter 4, §§243–427, begins with a critique of the idea of a private language, 'a language which describes my inner experiences and which only I myself can understand' (§256), and the related notion that our psychological concepts get their meaning by standing for objects in the mind. The principal concepts under discussion in §§243–315 are those of sensation and visual experience; the main topics of the remainder of this chapter are thought (§§316–62), imagination (§§363–97), and the self and consciousness (§§398–427). Chapter 5, §§428–693, is less focused and concerns a wide range of

to §300; the new material consists of approximately half of the remarks we now know as §§189–421. The typescript of a late draft, the basis for the published text of Part 1, was probably produced in 1946. There is little evidence that Wittgenstein regarded the material published as Part II, written during the years immediately after the Second World War, as the second part of *Philosophical Investigations*. For further discussion of the relationship between the Wittgenstein papers and the text of the *Philosophical Investigations*, see Stern 1996a, 1996b, forthcoming a.

interrelated topics, but intentionality is the principal topic of the opening part (§§428–65) and a theme that runs through the rest of Part I. Other topics include negation (§§446–8, §§547–57), meaning (§§449–68, 503–24, 558–70, 661–93), understanding (§§525–46), intending (§§629–60), and willing (§§611–28).

The three-stage argument of §§1–3 marks the beginning of an extended critique of the notion, prominent in §1, that every word has a meaning, the object for which it stands. This critique, which occupies much of §§1–64, can be divided into two distinct units. The first unit, §§1–38, is an attack on the idea that the meaning of a word consists in its standing for a familiar object of one kind or another. One of the principal approaches under discussion in §§1–38 is the view that ostensive definition – explaining a word's meaning by pointing at an object – is the basis of meaning. The second unit, §§39–64, looks at the view that words stand for simple objects, an approach that promises to avoid some of the difficulties that have arisen in §§1–38. Sections 39–45 consider the possibility that familiar things could be simples; §§47–64 examine the notion that ultimately words get their meaning by standing for 'simple objects', objects that we reach by analysing familiar objects, which are complex, into their ultimate, primitive components, or 'ur-elements', on an overly literal translation.

A three-stage argument starts from questions about something apparently unphilosophical – language learning, or giving a name to a thing; but this draws the narrator's alter ego into Stage 1, a preliminary formulation of a philosophical thesis. Stages 2 and 3 bring us back to earth, by first proposing as prosaic and simple an example as possible, and then pointing out its limitations. Still, the method of three-stage argument can only get us so far. Replying to Socrates with a list of different kinds of knowledge, or to the denotationalist with a list of different uses of words, may be a first step towards being suspicious of the idea that we must be able to give a unitary specification of knowledge, naming, or the use of words. On the other hand, a Socratic philosopher will reply that the only thing wrong with such theories is that they need refining. For this reason, Wittgenstein's narrator replies to many different Socratic lines of thought in §§1–38 and §§65–88, and raises different problems for each formulation of the idea under discussion. However, the problems and paradoxes

Wittgenstein's narrator produces provoke his alter ego to dig deeper, and look for something hidden, a structure that supposedly underlies, or a hidden process that somehow animates, our everyday lives and language. Wittgenstein speaks of this movement from the Socratic questions that typically initiate philosophical inquiry to the counter-examples and paradoxes that such questions inevitably produce, and from there to the Platonic vision of a reality behind the phenomena, as a 'tendency to sublime the logic of our language' (§38, cf. §89).[11] For this reason, the Socratic questions about naming and reference in the opening sections of the *Philosophical Investigations* lead up to the formulation of a paradox about ostensive definition: 'an ostensive definition can be variously interpreted in *every* case' (§28, §§26–31; see 4.3). This results in a discussion of 'sublime names': names that must stand for their objects, and so cannot be variously interpreted (§§39–64; see 4.4).

The larger argumentative cycle, beginning with initial puzzlement, leading up to the formulation of a paradox, out to the further reaches of the sublime, and then back to the everyday, provides an overarching plot for the principal units that make up Part I of the book. It will be convenient to speak of them as chapters in what follows: §§1–64 are the first chapter, discussed in 4.1–4.4; §§65–133 make up the second, discussed in 5.1–5.2; §§134–242 are chapter 3, discussed in 6.1–6.2; §§243–427 are the fourth, whose opening sections are discussed in 7.1–7.2; and parts of §§428–693, which, like Part II, address similar concerns, but do not have the same overall structure, are discussed rather more briefly in 4.4 and 5.2.

Within chapter 2, §§65–133 of the *Philosophical Investigations*, we can identify two principal units. The first turns on the idea that understanding a word or a sentence involves commitment to definite rules for its use (§§65–88; see 5.1). Wittgenstein's response to Socratic demands for an analysis of what words mean in terms of rules for their use culminates in the formulation of a paradox about explanation: any explanation hangs in the air unless supported by another one (§87). This, in turn, leads up to the second half of chapter 2, a discussion of 'sublime logic', the idea of rules that would state the essence of language (§§89–133; see 5.2).

---

[11] For further discussion of Wittgenstein's conception of 'subliming', see 4.3–4.4 and 5.2.

Here Wittgenstein criticizes the idea that because our use of language presupposes the rules of logic, we can distil a set of fundamental principles about the nature of language from pure logic. Chapter 3, §§134–242, concerns the 'paradox of rule-following': the problem that any rule can be interpreted in a number of mutually incompatible ways. Consequently, it can seem as if any interpretation – any statement of what a word or rule means – hangs in the air unless supported by another. Famously, Wittgenstein summarizes this predicament in §201: 'This was our paradox: no course of action could be determined by a rule, because any course of action can be made out to accord with the rule.'

Like the remarks that open the two principal topics in chapter 1 (§1: Augustine; and §46: Plato's Socrates), the remarks at the beginning of the two halves of chapter 2 and the opening of chapter 3 begin with a clear invocation of the words of another philosopher and a particular philosophical picture. In §65 and §134 it is the 'author of the *Tractatus Logico-Philosophicus*' (§23) and the notion of the 'general propositional form': a logical form that every meaningful proposition must share (*Tractatus* 5.47ff.). Section 65 concerns the *Philosophical Investigations*' rejection of the Tractarian view that every proposition shares the same general form, and §134 returns to this topic, quoting, without giving a citation, the words the *Tractatus* tells us state the general propositional form: 'This is how things are' (*Tractatus* 4.5). Section 89 returns to Augustine's *Confessions*, quoting a passage in which he tries to answer the question 'What, then, is time?' Another aspect of the intricate argumentative structure of this portion of the book is that in the first half of chapter 2, and throughout chapter 3, passages linked to §2 are key points in the argumentative structure of each unit. Sections 65–88 begin by making what appears to be a sharp break with the discussion of simples and §48. It responds to the *Tractatus*' quite general idea about the shared nature of all language by offering a close examination of the variety of ways we use a single word, the word 'game', but it culminates in a paradox that is set out using a language-game based on the one in §2, a paradox that reappears in a slightly different form as the leitmotif of §§134–242.

While it is generally recognized that the main theme of chapter 3, the 'rule-following' chapter, is a recapitulation of a previous train of argument, the full implications of the fact that it is a continuation of an argument that begins in the opening sections of the book are rarely acknowledged.[12] A key paradox that occurs over and over again, in one form or another, throughout the first two hundred sections of the *Philosophical Investigations* is that nothing is intrinsically meaningful, for all determination of meaning, by such means as definitions, rules, thoughts, or images, is dependent on interpretation. Given any candidate meaning-determiner, it is always, in principle, open to a further, deviant, interpretation. No act of defining or intending, grasping a rule or deciding to go on in a certain way, can give the supposed meaning-determiner the power to determine our future actions, because there is always the question of how it is to be interpreted. Only if we ignore the context can we think that some isolated act or event can have a determinate meaning regardless of its context. A change in the context of application can yield a change in meaning, and therefore meaning cannot be identified with anything independent of context. Leading examples include the wayward child who learns to add small numbers correctly but systematically miscalculates, all the while insisting that he is going on the same way (§143, §185), the drawing of an old man walking up a steep path, resting on a stick, that a Martian might describe as a man sliding downhill (PI, p. 54/46), and deviant ways of following arrows or signposts (§§85–6), or interpreting a drawing of a cube (§§139–41).

The resolution of these paradoxes, like the resolution of a three-stage argument, turns on considering the wider context in which our words are used. In response to a proto-philosophical theory, a three-stage argument draws our attention to the circumstances it fits and those it does not fit. Similarly, in replying to a philosophical paradox, Wittgenstein's narrator points out that the paradox does not arise in our everyday lives, and draws our attention to the way in which it turns on a failure to pay attention to the circumstances in which those words are ordinarily used. Ordinarily, the paradox does not arise, because it is already clear how the words or actions in question are to be understood. Thus Wittgenstein's reply to the paradox of ostension turns on the point that 'ostensive definition explains the use – the meaning – of a word when the overall role of the word in language is clear' (§30a). A parallel paradox about explanation – that

---

[12] See Kripke 1982, 81–4; Stroud 2000, 222–3.

any explanation of the meaning of a word hangs in the air unless supported by another one – receives a similar response: 'an explanation may indeed rest on another one that has been given, but none stands in need of another – unless *we* require it to prevent a misunderstanding' (§87a). Analogous paradoxes about understanding, interpreting, and following a rule are the principal concern of §§134–242; by the time Wittgenstein sums up the paradox of rule-following and provides his response in §201, he expects the paradox to be so familiar that his treatment takes the form of a summary that begins by referring back to the previous discussion.

1.3 SEEING THE *PHILOSOPHICAL INVESTIGATIONS* AS A DIALOGUE

The previous paragraph attributes a clear-cut set of answers to the paradoxes of ostension, explanation, and rule-following to Wittgenstein. There can be no denying that these answers are present in the text; they can be compared to a prominent and repeated pattern in the weave of the *Philosophical Investigations*' argumentative fabric. Most interpreters attribute this argumentative strand to Wittgenstein without any pause. But the connection between this train of thought and the author's intentions is far from clear, and so I will usually qualify this by attributing them to 'Wittgenstein's narrator'.

If we take Wittgenstein's narrator to be a behaviourist, or an ordinary language philosopher who maintains that the rules of our language guarantee that we are mostly right, then the sceptical paradoxes – namely, that ostension, explanation, and rule-following can always be undermined by sceptical possibilities – receive what Kripke calls a 'straight' solution: we really can provide a positive answer to the paradoxes, because the expressions in question can be defined in terms of public behaviour, or the rules of grammar that govern our use of language. If, on the other hand, we follow Kripke in taking Wittgenstein to be a sceptic who endorses the paradoxes he has formulated, then the appeal to what the community ordinarily does in its use of these terms is only a negative answer to the sceptical problem (Kripke calls this a 'sceptical' solution): recognizing that we cannot solve the problem, we instead appeal to what we ordinarily do as a way of indicating the best reply available, albeit one that does not really solve the paradoxes.[13]

Rather than seeing these arguments as exchanges between 'Wittgenstein' and 'his interlocutor', I propose that we approach them as an exchange between a number of different voices, none of which can be unproblematically identified with the author's. For these reasons, in discussing passages of dialogue in the *Philosophical Investigations*, I prefer to speak of dialogues between 'Wittgenstein's narrator' and 'an interlocutory voice', rather than between 'Wittgenstein' and 'the interlocutor'. In some places, and particularly in those parts of the text that are most critical of the *Tractatus* – principally §§39–142 – the narratorial voice sets out the case against philosophical positions set out in Wittgenstein's first book, in opposition to voices that express Tractarian convictions. In §§140–693, the narratorial voice is frequently used to set out behaviourist, verificationist, and anti-essentialist objections to traditional philosophical views, in opposition to an anti-behaviourist voice that expresses mentalist, verification-transcendent, and essentialist intuitions and convictions.

In addition to these opposing voices, voices that play different parts at different points in the text, we also meet with a third voice. This third voice, which is not always clearly distinct from the narratorial voice, provides an ironic commentary on their exchanges, a commentary consisting partly of objections to assumptions the debaters take for granted, and partly of platitudes about language and everyday life they have both overlooked.[14] Most readers treat both of these voices as expressions of 'Wittgenstein's' views, with the result that they are

---

[13] For further discussion of Kripke and rule-following, see chapter 6.

[14] The commentator's role is comparable to that of the leading character in Nestroy's plays; see the discussion of Nestroy in 3.2. The voices of the narrator, interlocutor, and commentator also play roles quite similar to Demea, Cleanthes, and Philo in Hume's *Dialogues Concerning Natural Religion*, another posthumously published work whose conclusions have been much debated. Cleanthes, a rather naive deist, unquestioningly believes in God much as the interlocutor believes in the mind and its powers. As Cleanthes is an advocate of the argument from design for God's existence, he sees evidence of God's handiwork everywhere he looks, and cannot comprehend how anyone could deny the plain fact of a Designer's existence. In much the same way, the interlocutor finds it incredible that anyone could deny the nature of his experience. Demea, a dogmatic rationalist, thinks the existence of God is established by a priori proof, not by an appeal to evidence for design. Demea considers Cleanthes' conception of God as the unseen cause of the order in our world to turn on a misunderstanding of God's nature, and his place in the world. The narrator treats the interlocutor's view of the

unable to reconcile the trenchant and provocative theses advocated by the narrator and the commentator's rejection of all philosophical theses.

Despite my emphasis on the variety, diversity, and ambiguity of the voices in the *Philosophical Investigations*, I do not aim to replace those black-and-white readings on which the *Philosophical Investigations* is an attack on a single 'Augustinian picture', or a continuous dialogue between 'Wittgenstein' and 'his interlocutor', by endless shades of gray or a kaleidoscopic hall of mirrors. On the contrary, I have outlined the argumentative strategies that structure the *Philosophical Investigations*, both at the micro-level of individual remarks or groups of remarks, and the macro-level of the themes and concerns that link these smaller units. On the reading advocated here, the 'straight' and the 'sceptical' solutions are equally misguided, for they both misunderstand the character and methods of the *Philosophical Investigations*. They mistakenly identify the viewpoint defended in a particular strand of argument – in one case, the reasons Wittgenstein's narrator gives us for thinking that the problem of rule-following can be solved, in the other, a sceptical problem that the narrator claims the interlocutor faces – as equivalent to the views that are advocated by the author, or the book as a whole. Wittgenstein, I contend, provided neither a straight solution nor a sceptical solution to the philosophical problems discussed in the *Philosophical Investigations*. Rather, he aimed to dissolve those problems by means of a dialogue between opposing voices, a dialogue in which the commentator comes closer to expressing the author's viewpoint than either of his leading protagonists do.

The following passage provides a convenient summary of the commentator's approach, not only to disputes over realism and idealism, but also to the exchanges between narrator and interlocutor, the voice of correctness and the voice of temptation:

mind as a rather similar misunderstanding of the nature of experience, and its place in the world. Demea thinks God's existence can be proved by rational argument; the *Philosophical Investigations*' narrator maintains that statements about the mind are logically linked – by means of 'criteria' – to public behaviour. Philo, often identified as the mouthpiece for Hume's own view by his readers, plays a role similar to the commentator's voice in the *Philosophical Investigations*, rising above the standard arguments offered by the others. Philo provides a minimalist standpoint that offers so little support to traditional approaches to proofs of God's existence that, despite his professions of deism, many have taken Hume to be using Philo to provide the coup de grâce to deism.

For *this* is what disputes between Idealists, Solipsists and Realists look like. The one party attack the normal form of expression as if they were attacking a statement; the others defend it, as if they were stating facts recognized by every reasonable human being. (§402b)

Most of the *Philosophical Investigations* does consist of a debate for and against 'the normal form of expression'. The narrator is usually taken to be arguing for Wittgenstein's own philosophical position, 'ordinary language philosophy', while the interlocutor attacks our ordinary way of speaking, arguing that it does not do justice to his intuitions and his arguments. While the *Philosophical Investigations* is, for the most part, made up of conversation, questions, jokes, and diagnoses, it is not straightforwardly identifiable as a dialogue, a confession, therapy, or philosophy of language, though it certainly contains elements of all these. The book plays upon, and offends against, multiple styles and genres, while resisting identification with any one of them. What kind of a book is the *Philosophical Investigations*, then? On the one hand, it is in large part made up of Socratic dialogues in which a hero aims to find the truth through rational argument with others. It certainly makes liberal use of both of the basic devices of Socratic dialogue: syncrisis – a debate between opposed viewpoints on a given topic – and anacrisis – forcing an interlocutor to express his opinion thoroughly and subjecting it to critical appraisal. Thus there certainly is good reason to read the book as belonging to the familiar philosophical genre of the dialogue.

On the other hand, unlike traditional philosophical dialogues, the *Philosophical Investigations* contains no named characters to whom parts are assigned. Jane Heal observes that while there is no uniform syntactic device that signals the beginning and end of parts in the dialogue, such as dashes or quotation marks, what does make the use of the term 'dialogue'

seem entirely apt is the strong impression that, from time to time, a voice other than Wittgenstein's speaks, i.e. that some thought other than one endorsed by Wittgenstein himself is being expressed.[15]

This is, I think, the right way to read the dialogues in the *Blue Book* and the *Brown Book*, which clearly do set out views endorsed by their author, interspersed with occasional objections, but not the

---

[15] Heal 1995, 68.

Philosophical Investigations, where matters are not always so simple. Most interpreters share Heal's assumption that the dialogue is between two clearly identifiable voices, and the leading voice expresses the author's considered convictions. But this prevents us from seeing how Wittgenstein's second masterpiece is not simply the result of simply putting together what he had already written, even though a good portion of the words of Part 1 of the *Philosophical Investigations* had been drafted by the time Wittgenstein finished dictating the *Brown Book*.[16] While it is certainly possible to construe certain selections from the *Philosophical Investigations* as exchanges between 'Wittgenstein' and 'his interlocutor', or a doctrinaire behaviourist and a querulous anti-behaviourist, we should not identify the outlook of the author with every passage that we attribute to his leading narrator. The closest the author of the *Philosophical Investigations* comes to expressing his own views is not in the person of his narrator, the aggressively anti-Socratic protagonist we meet in the book's three-step arguments, but rather in the moments when he steps back from this serio-comedy and offers us a striking simile, or draws our attention to platitudes that philosophers don't take seriously.[17]

For this reason, all this talk of Wittgenstein's argument and of the positions he opposes, while unavoidable, is potentially deeply misleading. For it implies that he thinks of the views he is opposing as intelligible, albeit mistaken. It also makes it tempting to suppose that Wittgenstein's distinctive contribution to philosophy turns on a clear distinction between unproblematic, 'everyday' uses of language, and their mirror image, the 'metaphysical' uses of language that are characteristic of traditional philosophy.[18] However, if Wittgenstein is correct, the accounts offered by all the participants in his dialogues are nonsense, and so cannot, in the end, be true or false. Ultimately, Wittgenstein's view is that the proto-philosophical accounts of meaning and mind that his interlocutor proposes and his narrator opposes cannot be understood, and that neither the descriptions of simple situations his narrator offers in Stage 2, nor the sublime truths

---

[16] At this point, most of the remarks in Part 1 had been written, but nothing resembling the *Philosophical Investigations* more closely than the *Brown Book* had been assembled; nearly all of §§1–188 was put in its present order around the end of 1936.

[17] This claim is discussed and defended at greater length in chapters 2–3.

[18] For further discussion of §116 on metaphysical and everyday language, see 5.2.

about the essence of the world and language his interlocutor aims for, will do justice to those ideas and intuitions with which philosophical discussion begins. On this reading, Wittgenstein is neither saying that a solution to the sceptical paradoxes or a 'private language' is possible, nor proving that such things are impossible. Rather, Wittgenstein holds that such words do no useful work at all:

> What we 'are tempted to say' in such a case is, of course, not philosophy; but it is its raw material. Thus, for example, what a mathematician is inclined to say about the objectivity and reality of mathematical facts, is not a philosophy of mathematics, but something for philosophical *treatment*.
> 255. The philosopher treats a question; like an illness. (§§254–5*)

If we follow the author's advice, rather than those of the protagonists in his dialogues, we will give up both behaviourism and anti-behaviourism. The result of his discussion of philosophical problems is not supposed to be an endorsement of one of the views he discusses; rather, 'a combination of words is being excluded from the language, withdrawn from circulation' (§500).

Nevertheless, in order to 'turn something that isn't obviously nonsense' – such as the initial expression of a philosophical account of meaning we find in §1 – 'into obvious nonsense' (§464*; cf. §524c), we must first try to make sense of it, and in so doing, come to see that we cannot. There are few better ways of beginning to do this than to try to think of cases the proposed account does fit as well as possible, and then seeing how it fails to fit when the context or circumstances change. Wittgenstein sums up this predicament and his response to it in the following words:

> 374. The great difficulty here is not to represent the matter as if it were a matter of inability . . . —— And the best that I can propose is that we should yield to the temptation to use this picture, but then investigate how the *application* of the picture goes.

However, in our investigation of what Wittgenstein has to say about yielding to philosophical temptation, I am proposing that we should not simply assume that everything that is said in opposition to these temptations must be taken as a straightforward statement of its author's philosophical convictions.

In my first book on Wittgenstein, I approached his post-*Tractatus* writing as a dialogue with various different stages of his own earlier work, stressing the extent to which the views that receive close critical attention in the *Philosophical Investigations* are not only the logical atomism of the *Tractatus*, but also ones that he himself had set out in writings from 1929 and the early 1930s.[19] In particular, I emphasized both the continuities and the contrasts between Tractarian logical atomism, the 'logical holism' of the 1929–34 period, and the 'practical holism' of the later 1930s. The principal continuity is that, in each of these phases, Wittgenstein emphasizes the primacy of context, but his conception of that context changes decisively in the course of his working out the implications of the language-game comparison. Tractarian logical atomism takes it for granted that every context is always governed by formal logic, and that logic, properly expressed, is self-explanatory: 'Logic must take care of itself.'[20] In the 'logical holist' work from the early 1930s, Wittgenstein frequently compares particular parts of our language with a calculus, a formal system governed by clearly defined rules, and the context in question is usually a matter of publicly verifiable behaviour. Language takes the place of logic: 'Language must speak for itself.'[21] In the later 'practical holist' work, Wittgenstein stresses the open-ended and interconnected character of language, and the context in question is much broader, including the whole range of human life and the various settings in which it takes place. Even formal rules depend on a practical background for their sense: 'rules leave loop-holes open, and the practice has to speak for itself'.[22]

The principal discontinuities separating the *Tractatus* and the subsequent phases of Wittgenstein's work have to do with his changing conception of the mind and meaning. The *Tractatus* has very little to say about the philosophy of mind, but in 1929, a dualism of a 'primary' mental world and a 'secondary' physical world took on a leading role in the further development of the main ideas he took from his previous work. If we look at the first post-*Tractatus* manuscripts, begun almost immediately after his return to Cambridge in January 1929, we find him developing a whole metaphysics of experience, barely hinted at in the *Tractatus*. It was based on a fundamental distinction between two realms, the 'primary' and the 'secondary'. The primary

---

[19] See 6.1 and Stern 1995, 4.4.　　[20] *Notebooks 1914–1916*, 2; *Tractatus*, 5.473.
[21] *Philosophical Grammar*, §2 and §27.
[22] *On Certainty*, §139. For further discussion of theoretical and practical holism, see chapter 6.

is the world of my present experience; the secondary is everything else: not only the 'external world', but also other minds, and most of my mental life. He repeatedly made use of a cinematic analogy, comparing the primary, 'inner' world to the picture one sees in the cinema, the secondary, 'outer' world to the pictures on the film passing through the projector. But by October of that year, he decisively rejected this whole approach. He came to see that the primary and secondary were not two different worlds, but rather two different ways of talking, and he thought of philosophy as a matter of clarifying those uses of language.

The anti-behaviourist views that are voiced by the interlocutory voice in the *Philosophical Investigations*, and especially the view that there must be intrinsically meaningful mental processes that give life to our use of language, have a great deal in common with the views voiced in Wittgenstein's writings from 1929. The behaviourist responses voiced by the narrator of the *Philosophical Investigations*, and especially the idea that mental processes only have the meaning that they do within a particular context, are first drafted in writings from the first half of the 1930s, writings that are often a direct response to the anti-behaviourist views one finds in Wittgenstein's 1929 manuscripts. However, this book attends to the dialogue between them as it takes place in the *Philosophical Investigations*. Although these voices first emerge within Wittgenstein's inner dialogue in his notebooks, they take on a life of their own in the published book, a life that calls for our response to those words.

The next two chapters may seem, at first sight, to move rather slowly: chapter 2 is about the prefaces to the *Tractatus* and the *Philosophical Investigations*, and chapter 3 is devoted to the motto to the *Philosophical Investigations*. However, because the preface and the motto amount to some of Wittgenstein's best guidance as to how to read the book, they are worth reading carefully. In the course of discussing how to read the *Philosophical Investigations*, chapters 2 and 3 also consider the question of the relationship between the *Tractatus* and the *Philosophical Investigations*, and some of the principal approaches to be found in the secondary literature. In presenting my approach to interpreting Wittgenstein, I also review the principal approaches to Wittgenstein interpretation.

CHAPTER 2

From the Tractatus *to the* Investigations: *two prefaces*

2.1 SEEING THE *INVESTIGATIONS* 'IN THE RIGHT LIGHT'

In the preface to the *Philosophical Investigations*, Wittgenstein wrote the following about the relationship between that book and his previous work:

> Four years ago I had occasion to re-read my first book (the *Tractatus Logico-Philosophicus*) and to explain its ideas to someone. It suddenly seemed to me that I should publish those old thoughts and the new ones together: that the latter could be seen in the right light only by contrast with and against the background of my old way of thinking. (PI, viii/x)

This raises a question that confronts every reader of the *Philosophical Investigations*: what was Wittgenstein's 'old way of thinking', and what is the relationship between his 'old thoughts' and the 'new ones'? Unfortunately, while there are a number of short and simple answers to be found in philosophical encyclopedias, none of them is satisfactory. The conventional wisdom is that there were 'two Wittgensteins', the 'early Wittgenstein' who wrote a logico-philosophical treatise, and the diametrically opposed 'later Wittgenstein', the author of the *Philosophical Investigations*. At first sight, the two books look very different, and the preface to the *Philosophical Investigations* speaks of Wittgenstein's recognition of 'grave mistakes in what I wrote in that first book' (PI, viii/x).

The *Tractatus* is forbiddingly formal and presupposes knowledge of Frege's and Russell's work on modern logic. Because every proposition in the book is numbered, and the book is so short, it looks like an analytical table of contents for a much longer book. Wittgenstein once said, 'Every sentence in the *Tractatus* should be seen as the heading of a chapter, needing further exposition.'[1] The seven most important statements are numbered 1 to 7; decimal numbers are used to indicate the structure of the supporting paragraphs.

While the *Philosophical Investigations* is written in a much more informal and accessible way than the *Tractatus*, and makes almost no use of technical terminology, it can often be difficult to see why Wittgenstein says what he does. Although Wittgenstein worked on the *Philosophical Investigations* from 1930 to 1948, and came close to publishing Part 1 on a number of occasions, it was only published after he died. The 'remarks' which make up Part 1 – passages that can be as short as a sentence and as long as a couple of pages – are numbered from 1 to 693; Part II is made up of pieces of text from one to thirty pages long, numbered from i to xiv.

Most interpreters start with the passages they find most interesting in each book, and use them to construct a pair of congenial theories. While the content of the theories varies greatly, one of them is usually very close to the interpreter's own views, while the other provides a convenient target for criticism. Consequently, interpretations of the *Tractatus* and *Philosophical Investigations* often tell us more about the interpreter than about Wittgenstein. However, it is also true that Wittgenstein invited such one-sided readings, thinking of them as a necessary first step towards self-understanding. In 1931, he wrote: 'I must be nothing more than the mirror in which my reader sees his own thinking with all its deformities & with this assistance can set it in order.'[2] Much of the *Philosophical Investigations* consists of fragmentary dialogues, dialogues that readers inevitably first make sense of in terms of their previous philosophical preoccupations; the book pulls us in by both speaking to our concerns and unsettling them. Because of this close relationship between the way Wittgenstein wrote and the way his readers have been stimulated to thoughts of their own, this chapter's reading of the prefaces to the *Tractatus* and *Philosophical Investigations* is also an introduction to some of the main approaches to Wittgenstein interpretation.

[1] Drury 1984, 159–60.
[2] Wittgenstein, *Culture and Value*, 1980a, 18; 1998, 25. This echoes an aphorism of Lichtenberg's, one of Wittgenstein's favourite authors: 'A book is a mirror: if an ape looks into it an apostle is unlikely to look out.' Lichtenberg 2000, F17, 81; cf. E49, 71.

The preface to the *Philosophical Investigations* informs the reader that it is not a conventional book, proceeding 'from one subject to another in a natural order and without breaks', but an 'album', made up of remarks:

—— And this was, of course, connected with the very nature of the investigation. For this compels us to travel over a wide field of thought criss-cross in every direction. —— The philosophical remarks in this book are, as it were, a number of sketches of landscapes which were made in the course of these long and involved journeyings.

The same or almost the same points were always being approached afresh from different directions, and new sketches made. Very many of these were badly drawn or uncharacteristic, marked by all the defects of a weak draughtsman. And when they were rejected a number of tolerable ones were left, which now had to be arranged and sometimes cut down, so that if you looked at them you could get a picture of the landscape. Thus this book is really only an album. (PI, vii/ix)

Consequently, most commentators have approached the *Investigations* as a book in need of an analytical table of contents.

Perhaps because of these contrasts, the idea that the 'right light' in which to read the *Investigations* is one that highlights the contrast with the *Tractatus* is usually taken for granted. The *Tractatus* is usually read as a metaphysical theory about the nature of mind, world, and language, on which language and mind mirror the world. 'One Wittgenstein' interpreters, on the other hand, maintain that the 'background of my old way of thinking' is much more important than the contrast between old and new, and that the similarities between the *Tractatus* and *Investigations* are more significant than the differences. Earlier exponents such as Feyerabend and Kenny argued that Wittgenstein never gave up many of the *Tractatus'* metaphysical doctrines; more recently, Cora Diamond has advocated a reading of both *Tractatus* and *Philosophical Investigations* on which he was always opposed to any kind of philosophical theory.[3]

The preface to the *Tractatus* informs the reader that it contains 'on all essential points, the final solution of the problems' of philosophy.[4] This is the philosophical promise that animates the book: the definitive solution to philosophy's problems. However, that preface

<hr />

[3] Feyerabend 1955; Kenny 1973. Diamond 1991a, 1991b, 1997.
[4] Wittgenstein 1961b, 4.

also says that those problems arise out of a misunderstanding of the logic of our language. The whole sense of the book, Wittgenstein says, could be summed up as follows: 'What can be said at all can be said clearly; and whereof one cannot speak thereof one must be silent.' Accordingly, the aim of the book is to 'draw a limit to thinking', or more carefully put, to draw a limit 'to the expression of thoughts'. For talk of drawing a limit to thought suggests we can think both sides of the limit, which is just what Wittgenstein denies. 'The limit can, therefore, only be drawn in language and what lies on the other side of the limit will be simply nonsense.' This is the complementary anti-philosophical aim: the 'definitive solution' is to take the form of drawing a boundary to language and philosophy.

The closing remarks of the *Tractatus* develop these themes in the following words:

> The right method of philosophy would be this. To say nothing except what can be said, i.e. the propositions of natural science, i.e. something that has nothing to do with philosophy: and then always, when someone else wished to say something metaphysical, to demonstrate to him that he had given no meaning to certain signs in his propositions. This method would be unsatisfying to the other – he would not have the feeling that we were teaching him philosophy – but it would be the only strictly correct method.
>
> My propositions are elucidatory in this way: he who understands me finally recognizes them as nonsense, when he has climbed out through them, on them, over them. (He must so to speak throw away the ladder, after he has climbed up on it.)
>
> He must get over these propositions; then he sees the world rightly.
>
> Whereof one cannot speak, thereof one must be silent. (*Tractatus* 6.53–7)[5]

How are we to make sense of a book that ends by saying it is nonsense, a ladder that must be climbed and then discarded? On the one hand, the 'framing' passages, which begin and end the book, are quite insistent that all philosophical doctrines must be discarded.

---

[5] There are two departures from the Ogden translation here: 'nonsense' replaces Ogden's mistaken translation of *unsinnig* as 'senseless', and I have replaced his archaic 'surmount' by the more colloquial 'get over'. Ogden's use of 'proposition' for the German *Satz* is also a problem, but less easily fixed, and so I have left it unaltered. The problem is that the German word can mean not only 'proposition' – the content expressed by a meaningful statement – but also a sentence, perhaps one with no meaning at all. However, English has no one word with the same range of meanings. So while Ogden's first use of 'proposition' is unproblematic, it is potentially misleading to talk about the metaphysician's 'propositions'.

On the other hand, the rest of the book appears to be advocating any number of distinctive and debatable philosophical doctrines. Because the book – or the part of the book that the frame surrounds – does appear to be full of arguments for philosophical doctrines, few readers have taken the book's opening and closing instructions at face value. For the remainder of the book seems to set out a sophisticated philosophical system of a quite traditional kind, whose principal innovation is that it is based on Fregean, not Aristotelian, logic. It presents us with a world composed of facts, each of which is made up of objects, a logically structured world that is mirrored in a language composed of propositions, each of which is made up of names.

If we turn to the *Philosophical Investigations*, we face an analogous problem in understanding its methods. Like the *Tractatus*, it maintains that philosophy can only be a matter of clearing up misconceptions; philosophy, as Wittgenstein conceives of it, should say nothing more than what everyone would agree to. Yet the *Philosophical Investigations'* critique of philosophical errors has inspired many of its readers to formulate positive philosophical theories, and to attribute those theories to Wittgenstein.

There are some striking parallels between this disagreement over Wittgenstein's methods and conception of philosophy and nineteenth-century debates among Hegel's followers, parallels which cast some light on the character of the dispute. Like the later Wittgenstein, Hegel was an opponent of foundationalism, a philosopher who aimed to bring philosophy's transcendental aspirations back to earth by reminding us of the ways in which our concepts belong within a social and practical setting. Bernard Williams summarizes these parallels between the later Wittgenstein and Hegel as follows:

> It is mistaken, on this picture, to try to ground our practices, whether ethical or cognitive; we must rather recognize that our way of going on is simply our way of going on, and that we must live within it, rather than try to justify it. This philosophy, in its rejection of the 'abstract', may itself remind us of a kind of Hegelianism, though without, of course, Hegel's systematic pretensions or his historical teleology.[6]

The principal disagreements among Hegel's followers concerned the political implications of his practical turn. Right-wing Hegelians

---

[6] Williams 1992, 38.

wanted far-reaching limits on the opportunities for political criticism of the established order, and often had a conservative attachment to monarchy and authoritarian rule. Left-wing Hegelians wanted a society that would embody what was best in both established traditions and a radical critique of those traditions, and were much more ready to support revolutionary change. Each side saw their political agenda as underwritten by Hegel's communitarian turn: conservatives were attracted to the idea of society as an organic whole that could only be changed piecemeal, while radicals saw that the tools Hegel had provided could be turned towards a far-reaching critique of the inequities of the modern world.

While there have been comparable disagreements over the implications of Wittgenstein's philosophy for political theory and practice, this has not, so far, been a central issue for Wittgenstein's interpreters.[7] The principal fault line separating Wittgensteinians is over a question of philosophical method: whether or not radical philosophical change – putting an end to philosophy – is possible. Robert Fogelin draws a helpful distinction between 'Pyrrhonian' readings of the *Investigations*, which see the book as informed by a quite general scepticism about philosophy and so as aiming at bringing philosophy to an end, and 'non-Pyrrhonian' readings, which construe the book as a critique of certain traditional theories in order to do philosophy better.[8] For Pyrrhonian scepticism, at least as it is represented in the writings of Sextus Empiricus, clearly prefigures this aspect of the *Philosophical Investigations* in its marshalling of reasons for doubting that any philosophical doctrine is coherent, let alone defensible. Fogelin reads Wittgenstein's later writings as a constant battle between two Wittgensteins: one is the non-Pyrrhonian philosopher

---

[7] One reason for this state of affairs is that Wittgenstein's own conception of philosophy did not leave any room for a distinctively political dimension. For philosophy, as he conceived of it, had to do with matters on which we would all agree: the 'we' in Wittgenstein's talk of 'what we would say' is not an appeal to one particular group as opposed to others, but an 'us' that aims to include anyone with whom we could converse. It has too often been taken for granted by Wittgenstein's most dismissive critics, such as Ernest Gellner and Herbert Marcuse, that his philosophy depends on a commitment to a conservative world view, and that Wittgenstein's philosophy was a displaced form of right-wing politics masquerading as impartiality. For an exchange on the place of conservatism in Wittgenstein's philosophy, see Nyíri 1982 and Schulte 1983. There is a discussion of Wittgenstein's relationship to social science in Stern 2002 and 2003.

[8] Fogelin 1994, 205; see also 3–12 and 205–222, Fogelin 1987, ch. 15, and Sluga 2004.

whose reply to the interlocutor's foundationalist intuitions is a non-foundationalist theory of justification; the other is the Pyrrhonian anti-philosopher who is equally dismissive of both foundationalism and anti-foundationalism.

According to leading non-Pyrrhonian interpreters (e.g. Hacker, early Baker, Pears, Hintikka and Hintikka, von Savigny), Wittgenstein replaces mistaken views with a quite specific positive philosophical position of his own. On this reading, Wittgenstein offers us a form of post-Kantian philosophy, one which turns on the logic of our ordinary language, rather than the logic of mind: a logico-linguistic critique of past philosophy that makes a new philosophy within the limits of language possible. The result of his critique of previous philosophical views about the nature and limits and language is supposed to be a 'clear view', an *Übersicht* of the grammar of our ordinary language. Just how the *Philosophical Investigations* provides a clear view of grammar, criteria, and language, is controversial. But the point is usually taken to be that we can give a definite refutation of traditional forms of epistemological scepticism: challenges to our knowledge of the external world or of other minds are shown to be wrong (say, because criteria, and the internal relations they constitute, are supposed to prove that the matter in question is known to be true).

Pyrrhonian Wittgensteinians (e.g. Diamond, Conant, later Baker) see Wittgenstein's contribution as therapeutic, a critique of all philosophy, including his own. According to these interpreters, Wittgenstein aims to get us to give up all philosophical views, not to provide a better philosophy. On this reading, Wittgenstein offers us a form of scepticism that is aimed not at our everyday life, but at philosophy itself, with the aim of putting an end to philosophy and teaching us to get by without a replacement.

To sum up: Pyrrhonian Wittgensteinians read Wittgenstein as putting an end to philosophy, while non-Pyrrhonian Wittgensteinians read him as ending traditional philosophy in order to do philosophy better. This controversy is, in turn, closely connected with the question of what Wittgenstein means by saying that past philosophy is nonsense. On a non-Pyrrhonian reading, Wittgenstein has a theory of sense (as based on criteria, grammar, or forms of life, say) and this is then used to show that what philosophers say doesn't accord with the theory. On a Pyrrhonian reading, there is no such theory of sense to be found in his writing, and to say that philosophy is nonsense is just to say that it falls apart when we try to make sense of it.

Another way of putting this distinction is to say that Pyrrhonian Wittgensteinians believe philosophy, properly conducted, should not result in any kind of theory, while non-Pyrrhonian Wittgensteinians maintain that Wittgenstein's criticism of traditional philosophy leads us to a better philosophical theory, albeit not the kinds of theorizing we find in the philosophical tradition. While Wittgensteinians rarely draw overtly political dividing lines, the parallels with the talk of left and right Hegelians, and the contrast between revolutionary and traditional factions, are apt.[9] Just as there were substantial disagreements among monarchists about what form the Restoration should take, so there are substantial differences among non-Pyrrhonian Wittgensteinians. Whether the positive view they extract is a scientific theory of some kind, or a theory of 'linguistic facts', forms of life, grammatical rules, or criteria, to mention some of the leading candidates, is not unimportant, but they all agree in reading Wittgenstein as teaching us how to be better philosophers. Pyrrhonian Wittgensteinians, on the other hand, opponents of the tradition, maintain that Wittgenstein's criticism of traditional philosophy leads us to stop philosophizing.

What makes the contrast less clear than it seems at first is that most Wittgensteinians oscillate, or vacillate, between these views. Although they would never admit it, they want both to be uncompromisingly opposed to philosophical doctrine, and still to make some sense of the non-Pyrrhonian view that giving up traditional philosophical theories can lead us to something better. Card-carrying Pyrrhonians are like the Jacobins, permanent revolutionaries opposed to any stable regime. Centrist Wittgensteinians are like the Girondins, those opponents of the old regime who wanted to put a firm constitutional system in its place.

There is some truth in all these approaches, but each of them gives us a Wittgenstein who was much more single-minded and doctrinaire than the books he actually wrote. What is really interesting about both the *Tractatus* and the *Philosophical Investigations* is neither a

---

[9] Goldfarb has compared resolute and irresolute readings of the *Tractatus* to various factions in the period of the French Revolution; the analogy can be extended to the present issue. See Goldfarb 2000.

metaphysical system nor a supposedly definitive answer to system-building, but the unresolved tension between two forces: one aims at a definitive answer to the problems of philosophy, the other aims at doing away with them altogether. While they are not diametrically opposed to one another, there is a great tension between them, and most readers have tried to resolve this tension by arguing, not only that one of them is the clear victor, but also that this is what the author intended.[10] In the case of the *Tractatus*, this tension is clearest in the foreword and conclusion, where the author explicitly addresses the issue; in the *Investigations*, it is at work throughout the book.

The split between non-Pyrrhonian and Pyrrhonian Wittgensteinians, between those who read him as 'doing philosophy' and those who see him as 'stopping doing philosophy', arises out of an unresolved tension in Wittgenstein's writing, a tension that helps to explain why each side finds ample support in his writing, yet neither side is able to make sense of the whole. Part of the problem is that both sides understand themselves in terms of a conception of philosophy that is itself in question in his writing. Rather than trying to enlist the author of the *Investigations* as a systematic philosopher or an impatient anti-philosopher, we will do better to see him as helping us understand that conflict – as a patient anti-philosopher who sees the need to work through the attractions of systematic philosophy.

Both sides of the debate over Wittgenstein's views about the nature of philosophy have been overly dogmatic. They have misread a book that has a profoundly dialogical character, mistaking voices in the dialogue for the voice of the author. But neither side does justice to the way in which these apparently incompatible aspects are intertwined. The standard approaches are best seen as partial insights, accounts that focus on different aspects of Wittgenstein's writing but lose sight of its character as a whole. Here I have in mind not just the way in which different philosophical positions and arguments are sketched without any definitive resolution, but also the ease with which Wittgenstein's stories and arguments can be interpreted in utterly incompatible ways.

---

[10] Here I am indebted to the wording of the conclusion of David Pears' *Wittgenstein*: 'Each of the two forces without the other would have produced results of much less interest . . . But together they produced something truly great' (Pears 1986, 197–8). But Pears, a leading exponent of the 'two Wittgensteins' interpretation, and the author of one of the canonical metaphysical readings of the *Tractatus*, only attributes this to the later philosophy.

However, this is not to dismiss the previous positions in the interpretive debate, which can best be seen as attempts to turn particular voices in the dialogue into the voice of the author.

While many writers on the *Philosophical Investigations* acknowledge its anti-doctrinal character, they nearly always go on to write about the book as though it were a traditional philosophical text that happens to be written rather oddly. Wittgenstein's ambivalent relationship to philosophy led him to write in many voices, undermining the traditional demand that the author be consistent. His narrator's debates with an interlocutory voice and the many unanswered questions are not an incidental stylistic matter, but a direct response to the distinctive character of the problems that preoccupied him. The *Philosophical Investigations* is a book that was written with an eye to being read out loud, and that calls for the reader to try out different ideas about what is going on in the text, ideally by discussing it with a group of other readers. Frequently, people first become acquainted with the book by reading it with others in a class, seminar, or reading group, in which everyone can learn from the different perspectives that other readers bring to the text. But this process of collaborative reading and re-reading, attending closely to each detail, is hardly ever explicitly discussed in the existing introductions, which are usually about the interpreter's results, not the process of reading the book. Because different readers will find very different things in the *Philosophical Investigations*, a group of readers will almost certainly explore a range of readings that any one person would be most unlikely to consider. Consequently, this book aims to provide an orientation for those beginning, or continuing, such a reading of the *Philosophical Investigations*.

The *Philosophical Investigations* contains an extraordinary number of questions, and few of them are easy to answer. Kenny counts 784 questions in the *Philosophical Investigations*, and only 110 answers, and by his count '70 of the answers are meant to be wrong' (1973, 20). It is always worthwhile to stop and think about Wittgenstein's questions; you may want to keep track of your answers, both before and after discussing them with others.

A further reason that the *Philosophical Investigations* lends itself to this kind of reading is the way that, like the best Socratic dialogue, it has the feeling of a serious but informal philosophical discussion, rather than the systematic exposition one expects from a conventional philosophical publication. The book is made up of an exchange between different voices, and the point is to work through the conflict, to come to a conclusion as a result of working out that argument. However, unlike a conventional philosophical dialogue, speakers are not usually explicitly identified; who is speaking, and why, are questions one always needs to bear in mind.

This book approaches the argument of the *Philosophical Investigations* as a whole, but concentrates on giving a close reading of key passages, one that brings out alternative readings and their connection with other parts of the text. This should not only help the reader make sense of those passages, but will also provide the tools needed to read Wittgenstein for oneself. While further information can be valuable, extensive background knowledge is not a precondition for the book's bringing 'light into one brain or another' (PI, viii/x). For Wittgenstein did not want his writing 'to spare other people the trouble of thinking. But, if possible, to stimulate someone to thoughts of his own' (PI, viii/x). The *Philosophical Investigations* is a book that calls for the reader's active engagement in thinking through the ideas it throws up, and is not the sort of treatise that lends itself to being read as a set of doctrines, arguments, or results.

One aim of this book is to free beginning readers of the *Philosophical Investigations* from the misunderstanding that it presupposes a great deal of arcane knowledge, and that the point of reading the *Philosophical Investigations* – or an introduction to it – is to choose between competing scholastic summaries of what Wittgenstein supposedly had to say. I propose we approach the *Philosophical Investigations* as a dialogue between different philosophical voices, rather than as an oddly written but otherwise conventional piece of philosophy. The first step that most readers take in turning the book into an exposition of a positive philosophical doctrine is to allocate each line of dialogue to one of two characters: 'Wittgenstein' and 'the interlocutor'. 'The interlocutor' defends a variety of familiar philosophical doctrines, such as a foundationalist theory of justification, or Cartesian views about privacy, which 'Wittgenstein' criticizes, replacing them with anti-foundationalist doctrines, such as a coherentist, holistic theory of justification, or the primacy of ordinary language and publicly accepted criteria. One way of summarizing this reading of the

Philosophical Investigations is to say that Wittgenstein raises sceptical doubts about certain traditional philosophical doctrines, substituting a new doctrine or an anti-foundationalist way of doing philosophy. But there are many voices at work, and many disagreements between them, disagreements that cannot be neatly allocated to two diametrically opposed doctrines. Indeed, this anti-foundationalist reading fails to do justice to one of the most important strands in the discussions, namely a scepticism *about* philosophy, the use of philosophical argument against philosophy altogether. One of these dialogues, particularly prominent in §§48–140, is a dialogue with the *Tractatus*. It is often taken for granted that Wittgenstein of the *Philosophical Investigations* treats the *Tractatus* as a prime example, or source, of the views he is now attacking. However, the tension between Pyrrhonian and non-Pyrrhonian approaches to philosophy is also at work in the *Tractatus*; in order to appreciate the relationship between the *Tractatus* and the *Philosophical Investigations*, we need to first consider the sources of these issues in the *Tractatus*.

2.2 PYRRHONISM IN THE *TRACTATUS*

From the 1930s to the 1950s, the *Tractatus* was usually seen as contributing to the Vienna Circle's verificationist and anti-metaphysical programme. The logical positivists found inspiration in the central role the book gave to the distinction between sense and nonsense, its reliance on modern logic, and its dismissal of previous philosophy as cognitively empty. While the verification principle – the doctrine that the meaning of a statement is whatever would show that it is true (or false) – is never explicitly mentioned in the *Tractatus*, Wittgenstein did stress it in his discussions with members of the Vienna Circle, and in his writing from the early 1930s. The logical positivists took the *Tractatus'* insistence on clearly distinguishing meaningful from meaningless discourse both as a proof that traditional philosophy is nonsense and as providing the blueprint for the anti-metaphysical and thoroughly scientific world view of the Vienna Circle.

In the 1950s, interpreters rediscovered the logico-metaphysical aspects of the *Tractatus*. Their principal criticism of the positivists' reading of the *Tractatus* was that they had not taken that book's distinction between what we can say in words, and what we can only show, seriously enough. True enough, what the *Tractatus* allows us to *say* – strictly speaking, no more than matters of empirical fact – is in accord with the positivist reading. However, the *Tractatus* does not stop there. Even if none of what the traditional philosopher wants to say can be *said*, much of it can still be *shown*. The metaphysical reading adds a crucial qualification to the positivistic view that the *Tractatus* sets out the limits of language, of what can be said: on the metaphysical reading, the limits are drawn in order to show what cannot be said. On this reading, there are certain insights expressed in his words that cannot be directly stated, and the attempt to do so inevitably leads to nonsense. Nevertheless, these insights can be expressed indirectly; the nonsense does succeed in showing what cannot be said.[11]

A letter Wittgenstein wrote to Russell in 1919, replying to Russell's first questions about the book, provides strong prima facie support for this criticism.

Now I'm afraid you haven't really got hold of my main contention, to which the whole business of logical propositions is only a corollary. The main point is the theory of what can be said by propositions – i.e. by language – (and, which comes to the same, what can be *thought*) and what can not be expressed by propositions, but only shown; which, I believe, is the cardinal problem of philosophy.[12]

Thus, the distinction between showing and saying became the key to understanding the book. It permits the interpreter to argue that while all sorts of doctrines are not actually put forward in the text, they are nevertheless shown. Thus, everything that is explicitly excluded can be let in the back door, as implicitly shown. This creates a great deal of leeway for the interpreter: the question of just what the *Tractatus* shows has led to enormous disagreement. As the *Tractatus* says so little about the nature of facts and objects, for instance, and Wittgenstein himself entertained a variety of different views, it is hardly surprising that able interpreters were able to find arguments for almost any ontology there.

[11] Two classic expositions of the 'two Wittgensteins' reading are Hacker (1986) and Pears (1986, 1987, 1988). Anscombe 1959, the first introductory book on the *Tractatus*, also provided an influential introduction to the metaphysical reading. Black 1964, the only line-by-line commentary on the *Tractatus*, is also part of this tradition. Most of the early debate over the metaphysical reading was in dense and closely argued journal articles; many of the best are collected in Copi and Beard 1966.

[12] Wittgenstein, *Cambridge Letters*, 124; translation slightly modified.

After the publication of the *Philosophical Investigations* in 1953, the *Tractatus* was also sifted for evidence of the views that Wittgenstein must have been refuting in his later work. If the later Wittgenstein objected in the *Investigations* to certain views, such as the theory that a name has meaning because it stands for an object, and the *Tractatus* and *Investigations* were diametrically opposed, then it seemed obvious that those theories should be attributed to the *Tractatus*.

Initially, the publication of three pre-*Tractatus* notebooks, which Wittgenstein had written while he was a soldier in the First World War, provided grist for this mill. But the extended discussion of ethical and religious themes in the last notebook, the basis for some brief but far-reaching remarks towards the end of the *Tractatus*, helped to redirect readers' attention to the question of their place in what had seemed to be an austere and analytical text. Paul Engelmann, an old friend of Wittgenstein's, argued that the book's purpose was really ethical. His case gained strong support from a letter Wittgenstein had written to an editor who he wanted to publish the *Tractatus*:

The book's point is an ethical one. I once meant to include in the preface a sentence which is not in fact there now but which I will write out for you here, because it will perhaps be a key to the work for you. What I meant to write, then, was this: My work consists of two parts: the one presented here plus all that I have *not* written. And it is precisely this second part that is the important one. My book draws limits to the sphere of the ethical from the inside as it were, and I am convinced that this is the ONLY *rigorous* way of drawing these limits. In short, I believe that where *many* others today are just *babbling*, I have managed in my book to put everything firmly in place by being silent about it. And for that reason, unless I am very much mistaken, the book will say a great deal that you yourself want to say. Only perhaps you won't see that it is said in the book. For now, I would recommend to you to read the *preface* and the *conclusion*, because they contain the most direct expression of the point of the book.[13]

This led to a new style of *Tractatus* interpretation, on which the book's argument was subordinated to an ethico-religious vision. Like the metaphysical interpretations, such readings still looked for a

---

[13] Engelmann 1967, 143–4; translation slightly modified. For further discussion of the relationship between Wittgenstein's life and philosophy, see McGuinness 1988, Conant 1989a, Monk 1990, and the papers in Klagge 2001.

hidden doctrine that cannot be stated but is implicitly present. But they shifted the interpretive focus from explaining how certain ontological and semantical doctrines are *shown* (*zeigen*) by the logic of our language, to the questions of how religious, ethical, or mystical insights *show themselves* (*sich zeigen*). Given that the book says even less about ethics, God, and the mystical than it does about the nature of objects, it is hardly surprising that these interpreters arrived at extremely diverse conclusions. While it had little effect on the broad consensus among analytic philosophers that the book was a metaphysical treatise, it did make Wittgenstein's writing attractive to a readership with little interest in logical analysis.

Recently, Cora Diamond, Peter Winch, James Conant, and others have challenged readings of the *Tractatus* that find a philosophical theory there, proposing that we take Wittgenstein at his word when he says that philosophy is nonsense.[14] Diamond takes Wittgenstein's 'insistence that he is not putting forward philosophical doctrines or theses'[15] as her point of departure, stressing the idea that the very notion of a thesis or a doctrine in philosophy is Wittgenstein's principal target in both the *Tractatus* and the *Investigations*. On this reading, Wittgenstein only sets out philosophical views and arguments in order to expose their incoherence. The passages that appear to set out the positivist, metaphysical, ethical, and religious views that most readers have taken to be Wittgenstein's message are there to draw us in, by setting out views that appear attractive, but prove in the end nothing more than cloud-castles, or nonsense. The real message of the *Tractatus* and *Investigations* is that *all* philosophy, including the philosophy ostensibly presented and endorsed within the *Tractatus* itself, is simply nonsense.

On this 'therapeutic' reading, Wittgenstein never believed philosophy could arrive at any kind of a positive doctrine. Consequently, Diamond maintains we must take the 'frame' of the *Tractatus* as our guide to the book. To say that the book really is nonsense, but then read it as advocating any doctrine, explicit or implicit, is to lack the courage of one's convictions. Diamond aptly observes that this problem is 'particularly acute' in *Tractatus* 6.54:

---

[14] Diamond 1991a, 1991b; Winch 1987, 1992; Crary and Read 2000; Conant 2002.
[15] Diamond 1991a, 179.

Let me illustrate the problem this way. One thing which according to the *Tractatus* shows itself but cannot be expressed in language is what Wittgenstein speaks of as *the logical form of reality* . . . What exactly is supposed to be left of that, after we have thrown away the ladder? Are we going to keep the idea that there is something or other in reality that we gesture at, however badly, when we speak of 'the logical form of reality', so that *it, what* we were gesturing at, is there but cannot be expressed in words? *That* is what I want to call chickening out. What counts as not chickening out is then this, roughly: to throw the ladder away is, among other things, to throw away in the end the attempt to take seriously the language of 'features of reality' . . . the notion of something true of reality but not sayably true is to be used only with the awareness that it itself belongs to what has to be thrown away.[16]

Diamond charges that other interpreters have been weak and indecisive, 'chicken', unable to choose between one approach and the other, and advocates consistently following the approach outlined in the *Tractatus*' frame. Warren Goldfarb has suggested that 'irresolute' might be a better expression than 'chickening out'.[17] Like Diamond's expression, it captures the idea that the standard reading involves a certain kind of weakness — one wants to do justice to Wittgenstein's claim that philosophy is nonsense, but also make sense of the content of the *Tractatus*. Talk of being 'irresolute' is less tendentious, and there is the convenient contrast with a 'resolute' reading. According to Goldfarb, Diamond has endorsed this turn of phrase, noting that it captures the 'failure-of-courage element' prominent in her epithet, while also emphasizing 'a kind of dithering, which reflects not being clear what one really wants, a desire to make inconsistent demands'.[18]

This use of morally charged epithets makes the right philosophical position sound like a matter of being tougher than the other kids on the playground, or having a stiff upper lip. In this respect, it is uncannily akin to the role played by 'resoluteness' in Heidegger's early philosophy. In *Being and Time*, Heidegger promotes resoluteness, the decisive taking of a stand, as the touchstone for an authentic life and the only way of getting beyond the meaningless alternatives offered by conventional conformity.[19] Heidegger, confronted by the

---

[16] Diamond 1991a, 181–2.   [17] Goldfarb 1997, 64.   [18] Goldfarb 1997, 98.
[19] Heidegger 1962, §60, 343ff.

seeming impossibility of giving a rational justification of the right way to live, embraces resoluteness; Diamond and Goldfarb, facing an analogous nihilism about philosophy, likewise make a virtue of necessity and encourage us to have the courage of their Wittgenstein's anti-philosophical convictions.

But what is the status of the notion of 'nonsense' in Diamond's reading of the *Tractatus*, a reading that turns on a great deal of painstaking and serious discussion of the view of nonsense she finds in Frege and the *Tractatus*? That very fact makes it clear that she takes climbing the Tractarian ladder almost as seriously as throwing it away. Like the logical positivists, she may, in the end, be committed to certain philosophical views about sense and nonsense. On this reading, 'nonsense' is not just an expression used to emphatically dismiss a view, but also part of a theory of meaning. If so, Diamond's Wittgenstein rejects certain metaphysical doctrines, but is left with a minimal semantic theory. We throw away some Tractarian doctrines (simples, realism) but keep others in order to do so (logical form, elucidation). These doctrines would then provide the basis for a Tractarian theory of philosophy as nonsense.

On the other hand, if Diamond is to be consistently resolute, she must be no more attached to the 'framing' Tractarian views about meaning and nonsense than the ontology and theology that other readers have found in the 'body' of the text. In that case, Diamond must regard the Tractarian theory of nonsense as just one more rung on a ladder that must be discarded, a further use of philosophical argument in order to do away with philosophical argument. In 'Ethics, Imagination, and the Method of Wittgenstein's *Tractatus*' she clearly commits herself to this approach:

When I began to discuss Wittgenstein's remarks about ethics, I called them remarks about ethics, because the idea that there is no such thing as what they present themselves as, the idea that we are taken in by them in reading them as about ethics – that idea we cannot start with. So too the *Tractatus* itself. The reading it requires requires that it take us in at first, requires that it should allow itself to be read as sense, read as about logic and so on, despite not being so. What I have just said about the *Tractatus'* remarks 'about ethics' goes then equally for its remarks about logic.[20]

---

[20] Diamond 1991b, 79.

Certainly there is no suggestion here that Wittgenstein's views about sense and nonsense are any more privileged than what he has to say about ethics or logic.[21] Warren Goldfarb raises a closely related issue when he asks whether there isn't already some irresoluteness in Wittgenstein's use of 'nonsense' as a term of criticism, for it presupposes certain 'transitional' semantic views that are supposed to be discarded at the end of the *Tractatus*. His response is that 'nonsense' should not be understood as a general term of criticism, but as a kind of shorthand for the particular ways of seeing how philosophical language falls apart when it is given a resolute push: 'the general rubric is nothing but synoptic for what emerges in each case'.[22]

2.3 PYRRHONISM IN THE *PHILOSOPHICAL INVESTIGATIONS*

On Diamond's reading, the author of the *Tractatus* had given up all philosophical theories: every doctrine that appears to be endorsed in its numbered propositions is ultimately to be discarded. While this is what Wittgenstein says in the preface and towards the very end of the book, it is not so clear that he was able to carry out his aim in the text framed by those words. Adopting a resolutely anti-metaphysical outlook, or attributing it to the author of the *Tractatus* – two distinct moves that therapeutic readings often run together – does ensure a certain consistency. But at a high price: it guarantees that one will miss much of the tension between opposing views that makes this an inconsistent text. If previous readers made the mistake of too quickly dismissing the framing statements as mere rhetoric, Diamond may have made the opposite mistake: taking them too literally.

The framed text appears to state various metaphysical theses, but on this reading, once we see the point of the frame, what its author meant by it, we see that the framed text is nonsense. Consequently, she makes much of the distinction between what is *said* within the text of the *Tractatus* and what Wittgenstein, its author, *meant* by that text. That contrast is particularly clear near the end of the book, where

---

[21] Conant has defended the same strongly resolute view: 'the propositions of the entire work are to be thrown away as nonsense' (Conant 1989b, 274 n. 16).

[22] Goldfarb 1997, 71.

Wittgenstein does not say that one must understand the propositions of the *Tractatus*, but that one must understand *him*: 'he who understands me finally recognizes [my propositions] as nonsense'.[23] However, what Wittgenstein actually said about the *Tractatus*, both in his own later writings and when he discussed the book with others, is quite different.[24] Wittgenstein spoke of the book as having advanced arguments and views about the nature of language and world, not as trying to show that those arguments and views were nonsensical. Instead of explaining his aims in therapeutic terms, he always talked about doctrine: insisting on the importance of the show/say distinction, reaffirming certain views and modifying others, stressing the unrecognized inconsistency in the notion of elementary objects in his later discussions, and so forth. In particular, his philosophical writings from 1929–30 are the work of a philosopher modifying his earlier views.[25] This does not prove that Diamond's reading is entirely wrong, but it does force us to clearly separate her Wittgenstein, the author of the frame of the *Tractatus*, from much of what the person in question said and wrote.

Diamond reads the image of throwing away the ladder as the key to understanding the *Tractatus*, and uses it to attribute a consistently anti-philosophical method to Wittgenstein. If this were so, one would expect the later Wittgenstein might have retained that image, or at least spoken positively of it. However, in a draft for a foreword, written in November 1930, he described himself as out of sympathy with what he called the 'spirit of the main current of European and American civilization' and the values of the positivists, namely progress and constructive activity in science, industry, and architecture. Rather than aiming at progress, at trying to get somewhere else, Wittgenstein was trying to understand where he was already:

I might say: if the place I want to reach could only be climbed up to by a ladder, I would give up trying to get there. For the place to which I really have to go is one that I must actually be at already.

Anything that can be reached with a ladder does not interest me.

---

[23] *Tractatus* 6.54. See Diamond 1991a, 19; 1991b, 57; Conant 1989a, 344–6; 1991, 145; 1995, 270, 285–6. See n. 5 above for discussion of the translation of *Unsinn* as 'nonsense' here.

[24] See Stern 1995; Hacker 2000, §4.

[25] Stern 1995, ch. 5 and 6.1.

One movement orders one thought to the others in a series, the other keeps aiming at the same place.

One movement constructs & picks up one stone after another, the other keeps reaching for the same one.[26]

The *Tractatus* had been constructive, linking 'thoughts with another in a series', and this aspect of his work had attracted the Vienna Circle. If the author of the *Tractatus* had once thought of those constructions as a ladder-language that would free his reader from the desire to climb ladders, he showed no sign of it now. Instead, he associated the image of a ladder with just that aspect of his earlier work that he now repudiated. Seven years later, shortly after writing the first version of the *Investigations*, Wittgenstein again rejected the notion of climbing a ladder in very similar terms:

You cannot write more truly about yourself than you *are*. That is the difference between writing about yourself and writing about external things. You write about yourself from your own height. You don't stand on stilts or on a ladder but on your bare feet.[27]

Wittgenstein also described the *Tractatus* as 'dogmatic': it was written as though he were writing about external objects from a distance, and he had failed to see that to write philosophy is to write about oneself.[28] In his post-*Tractatus* work, he gave up the pursuit of a single over-arching solution to the problems of philosophy in favour of a pluralistic variety of methods. Instead of climbing a ladder in order to get a clear view of our predicament, he now thought the task of the philosopher was to describe where we currently stand, in a way that would make ladder-climbing unattractive. The later Wittgenstein's writings contain an extended critique of the idea that philosophy can provide us with an objective vantage point, a 'view from nowhere', or a privileged perspective that shows us the world as it really is. He tries to show the incoherence of the idea that philosophy can rise above our everyday life in order to provide an objective verdict on it.

[26] Wittgenstein, *Culture and Value*, 1980a, 7; 1998, 10. (Variant wording, and Wittgenstein's wavy underlining, indicating his doubts about the choice of certain words, have been omitted.)

[27] Wittgenstein, *Culture and Value*, 1980a, 33; 1998, 38.

[28] For further discussion of Wittgenstein's critique of his earlier dogmatism, see Stern 1995, 101–4.

But he no longer thinks he has a final solution to the problems of philosophy.

On the standard metaphysical interpretations of the *Tractatus'* skeletal arguments, they lead up to some such Archimedian standpoint: wherever we end up after climbing the ladder, it is not where we started. The therapeutic reading cuts through the Gordian knot of choosing between the metaphysical readings of the book by construing the *Tractatus* as a self-deconstructing anti-philosophy. But this flies in the face of Wittgenstein's own insistence that he was arguing for specific philosophical doctrines in the *Tractatus*, and his commitment to views about logic, language, and the foundations of mathematics that he had developed on the basis of his reading of Frege and Russell. Recoiling from the dogmatic extremes of most previous *Tractatus* interpretation, Diamond ends up with an equally extreme reading, one that fails to do justice to the very irresoluteness about the possibility of traditional philosophy that is one of the strongest characteristics of Wittgenstein's writing, both early and late. Richard Rorty sees the issue as a stark choice between a systematic reading of Wittgenstein, on which he 'proposed one more dubious philosophical theory', and construing Wittgenstein as a satirical therapist, who 'was not "doing philosophy" at all'.[29] On his preferred reading, Wittgenstein only makes use of traditional distinctions in order to undermine and subvert them: 'When Wittgenstein is at his best, he resolutely avoids such constructive criticism and sticks to pure satire. He just shows, by examples, how hopeless the traditional problems are.'[30] Nevertheless, Rorty reluctantly acknowledges that Wittgenstein's radical rejection of traditional philosophical problems is only part of the story.

Unlike Rorty, Wittgenstein had a strong sense of the power and attractiveness of those problems, and insisted that one can only find one's way out of philosophical error by carefully retracing the steps that led one in. Wittgenstein saw himself not as cutting through the knots created by philosophers' arguments, but as painstakingly undoing them. In the final, post-war, version of a passage first drafted in 1930, this is captured in the following exchange:

---

[29] Rorty 1982, 22.   [30] Rorty 1982, 34.

How does it come about that philosophy is so complicated a structure? It surely ought to be completely simple, if it is the ultimate thing, independent of all experience, that you make it out to be. – Philosophy unties knots in our thinking; hence its result must be simple, but philosophising has to be as complicated as the knots it unties.[31]

Consequently, 'satire' and 'dubious philosophical theory', Pyrrhonian and non-Pyrrhonian philosophizing, are intertwined in Wittgenstein's post-*Tractatus* writing. On Diamond's therapeutic reading, the philosophical knots in the text are only there to be untangled. In that case, the voice that asks the question is Wittgenstein's 'interlocutor', the standard name for the un-Wittgensteinian 'fall guy', and the final sentence states Wittgenstein's own considered view. However, it is the unresolved struggle between these voices, the systematic and the satirical, that gives the book its hold over us, and makes it possible for different readers to attribute such different views to its author. 'Satire' and 'dubious philosophical theory' are intertwined not just in this passage, but also throughout much of the *Philosophical Investigations*. In a manuscript written while he was struggling with the question of how best to arrange the material in an early version of the *Investigations*, Wittgenstein drew a close connection between the two:

This book is a collection of wisecracks. But the point is: they are connected, they form a system. If the task were to draw the shape of an object true to nature, then a wisecrack is like drawing just one tangent to the real curve; but a thousand wisecracks lying close to each other can draw the curve.[32]

The *Investigations* sums up this relationship between traditional philosophy and what Wittgenstein has to offer in the following terms:

We must do away with all *explanation*, and description alone must take its place. And this description gets its light, that is to say its purpose, from the philosophical problems. These are, of course, not empirical problems; they are solved, rather, by looking into the workings of our language, and that in such a way as to make us recognize those workings: *in despite of* an urge to misunderstand them. The problems are solved, not by reporting new

---

[31] *Zettel*, §452. Earlier versions include *Philosophical Remarks*, §2, 1930; Big Typescript, §90, 422, 1933 (*Philosophical Occasions*, 182, 183).

[32] Wittgenstein, MS 119, 108–9; written in English, 14 Oct. 1937.

experience, but by arranging what we have always known. Philosophy is a struggle against the bewitchment of our understanding by means of our language. (§109*)[33]

Where does our investigation get its importance from, since it seems only to destroy everything interesting, that is, all that is great and important? (As it were all the buildings, leaving behind only bits of stone and rubble.) What we are destroying is nothing but cloud-castles and we are clearing up the ground of language on which they stood. (§118*)

The problem for Diamond's and Rorty's readings is that Wittgenstein is not simply content to make wisecracks, or even to mime the systematic philosopher in order to undermine what he or she has built. They take Wittgenstein to be contrasting traditional philosophy which, bewitched by language, aims at explanation, with his therapeutic philosophy, which describes our language in order to struggle against bewitchment and return us to ordinary language. But at times his own talk of the 'ground of language' (§118) or the 'workings of language' (§109) goes beyond this: he also conceives of the remarks in the *Investigations* as forming 'a system', as 'drawing the curve' that clarifies the familiar landscape of 'what we have always known'. In using description of the everyday in order to combat philosophical theories, Wittgenstein was inevitably drawn into what can look like proto-philosophical theorizing about the everyday – first steps towards an ordinary language philosophy or a coherentist epistemology.

In the *Tractatus*, this tension is most apparent in the problematic relationship between 'frame' and 'content' of the book, between what Wittgenstein says about the method of the book and the method he actually employs. In the *Investigations*, questions about the nature of philosophy are a principal concern of the book itself. The conception of philosophy as therapeutic and anti-doctrinal is most clearly and forcefully stated in the remarks about the nature of philosophy in §§89–133, two of which have just been quoted. That discussion leads up to §133, where Wittgenstein states that

The real discovery is the one that makes me capable of stopping doing philosophy when I want to. – The one that gives philosophy peace, so that it is no longer tormented by questions which bring *itself* in question. – Instead,

---

[33] See 4.1 for further discussion of the final sentence; see also Stern 1995, 24.

a method is shown by examples; and the series of examples can be broken off. —— Problems are solved (difficulties eliminated), not a *single* problem. (§133c*)³⁴

Note that this passage lends itself to two diametrically opposed readings, for each sentence in this passage can be read in a Pyrrhonian or a non-Pyrrhonian way. On a non-Pyrrhonian reading, Wittgenstein is announcing that he has found a way of 'drawing the curve', a way of bringing philosophy to a clear view of the ground of language that provides a philosophical basis for his therapeutic critique of traditional philosophy.³⁵ He is claiming that the methods of the *Investigations* amount to the 'real discovery . . . that gives philosophy peace' and so straightforwardly endorsing the aim of '*complete* clarity'. On a Pyrrhonian reading, Wittgenstein is mocking the notion of a 'real discovery', a definitive solution.³⁶ The very idea of such a discovery is an illusion, and Wittgenstein is warning us of its dangers.

The non-Pyrrhonian reading gains considerable support if we consider the history of this remark. This material was drafted in 1931; in the Big Typescript, produced around 1933, it begins a section entitled 'Method in Philosophy. Possibility of peaceful progress'.³⁷ There, Wittgenstein likens his previous approach to dividing an infinitely long piece of paper lengthwise, producing a small number of infinitely long strips. He compares his new method to dividing the same strip crosswise, into short strips. In other words, he had given up the Tractarian idea of philosophy as consisting of a few insoluble problems. Instead, he would divide them into many smaller ones, each finite and soluble. The old conception sets us impossible tasks; the new one turns the seemingly central problems into many tasks that can be done piecemeal. Philosophers who look at things the wrong way around produce

the *greatest* difficulty. They want as it were to grasp the infinite strips, and complain that it cannot be done piecemeal. Of course it can't, if by 'a piece' one understands an endless vertical strip. But it may well be done, if one

---

³⁴ See also the earlier version of this passage, part of §92 of the Big Typescript, in *Philosophical Occasions*, 195, or Wittgenstein 1994a, 276–7.

³⁵ This interpretation is defended in Baker and Hacker 1980a, 246–7, Glock 1991, Hilmy 1991, and Jolley 1993.

³⁶ This interpretation is defended in Read 1995, but for rather different reasons.

³⁷ Wittgenstein 1994a, 276.

sees a horizontal strip as a piece. – But then our work will never come to an end! – Of course not, for it has no end.

(We want to replace wild conjectures and explanations by calm weighing of linguistic facts.)[38]

A defender of the Pyrrhonian reading can reply that the existence of this passage, as part of a chapter on philosophy in the Big Typescript, can at the very most show that Wittgenstein did take this view seriously in the early 1930s. However, a defender of the non-Pyrrhonian construal can reply that Wittgenstein retained this passage in his later work; in the Early Investigations, it actually follows the text of the published §133, quoted above.[39] It is, I believe, misleading to think of Wittgenstein's thinking as undergoing a once-and-for-all turn, a point after which he achieved the insights of his later (or, as some would prefer, his entire) philosophy. Rather, it is a continual struggle between conflicting impulses that gives his thought its peculiar vitality and importance, one that is only fully achieved in his most carefully revised writings. It is this quite particular and exceptional process of composition that makes Part I of the *Philosophical Investigations* all the more important.

Certainly, Wittgenstein's own commitment to bringing philosophy under control was counterbalanced by the hold philosophy had over him. In a letter, Rush Rhees recalled a conversation with Wittgenstein that ended in the following way:

As he was leaving, this time, he said to me roughly this: 'In my book I say that I am able to leave off with a problem in philosophy when I want to. But that's a lie; I can't.'[40]

Wittgenstein aimed to end philosophy, yet in doing so, he was continually struggling with philosophical problems.[41] In order to understand the *Investigations*, we have to see that the tension between philosophy

[38] Wittgenstein 1994a, 277. Translation slightly revised.

[39] In the Early Investigations, it forms the basis for the second half of §118. As it is also part of *Zettel*, §447, assembled after the final version of Part I of the *Investigations*, there is reason to think that Wittgenstein had not given up this way of seeing things. On the other hand, the fact that he did include this passage in the 1937 version of the *Philosophical Investigations*, but not the final typescript, is reason to think that he might no longer have been satisfied with the story of the horizontal and vertical strips.

[40] Hallett 1977, 230. See also Rhees 1984, 219 n. 7.

[41] For further discussion of these passages, see Stern 1995, 1.3, esp. pp. 19ff.

as therapy and philosophy as constructive argument operates there in a number of different ways. First, as is well known, many passages take the form of a debate between different voices. Often, one proposes a certain philosophical argument or theory – Wittgenstein's interlocutor, or the 'voice of temptation' – and the other argues against it – the 'voice of the everyday'.[42] Second, the voice that argues against philosophical theorizing and attempts to return us to everyday life can also be read as articulating positive philosophical views. These passages have usually been the basis for the theories that commentators have attributed to the author of the *Investigations*. However, interpreting them as the key to the systematic philosophical views that supposedly lie behind the text of the *Investigations* immediately raises the problem faced by any irresolute reading: how can we do justice to Wittgenstein's scepticism about traditional philosophy and attribute a traditional philosophical theory to him? Indeed, many of Wittgenstein's harshest critics take these passages to show that he was inconsistent, and had a philosophical theory that he pretended was composed of platitudes about ordinary language. Instead, I propose that we approach them as further sketches of the landscape, examples of how 'ending philosophy' and 'doing philosophy' are interwoven in the *Investigations*.

If we give up our reliance on simple stories about how to do philosophy, or how to bring philosophy to an end, we are still left with all the hard questions. To paraphrase Wittgenstein, someone might object against me, 'You take the easy way out! You talk about all sorts of language-games, but have nowhere said what makes them Wittgenstein's philosophy. So you let yourself off the very part of the investigation that once gave you yourself most headache, the part about the *general form of Wittgenstein's philosophy*.' In reply, I would quote Wittgenstein's own answer to a similar question:

– Don't say: 'There *must* be something common . . .' but *look and see* whether there is anything common to all. – For if you look at them you will not see something that is common to *all*, but similarities, relationships, and a whole series of them at that. To repeat: don't think, but look! . . .

---

[42] These expressions are taken from Cavell 1979 and 1996a.

And the result of this examination is: we see a complicated network of similarities overlapping and criss-crossing: sometimes overall similarities, sometimes similarities of detail. (§66)

Most readers have taken the *Philosophical Investigations* and the *Tractatus* to offer opposed views about the nature of mind, world, and language; a small minority have argued that they are in basic agreement. But nearly all of them take Wittgenstein to be primarily interested in advocating some quite specific non-Pyrrhonian view about what there is and what philosophy should be. I have been proposing that we approach both books in a less dogmatic spirit, as two very different approaches to the question about the nature of philosophy.

One measure of the power of the *Investigations* is that it has inspired such a wide spectrum of readings. However, these readings can cast a long shadow on the text, and can make it seem much more forbidding and difficult than it really is. Rather than trying to adjudicate between those readings, this book aims to help the reader approach the text of the *Investigations* for himself or herself. While we will inevitably do so by discussing the views we find there, the *Investigations* is primarily about how philosophical theorizing gets started, not the polished theories professional philosophers usually produce. For this reason, it is best read by discussing the questions it raises, rather than beginning by trying to formulate a consistent theory about what its author must have meant. This is not to deny that it is possible to do so. However, 'the author' and 'what he must have meant' are themselves just the sort of problematic philosophical concepts that the *Philosophical Investigations* places in question.

CHAPTER 3

The opening of the Philosophical Investigations: *the motto*

3.1 BEGINNING AT THE BEGINNING

This chapter is devoted to questions raised by the opening words of the *Philosophical Investigations*, words that are usually ignored or passed over rapidly by most interpreters. The motto is not only of interest in its own right; it also provides a particularly direct introduction to some of the central themes of the *Philosophical Investigations* as a whole. It also allows us to contrast the strengths and weaknesses of the two main approaches to the text: a genetic approach, on which passages are elucidated by appeal to the author's intentions, as shown in his previous drafts, and an immanent approach, which focuses on a rational reconstruction of the arguments that the reader finds in the text of the published book. While both of these approaches are valuable, single-mindedly following either of them will not enable us to do justice to the dialogical and context-oriented character of the text that follows the motto. The motto is puzzling on first reading; I propose that Wittgenstein expected it to be puzzling, and wanted his readers to reflect on what it might mean, reflection that requires us to think about the different contexts it belongs to, and the sense it makes in each of those contexts. In so doing, we can see an anticipation of the central role that context and circumstance play in our understanding of language, a leading theme of the book as a whole.

In 'Notes and Afterthoughts on the Opening of the *Investigations*', Stanley Cavell tells us that the 'clearest unchanging feature' of his Wittgenstein course over the decades 'was the opening question: How does the *Investigations* begin?'¹ Cavell is on the right track, I believe, when he observes, 'There are many answers, or directions of answer.'² However, Cavell begins his answer as follows: 'One might say, uncontroversially: It begins with some words of someone else.' The uncontroversial answer rapidly becomes controversial, for he identifies that 'someone else' as St Augustine; Cavell never mentions the motto, or its Viennese author, Johann Nepomuk Nestroy (1802–62). While the first numbered remark of the *Philosophical Investigations* begins with a passage from Augustine's *Confessions*, the published book begins, strictly speaking, with a line taken from Act IV, scene 10 of Nestroy's play *The Protégé (Der Schützling)*.³

The motto in question, 'Überhaupt hat der Fortschritt das an sich, daß er viel größer ausschaut, als er wirklich ist', has received relatively little attention, especially when one considers how much ink has been spilled over the question of how the *Philosophical Investigations* begins. In part, this is because it has been left out of every English translation of the book to date. However, there are also principled reasons why philosophers have not taken it seriously; these usually take the form of an argument that the front matter is not part of the book, properly speaking.

Norman Malcolm's memoir of Wittgenstein contains the following translation of the motto:

It is in the nature of every advance, that it appears much greater than it actually is.⁴

But this is triply problematic. First, *Fortschritt*, like the English word 'progress', is not just any advance; it implies movement towards a goal, and especially the goals of modern science. Baker and Hacker's translation corrects this:

It is in the nature of all progress, that it looks much greater than it really is.⁵

The second problem is that the words immediately around 'Fortschritt', namely 'hat der . . . das an sich', have a plainer and rather

¹ Cavell 1996a, 261.
² Cavell 1996a, 261. For further discussion of this issue, see 4.1.
³ Even more strictly speaking, the very first word to appear in the final typescript after the title, namely the word 'Motto', is not to be found in any of the printed editions of the book prior to Joachim Schulte's critical-genetic edition. See Wittgenstein 2001, 741.
⁴ Malcolm 1984, 51 (1958, 60).   ⁵ Baker and Hacker 1980a, 4.

different sense than talk of 'nature' would imply; they are identifying an issue, not taking a position on it. This problem is addressed in Barker's translation:

The thing about progress is that it appears much greater than it actually is.[6]

Third, none of these translations does justice to the first word of the motto: 'überhaupt'. Depending on the context, 'überhaupt' can serve either as a qualifier, an intensifier, or to indicate an aside; it can often be translated as 'in general', 'besides', or 'at all'. The word can also be used conversationally to indicate that what follows is only a rough way of putting things. In the Nestroy play, where this sentence serves to conclude a soliloquy about progress and introduce a big song about how progress 'looks much greater than it actually is', the opening word both serves as a transition or link, connecting the final sentence with what precedes it, and emphasizes that the sentence in question is a summing-up. In the motto, where no further context is provided, the first word of Nestroy's German has the effect of making the sentence sound even less like a thesis than these translations would lead one to expect. Spiegelberg and von Wright both take the word to be qualifying the remainder of the sentence, saying that it is only generally true:

In general, it is characteristic of progress, that it looks much bigger than it really is.[7]

It is a thing about progress: it generally looks bigger than it really is.[8]

Both of these are fairly close to the sense of the Nestroy sentence, but neither conveys any of its folksy and conversational flavour. Perhaps 'anyway' is as close as one can come to translating 'überhaupt' here. They are both conversational words that can serve to indicate that what follows is connected with what went before, or that it is something new. 'Anyway' also carries the implication that what follows is an aside, not a thesis. Adopting this suggestion, and making the translation as conversational and plainly spoken as possible, leads to the following translation:

Motto: 'Anyway, the thing about progress is that it looks much greater than it really is.' (Nestroy)[9]

---

[6] Barker 1985–6, 165.   [7] Spiegelberg 1978, 56.   [8] von Wright 1982, 114.
[9] My translation, based on Wittgenstein 2001, 741.

3.2 THE MOTTO AS A GUIDE TO THE TEXT: GENETIC READINGS, IMMANENT READINGS, AND BEYOND

Given that the motto is left out of the standard translations, what reason do we have to take it seriously as the opening words of the *Philosophical Investigations*? Is the front matter really part of the book, and even if it is, how much does that matter?

Eike von Savigny once argued that as the prefatory material is dated January 1945 and the book was not finished at that point, it was written for the 'Intermediate Version' of the *Philosophical Investigations*.[10] However, it has since become clear that the motto and preface are part of the final text of the book. Although the typescript that was used in publishing the book has been lost, we have two heavily corrected copies of the typescript that was used, which very closely approximate to the published text. (Wittgenstein usually had at least two carbon copies made of his philosophical typescripts.) In both of these surviving typescripts, the prefatory material takes up the first three and a half pages; the beginning of section one is halfway down page four. In fact, the typescript, which dates from 1946, makes it clear that the motto was chosen only after the rest of Part 1 had achieved its final form. For the typescript contains a motto, later crossed out, from the introduction to Hertz's *Principles of Mechanics*.

The Nestroy passage was presumably added some time after Wittgenstein wrote this passage down in a manuscript notebook, in an entry dated 25 April 1947, the only Nestroy quotation in the Wittgenstein *Nachlass* that provides his name.[11] Baker and Hacker cite seven other passages that Wittgenstein considered as possible mottoes at one time or another.[12] However, the choice of the author and the words in question was no afterthought. Another motto from Nestroy, 'Here only stupidity helps the stupid', began the first manuscript volume from 1929.[13] There are a number of other Nestroy quotations in Wittgenstein's manuscripts. Indeed, Wittgenstein was not only well acquainted with Nestroy, but was already quoting the words he was to use as the motto for *Philosophical Investigations* from memory

---

[10] Wittgenstein 2001, 563–738.   [11] Wittgenstein, MS 134, p. 152.
[12] Baker and Hacker 1980a, 4–6.
[13] My translation; see Wittgenstein 1994b, 1. vii. Although the words were subsequently erased, they are still legible. They read 'Hier hilft dem Dummen die Dummheit allein', and are taken from Nestroy's play *Heimliche Liebe – Heimliches Geld* (Secret Love – Secret Money).

in a letter to Schlick dated 18 September 1930, and describing it as
'magnificent' (*herrlich*).

Very well, the motto is part of the book, but how important is
it? One could invoke a literary distinction here, and argue that the
epigraph and preface, to be found on the preceding, roman-numbered
pages of the published book, are part of the *paratext*, liminal material
that is not really part of the book itself, and that the *text* begins on
page 1 of the published book, not the first page of the typescript.
Baker and Hacker must have had something like this distinction
in mind when they decided to begin Part I of the first volume of
their commentary with the sentence: 'The *Investigations* opens with
a quotation in which Augustine describes how he learned language
as a child', for they devote three full pages of their exegesis in Part 2
to a discussion of the motto, and another nine pages to the preface.[14]
But how are we to understand the relationship between the text of
the *Philosophical Investigations*, its paratext, and other texts, an issue
to which Wittgenstein interpreters have only occasionally given their
full attention?

In this connection, Hans-Johann Glock draws a convenient distinction between 'immanent' and 'genetic' approaches to the interpretation of the *Philosophical Investigations*. Roughly speaking, the
'immanent' approach attends only to the text itself, while the 'genetic'
approach draws on other evidence as well. According to Glock,
the immanent approach turns on two key assumptions: [1] that
'the author's intentions are irrelevant and [2] that an interpretation
should only take into consideration what a reader can understand
by looking at the text itself'.[15] We might add: what the immanent reading rules out are extra-textual intentions, not intentions
as expressed in the text. A genetic reading, on the other hand,
holds that the author's extra-textual intentions are important for
an understanding of the text, and has no qualms about taking
into consideration additional evidence not to be found in the text
itself.

One might expect that those who take the immanent approach, a
method that stresses the authority and self-containedness of the text,

[14] Baker and Hacker 1980b, 1; 1980a, 4–6, 7–15.
[15] Glock 1990, 153; repeated in his 1992, 118.

would give considerable weight to those opening pages that precede §1, but this has rarely been the case. The reasons for this become much clearer if one turns to Gérard Genette's *Paratexts*, which includes a systematic and encyclopedic study of those texts that precede the beginning of the text. He speaks of paratexts in general, and prefaces, epigraphs, and mottos in particular, as a kind of threshold, 'a transitional zone between text and beyond-text'.[16] The chief role of this part of the front matter, he maintains, is to communicate the author's intentions, to 'ensure for the text a destiny consistent with the author's purpose'.[17]

In view of this, we can see why an immanent reader will be likely to overlook the motto and preface, for to pay attention to them is to attend to the author's intentions, and to be forced to consider the relationship between the 'text itself' and other texts. A commitment to concentrating on what an intelligent reader can make of the text, without drawing on evidence of authorial intentions that is not present in the text, is well served by the conviction that the text begins with §1. This becomes particularly clear if one considers the content of the preface to the *Philosophical Investigations*, which discusses Wittgenstein's previous writing, both in the *Tractatus* and work leading up to the *Philosophical Investigations*, his philosophical discussions with others, and his fears and hopes for his book. For this very reason, proponents of the genetic approach usually regard the preface as an important part of the book. Yet they, too, rarely attend to the motto, an oversight perhaps due to their more liberal method: with such a variety of other texts they can look to for guidance, the motto can seem like a decorative flourish that does not call for any particular attention.

However, we ignore the motto – and the preface – at our peril, for they 'set the stage' just as much as the opening sections. Indeed, Genette's anatomy of paratexts turns on what he calls the 'obvious fact' that the immanent reader, attending only to what is in the text itself, 'does not exist . . . and cannot exist'. The immanent reader, a familiar figure in the history of philosophy and modernist literary criticism, is an entirely fictional character, for in practice no one can

---

[16] Genette 1997, 407.   [17] Ibid.

bracket out everything they know or take for granted. Reflecting on this moral leads Genette to the following

advice à la Wittgenstein: what one cannot ignore, one is better off knowing – that is, of course, acknowledging, and knowing that one knows it. The effect of the paratext lies very often in the realm of influence – indeed, manipulation – experienced subconsciously. This mode of operation is doubtless in the author's interest, though not always in the reader's. To accept it – or, for that matter, to reject it – one is better off perceiving it fully and clearly.[18]

The main concerns of Wittgenstein's preface to the *Philosophical Investigations* are quite clear, even if there is great scope for disagreement about how to interpret it: it draws connections between the text and what lies beyond it and is clearly very important for our understanding of the character of Wittgenstein's philosophy in general, and the relationship between the *Tractatus* and the *Philosophical Investigations* in particular. Here I will focus on the motto, which has proved much more difficult for readers to notice at all, let alone 'fully and clearly'.

What does the motto mean? What could the motto mean? Here, Genette's chapter on the epigraph, or prefatory quotation, is helpful. Two of the tasks that Genette identifies as the work of an epigraph are clearly relevant when we look at the motto of the *Philosophical Investigations*. A motto can comment on the text, 'whose meaning it indirectly specifies or emphasizes',[19] thus orienting the reader, either by providing explicit guidance for the first-time reader, or by allowing someone who knows the book well to see how it hangs together. It can also work more obliquely, invoking the prestige or associations of the motto's author; in some cases, the main point of the motto is not what it says, but who says it. But how does Wittgenstein's motto orient us? What kind of a 'comment on the text' is it? And what is the significance of Wittgenstein's choice of an Austrian playwright and performer, who played the lead in over eighty of his own plays between 1827 and 1862, a man famous in his homeland – his admirers call him the 'Austrian Shakespeare' – but virtually unknown elsewhere, because his plays depend on virtuoso use of dialect and wordplay? How are

---

[18] Genette 1997, 409.
[19] Genette 1997, 157. Mottos can also serve to indicate the genre of the work.

we to understand these words, taken from Nestroy's play, and placed at the beginning of this book?

One way of avoiding the difficulties involved in attempting to make sense of a few words in isolation is the genetic approach; one can investigate what the line means in the Nestroy play from which it is taken, its significance in Nestroy's work as a whole, and what Nestroy might have meant to Wittgenstein. This strategy turns on attending to the original context that the words are taken from, and the sense they make there. However, that context is itself a contested terrain, for Nestroy's plays are themselves extraordinarily complex; one of the principal problems for Nestroy's critics is the question of the relationship between the author's views and the views expressed in his plays. A recent survey of the Nestroy literature summarizes the problem in these terms:

> The actor-dramatist is all too easily identified with his characters. Nestroy would appear on stage and deliver lines – often memorably pithy lines – which he himself had written, but which, whether within the plot proper or in the solo scenes, are spoken by fictional characters; anyone seeking to extract political implications enters a methodological minefield.[20]

Nestroy characterized almost all of his plays, including *The Protégé*, as 'Posse mit Gesang', or 'farce with singing'; they were part of a long-standing comic tradition in Austria and Europe, although regarded at the time as unconventional and challenging the limits of what was acceptable on the stage. They were written rapidly, as vehicles for himself and his company – he would play a witty and satirical figure, caught up in an improbable scenario with a variety of character types, but always coming to a happy end. Nestroy often used the ironic device of 'double perspective', such as delivering an ostensibly jingoistic speech in an ironically mocking manner, fully expecting that most of his audience would not get the joke. The farcical plot was usually lifted from a well-known model, often connected with current events in some way, and made as much merciless fun of all concerned as was permitted by the censor. All of this makes it extremely difficult to establish the 'moral' of what Nestroy has to say:

[20] Yates 1994, 68.

Above all else, we should never assume the opinions voiced by the characters are automatically shared by the dramatist, any more than we should confuse character, narrator, and author when dealing with a work of prose fiction. . . . while it is tempting to assume that whatever we consider to be reasonable opinions in the plays must be Nestroy's opinions, that in turn implies that we would agree about what is reasonable, an assumption that is itself unreasonable; and, equally, we have no right to impose our own particular views either on Nestroy or his works.[21]

A much-anticipated aspect of these performances were Nestroy's 'monologues and comic songs', set off from the main action, where the central figure would address the audience and the topic of the play more directly. *The Protégé's* first monologue and song introduces Gottfried Herb, the play's hero, and establishes his character.[22] The second of these dramatic interludes, which occurs just before the dénouement, in which Herb's career is rescued from calumny and he lives happily ever after, is the high point of the play. In it, Herb speaks the lines that lead up to the motto, in a monologue that begins by deploring how little evil has been removed from the world, despite all our inventions, and concludes as follows:

And yet we live in an era of progress, don't we? I s'pose progress is like a newly discovered land; a flourishing colonial system on the coast, the interior still wilderness, steppe, prairie. Anyway, the thing about progress is that it looks much greater than it really is.

This immediately introduces a six-verse satirical song, complete with a full score, which drives home the point of Herb's observations about progress with lurid examples.[23] Each verse divides into three parts: (1) how bad things used to be, (2) how much better they seem now, and (3) why they're actually worse than ever. The refrain at the end of (2) is always:

It's really *splendid*,
How progress is so great![24]

---

[21] McKenzie 1985, 126, 137–8.   [22] Nestroy 2000, 11–15 (Act I, sc. 2).
[23] Nestroy 2000, 90–6 (Act IV, sc. 10); the score is on pp. 427–31.
[24] Nestroy 2000, 91–6; my translation. ''s Is wirklich *famos*, / Wie der Fortschritt so groß!' The odd German in the first line is an example of Nestroy's use of Viennese dialect.

Similarly, the last two lines of (3) are always:

> So, progress examined more closely,
> Hasn't made the world much happier.[25]

Barker has drawn attention to the striking similarities between Wittgenstein's life and 'Herb's plight'.[26] The play begins with Herb living in a whitewashed room with barely room for a bed and a table, 'having just given up his job as a rural schoolmaster because he feels destined for higher things'.[27] Herb is a writer, considered by himself and his friends a genius, but facing the desolate fate that 'genius has lost its privileges'[28] in these times and preoccupied by suicide. Remarkably, Herb finds success in iron and steel technology, the very area where the Wittgenstein fortune began; the final act, from which the motto comes, is set in a wooded valley affected by the iron foundry: 'the ambivalence of the setting, showing nature and industry in uneasy juxtaposition, is reflected in Herb's view on the meaning of ["progress"]'.[29] Wittgenstein wrote about his concerns about his originality and whether he had been influenced on a number of occasions.[30] Herb wants, most of all, to make his own way in the world, to not be anyone's protégé, yet he is only given his job at the foundry because a noble lady takes pity on him out of the goodness of her heart, and while he proves himself worthy of the task, he only finds happiness at the end of the play thanks to a series of utterly implausible plot devices.

The critical edition of the play includes a history of the play's production and reception and its relationship to the revolutionary year of 1848.[31] First performed in 1847, it was later seen as anticipating the problems of the following year. Most interpreters have concentrated on Herb's, and Nestroy's, attitudes to progress, as a guide to Wittgenstein's use of the sentence. Some readers have regarded Herb as a proto-socialist, for his sympathy for the suffering of the workers; others have stressed his reactionary sentiments. Almost all nineteenth- and early twentieth-century critics took it for

[25] Ibid. 'Drum der Fortschritt hat beym Licht betrach't, / Die Welt nicht viel glücklicher g'macht.'
[26] Barker 1985–6, 162.   [27] Barker 1985–6, 162; see also Nestroy 2000, 9.
[28] Nestroy 2000, 13.   [29] Barker 1985–6, 163.
[30] Wittgenstein, *Culture and Value*, 1980a, 18–20, 36, 60; 1998, 16–17, 42, 68.
[31] Nestroy 2000, 119ff.

granted that Nestroy's views could be identified with the views of his protagonists, although there was great disagreement about what they were. Karl Kraus, another hero of Wittgenstein's, led a revival of interest in Nestroy, praising his creative use of language and the deeply satirical character of his work and arguing that Nestroy's genius lay in the way he attacked pretension and falsity wherever he found it.

While Baker and Hacker observe that 'in its original context [the motto] expresses such negative views on progress as would harmonize with W.'s own repudiation of this aspect, and this ideal, of European culture', they do not put any great weight on this.[32] However, for a reader approaching the *Philosophical Investigations* as a philosophy of culture opposed to the ideal of progress, a critique of 'the darkness of this time' (PI, viii/x), the Nestroy passage provides an opening to placing his philosophical writings within a cultural tradition. If Wittgenstein's views about progress had changed since 1930, they had only become more negative, as these two passages, written in 1947 attest:

The truly apocalyptic view of the world is that things do *not* repeat themselves. It is not e.g. absurd to believe that the scientific & technological age is the beginning of the end for humanity, that the idea of Great Progress is a bedazzlement, along with the idea that the truth will ultimately be known; that there is nothing good or desirable about scientific knowledge & that humanity, in seeking it, is falling into a trap. It is by no means clear that this is not how things are.[33]

It may be that science & industry, & their progress, are the most enduring thing in the world today. That any guess at a coming collapse of science & industry is for now & for a *long* time to come, simply a dream, & that science & industry, after & with infinite misery will unite the world, I mean integrate it into a single empire, in which to be sure peace is the last thing that will then find a home.[34]

Brian McGuinness' biography names Nestroy as part of a current against the mainstream of Austrian culture, a current opposed to 'nationalism, radicalism, progress, and so on', which Wittgenstein 'felt he belonged to and which accords with his nostalgia for the period before 1848'.[35] Barker follows J. C. Nyíri, McGuinness, and

---

[32] Baker and Hacker 1980a, 4.
[33] Wittgenstein, *Culture and Value*, 1980a, 56; 1998, 64.
[34] Wittgenstein, *Culture and Value*, 1980a, 63; 1998, 72.   [35] McGuinness 1988, 36.

von Wright in holding that Herb's 'attack on "progress" as expressed in the drama may . . . be regarded as typical of the "conservative style" of thought in its opposition to a world dominated by the material consequences of rationalist thinking'.[36] Jacques Bouveresse and Beth Savickey have drawn connections with Wittgenstein's admiration for Karl Kraus, who was fond of quoting that sentence from Nestroy.[37] Kraus was a great advocate of Nestroy's; many judge his *Nestroy and Posterity*, based on a speech he gave to commemorate the fiftieth anniversary of Nestroy's death, as his finest piece of work.[38] It is also possible to construe the motto as hinting at 'a moral dimension to the *Investigations*' and as expressing 'the thought that modern technical progress, whether in science or in philosophy, has not come to grips with our moral concerns'.[39]

On an immanent approach, one puts all this to one side and asks what the words mean to the reader when they are taken out of the context of Nestroy's play, placed alone on the first page of the book. Previous discussion of this issue has turned on the question of how this talk of 'progress' is to be applied to our understanding of the book as a whole, and to what extent the book itself amounts to philosophical progress. Malcolm took the motto to be an expression of Wittgenstein's mixed feelings about the *Philosophical Investigations*:

He did not think of the central conceptions of his philosophy as *possibly* in error. He certainly believed most of the time, that he had produced an important advance in philosophy. Yet, I think that he was inclined to feel that the importance of this advance might be exaggerated by those who were too close to it.[40]

On the other hand, Baker and Hacker find it 'unlikely' that Wittgenstein was intimating 'that the advance made in PI over the philosophy of TLP is less substantial than it appears'; but in the end, their own reading is not so different from Malcolm's.[41] For they immediately go on to propose the hypothesis that the 'intention behind the motto echoes the end of the Preface to TLP: the value of this work . . . is

---

[36] Barker 1985–6, 163. See also Nyíri 1976, 1982; McGuinness 1982; von Wright 1982.
[37] Bouveresse 1992, 33; Savickey 1999, 10.   [38] *Nestroy und die Nachwelt*, Kraus 1912.
[39] Tilghman 1987, 100.
[40] Malcolm 1984, 51 (1958, 60). Hallett (1977, 61) and Spiegelberg (1978, 56) both quote this passage from Malcolm, and follow his lead.
[41] Baker and Hacker 1980a, 4.

that it shows how little is achieved when these problems are solved'.[42]
This is odd, because if the intention behind the motto to the second
book can be seen as echoing the preface to the first, that would seem
to lend strong support to the reading they dismiss as 'unlikely'. One
way in which the two books' prefatory disclaimers of their respective
achievements differ is that the *Tractatus'* preface does not express any
doubts about its contribution to philosophical progress. The preface
to the *Tractatus* seems to be saying that even though in philosophical
terms a great deal has been achieved, this achievement may seem to
matter little in different terms. The *Philosophical Investigations* also
raises the possibility that here, even in philosophical terms, progress
may look greater than it really is.

In an essay on Wittgenstein's mottos, Spiegelberg includes an interesting discussion of his

> personal experience in reading Wittgenstein and the help I derived from his
> mottoes. In my repeated attempts to penetrate into Wittgenstein's philosoph-
> ical mazes I found myself constantly puzzled, stopped and frustrated . . .
> the almost total absence of chapters and chapter headings, of previews,
> summaries, indexes and other aids to the reader added to this frustration.
> Under these circumstances the presence of the mottoes served as a kind
> of clue for what lay ahead . . . adumbrative, directive, preparatory. Mot-
> toes are sentences meant to guide our understanding of a longer text that
> follows.[43]

While Spiegelberg sets out both the approaches I have sketched so far,
and there is surely something to be learned from each, it is a remarkably meagre harvest. Certainly, the words can be read both as expressing a certain pessimism about modernity, and a conventional modesty
about the book's achievement. The information about Nestroy's play
and Wittgenstein's affinities for Nestroy is valuable, but it is hardly
plausible that Wittgenstein expected his readers only to be guided
by such considerations in their reading of the motto: we would be
tone-deaf if we weren't aware of the significance of those words in the
play, but we must also think for ourselves about what those words
mean on the opening page of the *Philosophical Investigations*.

Philosophical Investigations §525, which begins by asking whether
we understand a sentence taken out of context, provides a good

---

[42] Ibid.   [43] Spiegelberg 1978, 57.

starting point for reflecting on what other guidance we might be able to take from Wittgenstein's motto:

525. 'After he had said this, he left her as he did the day before.' – Do I understand this sentence? Do I understand it just as I should if I heard it in the course of a narrative? If it were set down in isolation I should say, I don't know what it's about. But all the same I should know how this sentence might perhaps be used; I could myself invent a context for it. (A multitude of familiar paths lead off from these words in every direction.)

We can imagine how the quoted sentence could be used; but we don't know how it was used in the narrative. Nor do we have a sense of the quite particular significance that such a line can take on within a particular play or poem, a significance that it would not have if it were rephrased. In *Zettel*, there are similar remarks about a line from a play by Schiller.[44] Wittgenstein says that those words, together with their tone and glance 'seem indeed to carry within themselves every last nuance of the meaning they have'.[45] To this he replies that this is so 'only because we know them as part of a particular scene. But it would be possible to construct an entirely different scene around those words so as to show that the special spirit they have resides in the story in which they come.'[46] In an earlier version of this material, these remarks about Schiller's words are followed by the last, parenthetical, sentence of *Philosophical Investigations* §525b.[47] In these passages, among others, Wittgenstein acknowledges that words can seem to have a quite particular significance, akin to the meaning we associate with a phrase from a familiar tune, yet in a different context the same words could have a quite different meaning.

I propose that the motto prepares us for what comes ahead by forcing us to slow down, to think about what the sentence could mean, and to see that it can be set in a number of different contexts, has a number of different meanings, that our problems in understanding the motto are like our problems understanding 'After he had said this, he left her as he did the day before.' Philosophical readers of

---

[44] 'Gottlob! Noch etwas Weniges hat man geflüchtet – vor den Finger der Croaten.' 'Heaven be praised! A little slipped – out of the Croat clutches.' Schiller, *Wallenstein, Die Piccolimini*, 1.2.
[45] Wittgenstein, *Zettel*, §176. 'Meaning' translates *Bedeutung*.   [46] Ibid.
[47] Wittgenstein, MS 129, pp. 146–7.

Wittgenstein's motto have been too ready to assume that there must be one 'intention behind the motto'[48] instead of taking a broader perspective on the 'multitude of familiar paths' that 'lead off from these words in every direction' (§525). Philosophers have also been too ready to assume that the guidance in question must be clear and unambiguous; but as Wittgenstein points out, we are guided not only when we follow directions, but also when we 'walk along a field-track simply following it' (§172), a simile that should remind us of the criss-crossing journeyings across a landscape described in the preface. Yet no discussion of Wittgenstein and Nestroy, including Janik and Toulmin's, which dwells on the fact that Nestroy was famous as a satirist whose words commonly had multiple meanings, entertains the possibility that the motto's ambiguities might have appealed to Wittgenstein.[49]

Set in one context, the motto expresses pessimism as to whether scientific progress will improve our lives; set in another, it expresses the author's doubts about his own work. But at the beginning of this book, the Nestroy quotation has a broader significance, one that is missed by the single-minded reader, genetic or immanent.

First of all, as we have seen, we are confronted with the exercise of making sense of this sentence, taken out of context, an exercise that should lead us to see at least some of its ambiguities. Context will play a crucial role in Wittgenstein's subsequent investigations, for he thinks that philosophy goes wrong precisely when it tries to abstract from context, taking words that have multiple meanings in multiple contexts and trying to understand those words taken out the particular contexts in which they are used.

Second, we should consider the context in which Wittgenstein placed it: for it also serves as the first half of a double epigraph, the second half being the quote from Augustine that begins §1. Oddly, no discussion of Wittgenstein's use of Nestroy has attended to the idea that the pair of quotations, one at the beginning of the book, and one at the beginning of the opening remark, might be connected, or that the motto also serves as a comment on the quotation from Augustine. The motto warns us that we should not take what follows at face value, and that what seems like progress – whether it is the

<hr/>

[48] Baker and Hacker 1980a, 4.   [49] Janik and Toulmin 1996, 86–7.

progress that Augustine makes in learning to speak, or the progress we may think we have made since Augustine's time, or the progress Wittgenstein makes in responding to Augustine – may not be as great as it seems.

Third, the quotations from Nestroy and Augustine are appropriate beginnings for a text that contains a number of voices, and should alert the reader to the presence of a number of voices in what follows – not all of them 'Wittgenstein's' or 'the interlocutor's'. In particular, it is significant that in Nestroy's play, the words of the motto are spoken by Nestroy's leading character, whose role is closely analogous to that of the voice of the commentator in the *Philosophical Investigations*.

The next chapter begins by setting out an approach to §1 of the *Philosophical Investigations* that draws on this guidance.

CHAPTER 4

The critique of referential theories of meaning and the paradox of ostension: §§1–64

4.1 AUGUSTINE ON LANGUAGE LEARNING: §1

Most interpreters take the opening remarks of the *Philosophical Investigations* as an outline of Wittgenstein's answers to questions about the nature of language. However, the opening of the *Philosophical Investigations* invites a multiplicity of readings, readings of the words Wittgenstein quotes at the beginning of the book, and of his opening words. As we shall see, Wittgenstein's opening is best understood as raising questions and introducing us to a number of voices in the discussion that follows.

According to Malcolm, Wittgenstein

revered the writings of St Augustine. He told me he decided to begin his *Investigations* with a quotation from the latter's *Confessions*, not because he could not find the conception expressed in that quotation stated as well by other philosophers, but because the conception *must* be important if so great a mind held it.[1]

The oldest known source of the *Philosophical Investigations'* discussion of Augustine on language learning gives a similar explanation for the choice of Augustine. There, Wittgenstein parenthetically stresses the significance of the distance between our time and Augustine's:

(And what Augustine says is important for us because it is the conception of a naturally clear thinking man who, being far away from us in time, certainly doesn't belong to our particular intellectual milieu.)[2]

---

[1] Malcolm 1984, 59–60.

[2] Wittgenstein, MS III, pp. 15–16, 15 July 1931; the punctuation is Wittgenstein's. 'Und was Augustinus sagt ist für uns wichtig weil es die Auffassung eines natürlich-klar denkenden Mannes ist, der von uns zeitlich weit entfernt gewiß nicht zu unserem besonderen Gedankenkreis gehört.'

However, there is no quotation from Augustine in this passage, nor in any other of the many subsequent drafts of material that was used in §1, until 1936. Even the reference to Augustine that opens the *Brown Book*, written in 1934, simply provides a very brief summary: 'Augustine, in describing his learning of language, says that he was taught to speak by learning the names of things.'[3] Only when Wittgenstein translated the *Brown Book* into German in August 1936 did he add a few words from the *Confessions*, and it was not until he wrote up the final revisions to the Early Investigations that he decided to use such an extensive passage from Augustine.[4] The first drafts of §1a and §1b are part of that manuscript.[5] Thus, it was at a relatively late stage in the composition of the first 180 sections of the *Philosophical Investigations*, when nearly all of the other material had already been written, that Wittgenstein decided to begin with these words of Augustine's, and the particular response to them that we find in §1b.[6]

Wittgenstein's first sentence tells us that the opening quotation from St Augustine contains a definite picture of the essence of language, yet on first reading, Augustine's words can strike the reader as an entirely natural and unproblematic description of how he learned to speak:

My primary reaction to the citation from the *Confessions*, read by itself, is to think that what it expresses is obvious – it seems trivial, prosaic, well-nigh unobjectionable. It is just a harmless elaboration of the observations that early in life children learn what things are called, and learn to express their wants and needs verbally.[7]

Warren Goldfarb contends that Wittgenstein expected his readers to be shocked by his initial construal of Augustine, and those commentators who 'would have us meekly acquiesce to this sentence' have been too ready to take what he has to say at face value.[8] Instead,

---

[3] *Brown Book*, 77; cf. MS III, p. 15.   [4] Wittgenstein 2001, 51–204.
[5] Wittgenstein, MS 142.
[6] Schulte's edition of this material shows that the quotation from Augustine used in the first draft of MS 142, and probably in the first draft of the next version of that material, TS 220, omits the middle sentence of the passage we have in the published text, which is already included in the final revisions to MS 142 and TS 220. See Wittgenstein 2001, 1097; cf. 57 and 210.
[7] Goldfarb 1983, 268.   [8] Ibid.

Goldfarb proposes, the aim of these opening words is not to show us that Augustine's conception of language is wrong and Wittgenstein's right, but to throw us off balance, by challenging our preconceptions about what is involved in having a conception of language. Ultimately, the aim of this challenge is to get us to see that the same words can be understood in both a commonplace and a philosophical way, and thus to see the unclarity of the very idea of our having a 'conception of language'. Talk of naming objects, pointing things out, and states of mind can be quite unproblematic, yet in certain contexts these notions 'come to have a weight that our ordinary understanding of them does not support'.[9] For Augustine's words can also be read as intimating a number of different conceptions of how language works, conceptions that can provide a starting point for philosophical theorizing about language and meaning. Wittgenstein's primary concern is not with the sophisticated statement of philosophical problems and theoretical solutions that they lead to, but how those problems arise. He begins not with systematic philosophy, or the history of philosophy, but with the patterns of thought, the ways of speaking, which can lead us into formulating such philosophical theories.

Cavell proposes that the *Philosophical Investigations* is about 'the argument of the ordinary'.[10] He approaches the book as an argument between two opposing voices: the 'voice of temptation', which begins to formulate various philosophical theories, and the 'voice of correctness', which replies to these theories by reminding us of what we ordinarily say and do. Most interpreters take the 'voice of correctness' to be a mouthpiece for Wittgenstein's own views. Most Wittgensteinians provide a systematic account of the views they attribute to the voice of correctness, and most anti-Wittgensteinians argue against them, usually in defence of 'Wittgenstein's interlocutor'. However, Cavell replies that *neither* voice is straightforwardly Wittgenstein's; he emphasizes the ways in which the book is more like a dialogue, a conflicted monologue, or a confession, than advocacy for any systematic position. Like Augustine in the *Confessions*, Cavell's Wittgenstein struggles with temptation and correctness. Rather than seeing the multiplicity of voices, the lack of clear demarcation between voices, the frequent shifts in topic, the fragmentary arguments, the multitude

9 Ibid.   10 Cavell 1979, 1996a.

of questions, suggestions, instructions, stories, and far-fetched imaginary examples as all advancing a single, authorial point of view, he proposes that we approach them as an invitation to explore the deep difficulties that arise when we start to philosophize.

On the other hand, nothing can stop a philosopher from taking Wittgenstein's arguments and drawing his or her own positive conclusions; indeed, the book both invites and resists such a reading. Because the voices are never explicitly identified, and often permit, or even invite, multiple readings, the reader is continually forced to work out who is speaking, where the discussion is going, and what larger context or contexts these words belong to. As von Savigny puts it, Wittgenstein's text continually raises the following three questions: (1) 'Who speaks?' (2) 'Where is it going?' and (3) 'Where does that belong?'[11] One of the ways in which Wittgenstein forces his readers to 'thoughts of [their] own' (PI, viii/x) is that we are continually brought up short by the 'Who speaks?' question: the problem of identifying the voices in these exchanges. To make matters worse, 'Who speaks?' expresses two related, but rather different, questions. It is not only a matter of identifying *speeches* – where one voice stops and another starts – but that the very identity of the *speakers* is unclear. Indeed, in certain cases, such as the opening words of the *Philosophical Investigations*, those words are open to a number of quite different construals.

Both the Nestroy motto and the book's opening paragraphs are like those ambiguous drawings which at first sight can seem quite straightforward, yet on closer examination are open to a number of incompatible interpretations. Such drawings fascinated Wittgenstein and are repeatedly discussed in his writings; two prominent examples are the line drawing in *Tractatus* 5.5423 and near the beginning of *Philosophical Investigations* II. xi, which can look like a cube sticking out of the page, a cube sunk into the page, or an assembly of flat geometric shapes, among other possibilities, or Jastrow's 'duck-rabbit', which can be seen as a duck facing left or a rabbit facing right (PI II. xi, 194/166; on the drawing of a cube, see also §139 and 6.1).

What, precisely, is the 'particular picture of the essence of human language' that Wittgenstein speaks of in the first sentence of his own words in the book, or 'the conception expressed in that quotation', as

[11] Von Savigny 1994–6, I. 1–2.

Malcolm puts it?[12] To many philosophers, §1b provides a clear outline of the mistaken view of the nature of language that Wittgenstein finds in Augustine, a view that is presupposed in §1a, and that forms one of the principal targets in what follows. One line of interpretation concentrates on the question of the nature of this 'particular picture' and its place in the overall project of the *Philosophical Investigations*. While I cannot do justice to the full range of such readings of §1b, the main disagreements concern the scope and character of the picture in question. On a 'big picture' reading of Augustine's words, they serve to introduce the paradigm, or world view, that Wittgenstein opposes throughout the book.[13] On a 'small picture' reading, they set out a quite specific philosophical theory, the topic of the opening sections of the book.

While there is some support for each of these approaches in §1b, Wittgenstein's words are more equivocal than they may seem at first sight. He does say that the 'particular picture' suggested to him by Augustine's words is that (1) 'individual words in language name objects' and (2) 'sentences are combinations of such names'. However, Wittgenstein qualifies all this by an 'it seems to me', one of the expressions he repeatedly uses as a warning that he is introducing or entertaining an idea, rather than giving it his full support. These words (§1b1–2) are followed by a long double-dash, used by Wittgenstein to indicate either a change of topic, or a new voice (unlike a single dash, which often indicates a brief pause within a single train of thought). Only then are we introduced to a further idea, which, we are told, has its roots in this picture: that (3) 'every word has a meaning [*Bedeutung*]', and it 'is the object for which the word stands'. Thus we are introduced to at least two views of the Augustine passage: the 'particular picture', which concerns the role of words in language, and a further development of this conception, which introduces the notion of a word's meaning.

Exponents of a 'small picture' reading of these words are often attracted to the idea that the *Tractatus* is the real target. For instance, according to Jaakko and Merrill Hintikka, the passage from Augustine

---

[12] See Malcolm 1984, 59–60, cited above, p. 72.
[13] Baker and Hacker 1980b 14; see also 1–27.

is Wittgenstein's starting point because it sets out the view that ostension – naming objects and pointing to them – is the 'prime vehicle of language teaching and learning'.[14] This view supposedly follows from an 'idea embraced by Wittgenstein in the *Tractatus* . . . the basic links between language and the world are simple two-place relations of naming'.[15] On the Hintikkas' construal, the links in question are ineffable; nothing more can be said about them within the Tractarian framework. A related reading maintains that the picture is a little bigger, for the Tractarian conception of naming can be specified – and criticized – in more detail. Thus, according to Hacker, it is part of the *Tractatus* view of naming that it requires a mental act 'that injects meaning or significance into signs, whether in thought or in language'.[16] But such crude and simple views of language and mind fail to do justice to the subtlety of the *Tractatus*, a book that takes as its 'fundamental thought' the idea that certain words do not stand for anything (*Tractatus*, 4.0312). Neither of these remarkably naive views of naming and the role of mind in meaning are of much independent philosophical interest, either. It is implausible, to say the least, that these are the principal topics raised by the *Philosophical Investigations*' opening.[17]

Consequently, most of those who begin by spelling out the rather limited views they find in §1b go on to say that their real interest lies in the bigger picture that they give rise to, or otherwise support. For instance, Baker and Hacker hold that this passage introduces the 'Augustinian picture',[18] which proves to be nothing less than an entire world view or philosophical paradigm, the principal target throughout the *Philosophical Investigations*, and this interpretation has seemed obviously right to many. However, much of the attractiveness of this view depends on the way its expositors trade on the open-ended and vague character of the picture in question, moving between a relatively small and specific view in the initial exposition, and the much larger theoretical positions it supposedly underwrites. Glock's *Wittgenstein Dictionary* entry on the 'Augustinian picture of language' is a good example of this:

---

[14] Hintikka and Hintikka 1986, 179.　　[15] Ibid.　　[16] Hacker 1986, 75.
[17] Cf. Fogelin 1987, 108–9 (1976, 96); Goldfarb 1983; Wilson 1998, 1.
[18] See Baker and Hacker 1980b, ch. 1.

[Wittgenstein] treated Augustine's view not as a full-blown theory of language, but as a proto-theoretic paradigm or 'picture' which deserves critical attention because it tacitly underlies sophisticated philosophical theories . . . The Augustinian picture comprises four positions: a referential conception of word meaning; a descriptivist conception of sentences; the idea that ostensive definition provides the foundations of language; and the idea that a language of thought underlies our public languages.[19]

Indeed, less sympathetic readers of Baker and Hacker have noted that 'most of the leading ideas of the [*Philosophical Investigations* are] interpreted as so many aspects of an extended critique of the Augustinian Picture'.[20] However, the 'big picture' reading has a slender textual basis: the very expression 'Augustinian picture' is an artefact that occurs nowhere in Wittgenstein's writing, and the 'particular picture' of §1b is only one of many quite specific philosophical mistakes and temptations that Wittgenstein discusses in the pages that follow. Indeed, Wittgenstein's explicit references in the *Philosophical Investigations* to the conception of language that he finds in Augustine are outnumbered by his references to other passages from the *Confessions*, each of which serves to introduce other philosophical pictures. Running these pictures, and others, into a single over-arching 'big picture' runs contrary to Wittgenstein's emphasis on the diversity and multiplicity of the ways in which we go wrong.

Furthermore, the significance of the passage from Augustine for the *Philosophical Investigations* is not simply that the opening quotation is a convenient point of departure for a critique of mistaken views about meaning and language learning. For the very words from Augustine that Wittgenstein quotes do not lend unambiguous support to the particular interpretations he advances in §1ff., either. In fact, Wittgenstein's reading of the Augustine passage is itself remarkably one-sided. While the quotation from Augustine does begin with his learning that certain sounds his elders made were signs for things, and ends with his learning to use these signs to express his own desires, much of it does not fit Wittgenstein's description at all. Augustine does not claim that this gives a model for understanding all word

[19] Glock 1996, 41; the last idea is not present in §1b, but something like it is attributed to Augustine in §32.
[20] Carruthers 1984, 451; cf. von Savigny 1994–6, I. 37.

meaning, and actually connects understanding words with grasping their 'proper places', not only in the structure of sentences, but also the context in which they are used. He also draws our attention to the role of facial expression, the play of the eyes, and tone of voice in expressing intention.

Augustine scholars have repeatedly pointed out that Augustine's philosophical views on language and naming are much more sophisticated than those Wittgenstein attributes to him.[21] As Anthony Kenny puts it:

Augustine is a curious choice as a spokesman for the views which Wittgenstein attacks since in many respects what he says resembles Wittgenstein's own views rather than the views that are Wittgenstein's target.[22]

Kenny argues that Augustine anticipates important aspects of Wittgenstein's treatment of language learning, for they both hold that understanding ostension presupposes a certain mastery of language, and that ostension by itself cannot make clear a word's linguistic role.[23] The main problem, however, is not just that Wittgenstein's Augustine isn't the historian of philosophy's Augustine, but that Wittgenstein's description of Augustine leaves out a large part of what Augustine says in the opening quotation:

Nothing is said about those 'bodily movements' which are, as it were, 'the natural language of all peoples'. Later Wittgenstein himself will say that 'words are connected with the primitive, the natural, expressions of [a] sensation and used in their place' (§244). For Wittgenstein, it is important that language arises through shaping various 'primitive and natural' human responses, but a similar notion in the Augustinian passage is ignored. Nor does Wittgenstein notice Augustine's reference to the use of these words 'in their proper places in various sentences' even though a parallel idea was important to him throughout his philosophical development. Instead, Wittgenstein simply discusses 'a particular picture' that this passage suggests – a picture more naive than the view actually presented by Augustine.[24]

Kenny maintains that Wittgenstein's misrepresentation of Augustine in the opening of the *Philosophical Investigations* shows

---

[21] Burnyeat 1987; King 1998; Kirwan 2001.   [22] Kenny 1984, 10.
[23] Ibid.   [24] Fogelin 1987, 108–9 (1976, 96).

that he was 'unreliable as an historian of philosophy . . . even great admiration for a thinker did not ensure that Wittgenstein would represent him accurately'.[25] True, Augustine is misrepresented in §1b. But is it really plausible that Wittgenstein was such a bad reader of Augustine that he failed to notice the misfit between the first two paragraphs of his own book? We know that Wittgenstein had thought long and hard not only about how to start his book, but also about the opening chapter of the *Confessions*. The *Nachlass* contains a number of other quotations from the *Confessions*, including at least three others from Book I. The Bergen edition of the Wittgenstein papers shows 105 hits for Augustine; the only philosophers whose names occur more frequently are Russell, Frege, and Ramsey, and a search for 'Plato or Socrates' yields 111 hits. In the *Philosophical Investigations*, a book that only mentions a few other philosophers by name (Lewis Carroll, Frege, William James, Moore, Ramsey, Russell, Socrates, and the Wittgenstein of the *Tractatus*), Augustine's is the name that occurs most frequently, and the *Confessions* is the most frequently cited text. Among the few books in his possession when Wittgenstein died were Latin and German editions of the *Confessions*, which he usually read in Latin.

The first Augustine quotation in the *Nachlass* is the motto to the *Philosophical Remarks*, a typescript Wittgenstein put together in March 1930 so that Russell could read his work and write a fellowship report.

[A]nd many, passing the same way in days past, had built a sorrowful road by which we too must go, with multiplication of grief and toil upon the sons of Adam.[26]

In the *Confessions*, these words come shortly after the passage that opens the *Philosophical Investigations*: Augustine describes how he first learned Latin in school, and the painful discipline it involved. Sheed translates the words leading up to this earlier motto as follows:

---

[25] Kenny 1984, 10, 11.

[26] Augustine 1993, 10. As with all of Wittgenstein's quotations from Augustine, with the exception of §1a, he provides the Latin, without any translation: 'Et multi ante nos praestruxerant aerumnosas vias per quas transire cogebamur multiplicato dolore filiis Adam.' Augustine 1992, 1.9.14.

O God, my God, what emptiness and mockeries did I now experience: for it was impressed upon me as right and proper in a boy to obey those who taught me, that I might get on in the world and excel in the handling of words to gain honor among men and deceitful riches. I, poor wretch, could not see the use of the things I was sent to school to learn; but if I proved idle in learning, I was soundly beaten. For this procedure seemed wise to our ancestors: and many . . .[27]

Augustine's 'sorrowful road' is not only the lessons he learned in school, but also the sin of idleness and the punishment decreed by his elders; there is, in the talk of Adam, an allusion to original sin. Wittgenstein's 'sorrowful road' is left unspecified. The preface to the *Philosophical Remarks*, which stresses his mistrust of scientific and technological progress and the great distance between scientific philosophy and Wittgenstein's own, suggests a reading on which the many who have preceded him are the generations from which he received his cultural inheritance. But the inheritance in question is also the language we speak, and the ways in which it is both the source of philosophical problems and the source of their solution, a prominent theme throughout Wittgenstein's writing. There is a close connection here with the way in which Wittgenstein speaks of philosophy as a 'struggle against the bewitchment of our understanding by means of language' (§109*), a construction that invites us to consider language both as the means of bewitchment and of struggle against bewitchment. This ambiguity is present in Augustine's Latin, and especially so when it is quoted out of context, for *praestruxerant*, the word that Sheed quite naturally translates as 'built', can also mean 'blocked'.

Given the amount of thought Wittgenstein clearly gave to the question of how best to start, and given his intimate acquaintance with Augustine, is it not much more likely that he expected the reader to be initially impressed by the reading offered in §1b, but then come to see its limitations? These are multiple: §1b is only a very partial description of what Augustine says, and the picture that it does sketch is only a first example of how we can go wrong in philosophy, not the outline of an overarching 'big picture'. After all, in §1c and §2a, Wittgenstein suggests that it can help us to understand the

[27] Augustine 1993, 10.

over-simple conception of language attributed to Augustine in §1b
if we see it, not as a misdescription of our language, but rather as a
description of a language simpler than our own. Surely Wittgenstein expected the careful reader eventually to see that §1b is an
over-simple, one-sided, and provocative reading of §1a. Yet many of
Wittgenstein's readers have either, like Hintikka or Hacker, taken §1b
to be an unproblematic exposition of what Augustine says or presupposes or, like Kenny, as proof that Wittgenstein missed Augustine's
point.

Wittgenstein's opening words, like Nestroy's and Augustine's, are
not as simple as they seem. Like the motto, they offer orientation in
several different directions. Clearly, they do introduce us to a family
of views about how language is learned, and what words mean, that
will be Wittgenstein's principal target in the first sixty-four sections
of the book. Along these lines, Anscombe observes that the 'main
purpose' of the opening of the *Investigations* is negative, namely

> to persuade us not to look at the connection between a word and its mean-
> ing either as set up or as explained by (a) ostensive definition, or (b) by
> association, or (c) by mental pictures, or (d) by experiences characteristic of
> meaning one thing rather than another, or (e) by a general relation of refer-
> ence or naming or designation or signifying which has (logically) different
> kinds of objects as its terms in different cases.[28]

However, while there is a good deal of argument along these lines
in the sections that follow, much of it, like §1b, is directed at positions that are remarkably naive. Baker and Hacker's explanation of
this is that the real target is the big picture that lies behind the particular topics that are discussed. There is something right about this:
Wittgenstein is trying to get at the preconceptions and unexamined
assumptions that lead philosophers to argue as they do. However,
Wittgenstein does not see those preconceptions as something else,
over and above these particular lines of argument, along the lines
of the 'Augustinian picture', the true motives hidden behind what
philosophers say and do, but rather as present in the moves that
begin philosophical reflection. For this reason he begins with particular examples of deceptively simple philosophical arguments, of the

[28] Anscombe 1981, 154.

kind that are more likely to come up in a classroom discussion than a philosophical article or book; yet his main aim is not so much to show that they are wrong, as to get us to think about what is involved in beginning to look for a philosophical account of language and meaning. As Robert Fogelin puts it, 'for the most part the work is not a criticism of the results of philosophizing, but an interrogation of its source'.[29]

This question about the character of Wittgenstein's critique of philosophy, in turn, is connected with the question of what Wittgenstein means by saying that past philosophy is nonsense. On Hacker's reading, Wittgenstein appeals to the grammar of our language to show that what philosophers say makes no sense. While it is true that there is a strand in the book's dialogue – Cavell's 'voice of correctness' – that does make use of grammar in just this way, I take it that the point of the book is not to get us to cheer on this side of the debate. Rather, to say that philosophy is nonsense is just to say that it falls apart when we try to make sense of it:

> The results of philosophy are the discovery of one or another piece of plain nonsense and of bumps that the understanding has got by running up against the limits of language. These bumps make us see the value of this discovery. (§119*.)

But this must emerge out of the reader's involvement in the dialogue of the *Philosophical Investigations*, our being tempted into particular philosophical theories, and our coming to see that those particular attempts at theorizing are nonsensical, rather than as a more general principle, or overarching method, that any one voice in the dialogue is advocating.

In §1d, Wittgenstein describes the first of his 'language-games', patterns of language and action that he imagines or draws our attention to. The paragraph begins with an instruction and a story:

> Now think of the following use of language: I send someone shopping. I give him a slip marked 'five red apples'. He takes the slip to the shopkeeper, who opens the drawer marked 'apples'; then he looks up the word 'red' in a table and finds a colour sample opposite it; then he says the series of cardinal

---

[29] Fogelin 1987, 110 (1976, 97–8).

numbers – I assume that he knows them by heart – up to the word 'five' and for each number he takes an apple of the same colour as the sample out of the drawer. (§1d1–3)

A dialogue between a pair of opposed voices follows the story. The first voice has an authoritative tone, gets in the first and the last word, and refuses to answer the other's questions.

—— It is in this and similar ways that one operates with words. —— 'But how does he know where and how he is to look up the word "red" and what he is to do with the word "five"?' —— Well, I assume that he *acts* as I have described. Explanations come to an end somewhere. – But what is the meaning of the word 'five'? – No such thing was in question here, only how the word 'five' is used. (§1d4–9)

Identifying speeches and speakers may seem to be a straightforward matter here: 'the imaginary interlocutor to whom W. replies is spokesman for a "philosophical concept of meaning"'.[30] On this construal, Wittgenstein begins the exchange by drawing a moral about the point of his story: look to everyday examples like this one if you want to understand our use of words. The interlocutor is dissatisfied, convinced that something essential is missing from Wittgenstein's story, for the grocer's grasp of these procedures has been taken for granted. Wittgenstein denies that he has left out anything essential; explanations have to come to an end somewhere, and here all one can say is that the grocer uses the words appropriately.

Like Hallett, Baker and Hacker are in no doubt that the passage is an exchange between the author and his interlocutor. They see the replies as encapsulating and anticipating his positive views about meaning and use: once the use of a word is specified, there is nothing further to be said about its meaning.

Of course, W.'s point is that there is nothing left to say about the meaning of 'five' (properly understood) after its use has been described. The meaning of a word is given by specification of its use, and this can be done without answering questions such as 'Of what is "five" the name?' or 'What does "five" stand for?'[31]

On this reading, the grocer's story plays the same role as it does in the *Blue Book*, where a slightly different version is described as a 'simple

[30] Hallett 1977, 75.   [31] Baker and Hacker 1980a, 24.

example of operating with words'.[32] There, the story is introduced as part of Wittgenstein's refusal to give a direct answer to questions such as 'What are signs?'; instead, he recommends that we 'look closely at particular cases'.[33] From this perspective, the main point of the grocer's story is that it provides a strikingly simple illustration of some of the leading points of Wittgenstein's discussion of Augustine: different words play different roles in our language and activities. Consequently,

> it is unimportant that greengrocers do not actually go through this rigmarole . . . It would make no difference to the tale (but only complicate it) if the order were for 25 reels of ultramarine cotton thread or 17 swatches of eau-de-nil silk (here the colour identification would typically require a colour chart, and the number requires counting).[34]

But is it really unimportant that grocers never do identify apples on a chart, or the colour red by means of a sample? On closer examination, the story of §1d seems better suited to a Beckett play, or the theatre of the absurd. Wittgenstein's story is surreal precisely because it concerns ordinary skills that are taken for granted by any competent speaker, let alone a shopkeeper, and because it describes a quite extraordinary set of procedures for exercising those skills: 'Surely nothing could be more extraordinary than this scene of supposedly ordinary life.'[35] However, the strangely wooden procedures that Wittgenstein describes are not only there to highlight the differences between words for colours, numbers, and fruits. They also serve as a kind of behavioural pantomime, an acting out on the public stage of just those mental processes that philosophers have often thought must underlie our public performance: correlating the word 'red' with a mental image of the colour red, correlating number words with imagined counting procedures. Once those processes are turned into public procedures, they seem quite lifeless; but then why should

---

[32] *Blue Book*, 16.

[33] *Blue Book*, 16. However, the *Blue Book* also claims that we can make a continuous transition from these simple cases to the more complicated ones, and that 'we see that we can build up the complicated forms from the primitive ones by gradually adding new forms' (*Blue Book*, 17). This idea is explored at length in Part 1 of the *Brown Book*, which continually builds up language-games in this way, and is clearly repudiated in *Philosophical Investigations* §§130–1.

[34] Hacker, emailed draft of revised version of commentary on §1d, March 2002.

[35] Mulhall 2001, 44.

we suppose that they are able to give our words meaning once they are placed inside the mind?[36] One of Wittgenstein's ways of exorcising the belief that a mental mechanism must animate our use of language is to bring the supposed mechanism into the light by asking us to imagine a comparable public procedure.[37]

In other words, Wittgenstein's tale is not a description of ordinary life, but a realization of one of our fantasies of it: the drawers and tables of his grocer's shop reflect the architecture and furnishings of the mental theatre we attribute to ourselves, and the robotic, chanting shopkeeper is the homunculus who occupies its stage.[38]

The story is a peculiarly muted fantasy; there is no conversation between shopkeeper and shopper, and the story is entirely about behaviour and the use of signs. This leads to a rather different reading of the dialogue in the second half of §1d. Instead of a description of ordinary cases of language use (§1d1–3), followed by an exchange between the voice of correctness (§1d4, 6–7, 9) and the voice of temptation (§1d5, 8),[39] the passage begins with a behaviouristic story (§1d1–3), followed by an exchange between a behaviourist (§1d4, 6–7, 9) and an anti-behaviourist (§1d5, 8). At first sight the two readings may seem entirely at odds. On the first reading, the first sentence of the dialogue: '—— It is in this and similar ways that one operates with words' (§1d5) is an injunction to return to our ordinary use of language, which presumably includes talk of people's thoughts and actions, while on the second reading, that sentence proposes that our ordinary use of language is best understood in terms of public behaviour. Furthermore, the second reading can easily lead one to think that if this is one of Wittgenstein's leading examples of the everyday use of language, then he must be a behaviourist. Certainly, such passages help to explain why Wittgenstein has so often been pigeonholed as a behaviourist, despite his repeated insistence that he was nothing of the kind. Because he repeatedly attacks certain misconceptions about our mental lives, he is frequently taken to be

---

[36] This is one of the leading themes of the opening of the *Blue Book*; see pp. 3–6, and esp. p. 5.

[37] This strategy is pursued at much greater length in the discussion of 'reading machines' in §§156ff. (see 6.2).

[38] Mulhall 2001, 46.

[39] It is also possible to construe §1d8 as spoken by the voice of correctness (or the behaviourist), in anticipation of what the voice of temptation (or the anti-behaviourist) would say.

denying that they exist altogether: 'the impression that we wanted to deny something arises from our turning away from the picture of the "inner process"' (§305*). However, the appearance of behaviourism here is best understood as a methodological device, a voice in the dialogue, and a way of challenging our fantasies about the powers of the mind, rather than as a doctrinal commitment.

4.2 LANGUAGE-GAMES: §§1–25

The elementary exposition in 1.2 presents the argument of the *Philosophical Investigations* as the articulation of two basic argument schemes – the method of presenting a paradox and dissolving it by logico-linguistic means, and the three-stage 'method of §2'. However, we also saw that the *Philosophical Investigations* is not simply the sum of these parts. For each of these argument schemes, if taken by itself, lends itself to a considerably simpler and much more dogmatic way of doing philosophy than the approach Wittgenstein takes in the *Philosophical Investigations*. If we imagine an instance of either of these arguments as a dialogue, it would have to be a Socratic dialogue between a didactic author and a naive interlocutor. In fact, both argument schemes do lend themselves to a didactic and rather doctrinaire exposition, and that is just what one finds if one looks at the principal attempts at an exposition of Wittgenstein's thought from the first half of the 1930s.

The method of dissolving paradoxes by clarifying the logic of our language plays a very large role in the *Tractatus* and Wittgenstein's work in the early 1930s: it is particularly prominent in the 'Philosophy' chapter of the Big Typescript and the *Blue Book*. The central idea here is:

It is the business of philosophy, not to resolve a contradiction by means of a mathematical or logico-mathematical discovery, but to make it possible for us to get a clear view of the state of mathematics that troubles us: the state of affairs *before* the contradiction is resolved. (And this does not mean that one is sidestepping a difficulty.)

The fundamental fact here is that we lay down rules, a technique, for a game, and that then when we follow the rules, things do not turn out as we had assumed. That we are therefore as it were entangled in our own rules.

This entanglement in our rules is what we want to understand (i.e. get a clear view of). (§125a–c)

This aspect of Wittgenstein's work is clearly influenced by Lewis Carroll's fascination with using word play and far-fetched examples as a way of drawing our attention to logical errors, and there are far-reaching parallels between the two.[40]

The method of §2, the three-stage argument, and the notion of a language-game first emerge in the early 1930s, and reach their high point in the *Brown Book*, where each of the seventy-three numbered remarks in Part I introduces another language-game. The central idea that motivates this method is that of drawing our attention to the context in which our use of language takes place. In some cases that context consists of the rules for the use of certain terms, and in these cases there is little difference from the method of paradox; but often, and especially in work after the early 1930s, the context is a much broader one. Certainly, there is no clear distinction between the notion of a 'calculus', a formal system of rules, and a 'language-game' in Wittgenstein's work from the early 1930s, and at first the two expressions were used interchangeably. However, by the time he wrote the early version of the *Philosophical Investigations* the two terms are quite clearly contrasted with each other: 'in philosophy we often *compare* the use of words with games and calculi which have fixed rules, but cannot say that someone who is using language *must* play such a game' (§81a).

What is a language-game? In the *Philosophical Investigations*, the term is introduced by describing some examples of simple practices, both real and imaginary: Wittgenstein's 'builders', children's games with words, such as 'ring-a-ring-a-roses' (PI §7c), and the ways children learn words. But he also applies the term to almost any practice in which language is involved in some way, any interweaving of human life and language:

I shall also call the whole, consisting of language and the actions into which it is woven, a 'language-game'. (§7d)

But how many kinds of sentence are there? Say assertion, question, and command? – There are *countless* kinds: countless different kinds of use of what we call 'symbols,' 'words,' 'sentences'. And this multiplicity is not something fixed, given once for all; but new types of language, new

---

[40] See Pitcher 1967, Carroll 1895, Carroll 1974; for an interpretation of Wittgenstein's method along these lines, see Pitcher 1964, ch. 8.

language-games, as we may say, come into existence, and others become obsolete and get forgotten. (We can get a *rough picture* of this from the changes in mathematics.)

Here the term 'language-*game*' is meant to bring into prominence the fact that the *speaking* of language is part of an activity, or of a form of life.

Review the multiplicity of language-games in the following examples, and in others:

Giving orders, and obeying them –
Describing the appearance of an object, or giving its measurements –
Constructing an object from a description (a drawing) –
Reporting an event –
Speculating about the event –
Forming and testing a hypothesis –
Presenting the results of an experiment in tables and diagrams –
Making up a story; and reading it –
Play-acting –
Singing catches –
Guessing riddles –
Making a joke; telling it –
Solving a problem in practical arithmetic –
Translating from one language into another –
Requesting, thanking, cursing, greeting, praying. (§23)

Wittgenstein conceives of both language and activities here in a broad sense, one that includes not just the uttering of words and the movement of limbs, but also covers much of what we might ordinarily consider their surroundings: broader patterns of action, the equipment used (such as colour samples and blocks), and even the sites where the activities in question take place.

While 'game' is the best translation for *Spiel*, it is worth remembering that the German word is rather broader in scope than our 'game', and covers freeform activities that in English would be called 'play' rather than 'games'.[41] Clearly, Wittgenstein intends to draw an

---

[41] This is an important point to bear in mind when evaluating the claim that language, like games, forms a family of related cases that cannot be given a unitary definition (see §§65ff.). One important point of the comparison with games only emerges in §65ff., where Wittgenstein responds to the objection that he has never said what's 'essential to a language-game, and thus to language' (§65). In §66, he asks us to consider the wide variety of activities that we call 'games', and contends that if we carefully consider a wide enough variety of games, we will see that they have no one thing in common; instead, they share a variety of 'family resemblances' – games 'form a family' (§67).

analogy between language use and playful activity, but the nature of
the analogy has often not been appreciated. As we have already seen,
one of its functions is to mark a contrast with the notion of language as
a calculus, a system that is governed by a set of formally defined rules,
by stressing the involvement of language use with practical activity,
activity which may well involve rules, but is not wholly determined
by them. However, language-games are not supposed to provide the
basis for a new, practice-oriented model of language, to supplant the
logico-mathematical calculus model, but rather to serve as '*objects of
comparison*' (§130), examples that help us to get clear about difficult
cases by looking closely at their details, comparing both the similarities and differences between them. Wittgenstein is not claiming that
language is nothing more than a game, or that we can change our
language as easily as we can change a game. Rather, he is advocating
a close comparison between language and games, a comparison that
can help us see aspects of our use of language – its connection with
activity, its diversity, and the role of rules – that are often obscured by
other approaches. By getting us to attend in this way to how language
is actually used, he aims to dispel the illusions that arise when, guided
by the model of an abstract system of rules, we try to work out how it
'must' work: 'In order to see more clearly, here as in countless similar
cases, we must focus on the details of what goes on; must look at
them *from close to*' (§51b).

4.3 THE PARADOX OF OSTENSIVE DEFINITION: §§26–38

In §6, where Wittgenstein's narrator asks us to imagine a tribe whose
whole language consists in the game of §2, he suggests that the teaching of the words for the blocks will presumably consist in such activities as the teacher's repeatedly pointing to the various kinds of blocks
and saying the appropriate words. However, he observes ostensive
definition is not yet possible for a child learning the vocabulary of §2:
'I do not want to call this "ostensive definition", because the child cannot as yet *ask* what the name is' (§6b). That words have the meaning
they do is never simply the product of a single connection between
word and thing, for even when one makes such a connection, its effect
depends on the larger context:

But if the ostensive teaching has this effect, – am I to say that it effects an understanding of the word? Don't you understand the call 'Slab!' if you act upon it in such-and-such a way? – Doubtless the ostensive teaching helped to bring this about; but only together with a particular training. With different training the same ostensive teaching of these words would have effected a quite different understanding.
'I set the brake up by connecting up rod and lever.' – Yes, given the whole of the rest of the mechanism. Only in conjunction with that is it a brake-lever, and separated from its support it is not even a lever; it may be anything, or nothing. (§6c–d)

Section 8 introduces a new language-game by making additions to the game described in §2: words for numerals, colours, 'this', and 'there'. The subsequent discussion emphasizes the great differences between these words, and the even greater differences between the variety of words commonly used in everyday language. Wittgenstein's narrator stresses how the differences between these words are not simply a matter of the different ways in which they are used, but also the larger context of use and training within which they are located. One of the morals of the intricate discussion in §§19–20 of the question whether 'the call "Slab!" in example (2) [is] a sentence or a word' (§19) is that the answer depends on the resources of the language in question, and the interests and concerns of the speaker.[42] Only after an extended introductory discussion of the diversity and multiplicity of language (§§21–5) is Wittgenstein ready to turn to the topic of ostensive definition.

Section 15 first introduces an extension of the game of §2, which includes names for particular objects, by putting distinctive marks on certain objects; the builder can then use those marks as a way of getting his assistant to bring the object:

It is in this and more or less similar ways that a name denotes and is given to a thing. – It will often prove useful in doing philosophy to say to ourselves: naming something is like attaching a label to a thing. (§15*)

However, this train of thought is allowed to lapse until §26, when it is explicitly taken up again, in the context of a discussion of the view that learning language consists in naming objects, where 'object'

---

[42] For further discussion of §§19–20, see Goldfarb 1983.

covers such diverse entities as people, shapes, colours, pains, moods, numbers, and so forth. Wittgenstein writes:

> To repeat – naming is something like attaching a label to a thing. One can say that this is preparatory to the use of a word. But *what* is it a preparation *for*?

An interlocutory voice immediately answers this question at the beginning of §27, in a tone that implies the answer is entirely unproblematic:

> 27. 'We name things and then we can talk about them: can refer to them in talk.'

This provides the jumping-off point for a correction by Wittgenstein's narrator:

> – As if what we did next were given with the mere act of naming. As if there were only one thing called 'talking about a thing'. Whereas in fact we do the most various things with our sentences. Think of exclamations alone, with their completely different functions. (§27a)

The first point the narrator makes here is sceptical: that, by itself, the act of naming settles nothing, for much depends on what happens afterwards (and before). The second point is that we have many ways of talking about things, and many ways of talking that are not a matter of talking about things at all. But Wittgenstein's principal point at this stage in his discussion of naming is neither the multiplicity of ways we talk about objects, nor the many ways in which we do things with words, but how these various uses of words depend on a taken-for-granted context.

Sections 26–8 build up to Wittgenstein's paradox of ostensive definition: 'an ostensive definition can be variously interpreted in *every* case'. Given any definition of a word that involves pointing to something, one can always come up with more than one interpretation of the definition, because there will be more than one way of interpreting the act of pointing. The dialogue begins with a platitude and puzzle that could have been spoken by the Queen in *Alice Through the Looking Glass*:

> 28. Now one can ostensively define a proper name, the name of a colour, the name of a material, a numeral, the name of a point of the compass and so on. The definition of the number two, 'That is called "two"' – pointing to two nuts – is perfectly exact.

The sensible voice that replies to the puzzle fails, as Alice usually does, to see the point:

– But how can two be defined like that? The person one gives the definition to doesn't know what one wants to call 'two'; he will suppose that 'two' is the name given to *this* group of nuts! (§28a)

This sets the Queen up for her claim that the puzzle is quite general: the problem doesn't only arise for the unusual case of ostensively defining a number, but even for the most seemingly straightforward cases of ostensive definition, such as naming objects or people:

—— He *may* suppose this; but perhaps he does not. He might make the opposite mistake; when I want to assign a name to this group of nuts, he might understand it as a numeral. And he might equally well take the name of a person, of which I give an ostensive definition, as that of a colour, of a race, or even of a point of the compass. That is to say: an ostensive definition can be variously interpreted in *every* case. (§28a)

At this point, the Queen makes the next move on Alice's behalf:

29. Perhaps you say: two can only be ostensively defined in *this* way: 'This *number* is called "two".'

This is one of the ways that Wittgenstein's dialogues frequently segue into a monologue of sorts: the voice criticizing a philosophical position or intuition begins to say what the philosopher will say next. Here, this is only an opportunity for the Queen to spell out the consequences of what has just been said:

For the word 'number' here shows what *place* in language, in grammar, we assign to the word. But this means that the word 'number' must be explained before the ostensive definition can be understood. – The word 'number' in the definition does indeed show this place; does show the post at which we station the word. And we can prevent misunderstandings by saying: 'This *colour* is called so-and-so', 'This *length* is called so-and-so', and so on. That is to say: misunderstandings are sometimes averted in this way. (§29a)

At first it may look as if the Queen has conceded too much to Alice: hasn't she just said that we can settle how an ostensive definition is to be understood, by specifying the appropriate category or type the name belongs to? In practice, she concedes, misunderstandings are sometimes averted in this way. In principle, however, the problem of multiple interpretations has not gone away, for the same questions can always be raised about the classifying terms that are used in specifying the word's 'post':

But is there only *one* way of taking the word 'colour' or 'length'?
– Well, they just need explaining.
– Explaining, then, by means of other words! And what about the last explanation in this chain? (Do not say: 'There isn't a "last" explanation.' That is just as if you chose to say: 'There isn't a last house in this road; one can always build an additional one.') (§29a*)[43]

This should remind us of the end of §1: 'explanations come to an end somewhere'. We can give explanations, but somewhere, usually sooner rather than later, our explanations will give out. The beginning of §30 provides a preliminary summary of the moral to be drawn:

30*. So one might say: an ostensive definition explains the use – the meaning – of a word when the overall role of the word in language is clear. Thus if I know that someone means to explain a colour-word to me, the ostensive explanation 'That is called "sepia"' will help me to understand the word. – And you can say this, so long as you do not forget that all sorts of problems attach to the word 'to know' or 'to be clear'.

One has already to know (or be able to do) something in order to be capable of asking a thing's name. But what does one have to know?

In a way, the question at the end of §30 is a restatement of the questions that opened this part of the discussion in §26. A minimal answer here would be the one canvassed above: we have to know what kind of thing you are talking about – a number, a colour – its '*place* in language, in grammar', as Wittgenstein puts it in §29.

At this point in the discussion, Wittgenstein's narrator is particularly didactic and insistent, devoting §31 to answering the question posed at the end of §30, by way of a discussion of a simple example taken from chess. Chess is one of Wittgenstein's favourite 'objects of comparison', a familiar game that can 'throw light on the facts of our language by way not only of similarities, but also of dissimilarities' (§130). Like many of Wittgenstein's imaginary language-games, chess

---

[43] I have introduced line breaks to emphasize the changes of voice.

is a game that has a clearly stated set of rules, but one can learn the game without explicitly stating them.[44]

Section 31 considers a variety of cases in which someone might be shown a chess-piece and told 'This is the king', and uses this as a way of asking what you have to know before I can explain the use of a chess-piece to you by pointing to it and saying 'This is the king.' In the first paragraph, Wittgenstein describes a straightforward, if unlikely, scenario in which you have explicitly learned the rules, but have not yet been told what a king looks like. The second paragraph considers the case in which you pick up the game without ever hearing or stating the rules. Here, you would have learned what a king looks like as you picked up the game, but perhaps because I own one of those novelty chess sets, I might need to tell you which piece in *this* set is the king. In either case, the explanation can only work if it connects my previous knowledge with the current circumstances.

This explanation again only tells him the use of the piece because, as we might say, the place for it was already prepared. Or even: we shall only say that it tells him the use, if the place is already prepared. And in this case it is so, not because the person to whom we give the explanation already knows rules, but because in another sense he has already mastered the game. (§31b)

In both of these cases, the words 'This is the king' only do their work because I already know the rules of the game, and only need to find out which chess-piece is the king. Finally, Wittgenstein turns to the case where someone is learning how to play chess, and the teacher uses 'This is the king' to introduce the piece by pointing to it, indicating how it moves, and so forth. Here, at last, one might think, the words do more work than in the previous cases. However, Wittgenstein observes that this case, just like the others, presupposes a great deal of prior knowledge, knowledge of how games are played and taught, if not knowledge of chess itself:

– In this case we shall say: the words 'This is the king' (or 'This is called the "king"') are an explanation only if the learner already 'knows what a piece in a game is'. That is, if he has already played other games, or watched 'with understanding' other people playing – *and similar things*. Further, only under these conditions will he be able to ask relevantly in the course of learning the game: 'What do you call this?' – that is, this piece in a game.

---

[44] Note also the role of the chess example in §108cd.

We may say: only someone who already knows how to do something with it can significantly ask a name. (§31cd*)

To sum up: ostensive explanation cannot be the foundation for learning a first language, because ostensive explanation presupposes a knowledge of how names work, and more generally, a grasp of their place in language, a grasp which will include familiarity with how they are used in a variety of cases. On the other hand, ostensive explanation is likely to be a large part of language learning for someone learning a second language, for here the preconditions for ostensive explanation are already in place. In §32, this leads Wittgenstein back to Augustine, and the suggestion that the Augustinian conception of language learning is modelled on the way we learn a second language, not a first.

With the statement of the paradox of ostension, and its connection, in §32, with the issues raised at the very beginning of the book, the main business of the first half of the first 'chapter' of the *Philosophical Investigations* has been completed: we have been led from the initial expression of philosophical intuitions and proto-theories about language to a clear statement of one of the paradoxes that arise if such trains of thought are pursued. Sections 33–5 explore a variety of possible responses to this paradox, all of which turn on the idea that something in the speaker's or hearer's mind allows him or her to pick out just what's intended – such as guessing correctly, attending to the correct aspect, having a certain characteristic experience. In each case, Wittgenstein's narrator points out that the supposedly disambiguating experience won't do the job, for such experiences are neither necessary – for we can think of cases in which the experience in question occurs, but we don't pick out what's intended – nor sufficient – for we can think of cases where the experience in question doesn't occur, but we do pick out what's intended. Once again, this is a further application of the familiar three-step argument we met in chapter 1.

The point of the train of argument in §§33–5 partly lies in the details, in the careful consideration of the very wide range of cases in which we may attend to a colour, or a shape. But it also serves to lay the groundwork for the next stage of Wittgenstein's discussion of naming. Sections 36–7 sum up the principal negative and positive conclusions that emerge from what has been said so far. Negative: when we are unable to find any one bodily action that guarantees one is pointing to a shape, rather than a colour, we find ourselves thinking that something in the mind, something 'spiritual', must do the trick. Positive: the relation between name and thing named is in clear view, and consists of a variety of quite familiar activities that we engage in when using names. Wittgenstein is quite happy to refer to both physical activities, such as writing the name on the thing, or saying the name when pointing at it, as well as mental activities, such as calling the picture of the object to mind. He is not denying that we do call pictures of objects to mind, or that the particular ways of looking and attending discussed in §§33–5 do occur, and can help us identify what we're talking about; what he is denying is that 'the mind' has the peculiar, quasi-magical ability to disambiguate, to guarantee that words and things are rigidly attached to each other, in the way that the paradox of ostension can lead us to wish for.

Sections 36–7 thus wrap up the discussion of the interlocutor's initial attempts to overcome the paradox of ostension, and lead in to §38, which lays the ground for the discussion of the strategies philosophers turn to when they fail to identify everyday solutions to their problems in understanding how names work and so are driven to postulate 'spiritual' solutions. Wittgenstein speaks here of a 'tendency to sublime the logic of our language' (§38b), and says 'philosophical problems arise when language *idles*' (§38d*).[45] Philosophers have often found this diagnosis puzzling or unsatisfying: why, they ask, does Wittgenstein regard philosophical uses of language as illegitimate? Why can't we simply say that the philosopher's use of language is another language-game, no less legitimate than the ones Wittgenstein offers as examples? The nub of Wittgenstein's reply is that the philosophical uses of language he opposes are not really uses of language at all, and that appealing to philosophers' intuitions about the use of language is like appealing to our fantasies or our dreams, if we want to understand our relation to the world around us. While there are places where Wittgenstein's voice of correctness does lay down the rules of grammar, and says that philosophical mistakes consist in

---

[45] Here I follow Rhees' pre-war translation, rather than Anscombe's somewhat more literal *'goes on holiday'*; the advantage of this translation is that it makes it a little clearer that Wittgenstein's point is that the language in question is not doing any work at all.

breaking them, this is not the considered position of the author of
the *Philosophical Investigations*. Talk of language's 'idling' or 'going on
holiday' should not be understood as a matter of breaking the rules
of sense or offending against certain pragmatic principles, but rather
as summing up the way philosophical language can conjure up an
illusion of sense, a fantasy that creates the appearance of solidity.

Wittgenstein supports this diagnosis by a detailed account of how
we go wrong, how we may be led from the desire to specify what
naming consists in to the Russellian illusion that I best capture the
essence of naming when I apply the word 'this' to an object directly
in the centre of my visual field. Failing to identify a single uniform
connection in plain view that links word and thing, we are misled
into thinking that there must be something 'spiritual', a mental or
intellectual process that does the job. But this 'spiritual' process is,
as Wittgenstein puts it, a 'queer conception', for it is an unexplained
explainer that has been introduced to fill a gap of our own making.

One way of understanding Wittgenstein's talk of 'subliming' here
is as a way of talking about the 'elevated' and mysterious character of
the appeal to 'spirit'. One can also draw a connection here with the
Kantian or Romantic notion of the aesthetic sublime, a realm above or
beyond the ordinary that only the gifted visionary can reach; certainly
the suggestion that the philosopher is reaching for a spurious profun-
dity is appropriate.[46] However, the word Wittgenstein uses here is
sublimieren. While it does, like the cognate English word, mean to
elevate or to purify, German, unlike English, has a different word for
the Romantic sublime, namely *erhaben*, which would have been a
much more natural choice if Wittgenstein had meant to emphasize
this connection. There is a stronger connection here with the notion
of 'subliming' as a physical process, one that Wittgenstein, as a trained
engineer, would have found quite familiar: the direct transition from

---

[46] Usually, it is taken for granted that 'sublime' means 'elevated' or 'pure'; Cavell (1989, 56–8) is
the leading advocate of a Romantic reading. Two interpreters that do give due consideration
to the question of how to understand Wittgenstein's use of *sublimieren* are von Savigny
1991, 309–12 and 1994–6, I. 148–9, and Bearn 1997, 86–9. There are also parallels with
the psychoanalytic use of the term: Freudian sublimation is a matter of giving displaced
artistic expression to repressed drives that would otherwise be inexpressible; Wittgensteinian
sublimation is a matter of providing a metaphysical response to philosophical problems that
cannot be given a more direct solution. In both cases, the result, however beautiful it may
be, does not solve the problem that gave rise to it.

a solid to a gas, without a liquid phase – a good example would be the clouds produced when dry ice (frozen carbon dioxide) vaporizes. One way of reading this talk of 'subliming' our language is to take it to be about a mistaken attempt to purify or refine the motley material of our everyday activities into something pure and simple, much as a distillation extracts pure alcohol from a fermented liquid, or pure crystals can be formed directly from a cloud of vapour.[47] This reading enables us to draw a connection with the talk of the interlocutor's requirement of 'crystalline purity' (§97, §§107–8). A related but rather different possibility is that the transition in question is not from (impure) solid to (pure) solid, by way of a gaseous process of distillation, but rather from something everyday and solid to something cloudy and diffuse.[48] On this reading, Wittgenstein is characterizing what the philosopher does as a matter of turning something solid – our ordinary use of words, the 'working of language' (§5a) – into a gas – the mysterious 'spiritual' processes supposedly at work, 'a haze which makes clear vision impossible' (§5a). This is connected with his disparaging parenthetic reference in §109 to 'the conception of thought as a gaseous medium'. Wittgenstein's talk of condensing 'a whole cloud of philosophy . . . into a drop of grammar' (II, 222/189) would then be a way of summing up the reverse process that takes us away from these cloud-castles and back to something more definite. The 'distillation' reading is an apt summary of what the interlocutor is trying to do; the 'gaseous' interpretation captures the narrator's assessment of what the interlocutor actually does.

4.4 SUBLIMING NAMES: §§39–64

In §39 and the sections that follow, the Stage 1 formulation of the position under attack is '*A name ought really to signify a simple*' (§39). Section 39 opens the discussion by sketching an argument for the conclusion that a name must correspond to an object in order to have a meaning, an object that must exist for the name to have a meaning. The motivation for saying that '*a name ought really to signify a simple*' is that otherwise it would be contingent whether a given proposition

---

[47] This appears to be the reading that von Savigny favours.
[48] Bearn advocates this construal.

makes sense or not, for it might be the case that the things it appears to refer to don't actually exist. Section 39 sets out this Tractarian line of reasoning: if the object a name refers to doesn't exist, then the name would have no meaning. But the proposition does have meaning, and so the object in question must exist. However, §40 replies that this confuses the meaning of the name with the bearer: when Mr N. N. dies, his name is still meaningful. In other words, this account manifestly fails to fit the way we use names of everyday people and equipment, which still have a meaning when their object ceases to exist. Sections 41–2 point out that we can construct language-games that follow the Tractarian model, but that this is only one possibility. This problem leads to the idea that we must first identify those names that do stand for simples. The critique of this idea by Wittgenstein's narrator involves at least two applications of the three-stage argument. In the first he examines the idea that ordinary names signify simples (§§40–5); in the second he turns to the view that we must first analyse ordinary names into real names, names that signify 'primary elements', simple objects that must exist (§§46–64). This movement back and forth between turning to familiar words and objects as the terminus of theorizing and looking for something hidden and unfamiliar is a recurrent feature of the *Philosophical Investigations*. Pears aptly sums up this aspect of the interlocutor's predicament as follows:

[T]here are two equally slippery paths leading to the limbo in which so many philosophical theories terminate: one is to postulate something remote and recondite to play an impossible role, and the other is to give an equally impossible role to some perfectly familiar kind of thing . . . They both make the same impossible demand: when a word is attached to a thing, it must immediately slot into a pre-existing grid or lock on to rails extending indefinitely into the future.[49]

Section 41 begins a reply to the idea that ordinary names signify simples: we are asked to imagine an extension of the language-game of §2 that includes names, and to consider the case where the builder calls out the name of a broken object. What will the assistant do? First, we get a Stage 2 response, a description of a situation that fits the position under discussion:

[49] Pears 1988, 209–10. In a footnote and the surrounding text, Pears draws a connection with the concerns of §218, but the point is considerably more general.

Well, perhaps he will stand there at a loss, or show A the pieces. Here one *might* say: 'N' has become meaningless; and this expression would mean that the sign 'N' no longer had a use in our language-game (unless we gave it a new one). 'N' might also become meaningless because, for whatever reason, the tool was given another name and the sign 'N' no longer used in the language-game. (§41)

Stage 3 follows immediately – the narrator describes a different case, which the Stage 2 interpretation does not fit:

– But we could also imagine a convention whereby B has to shake his head in reply if A gives him the sign belonging to a tool that is broken. – In this way the command 'N' might be said to be given a place in the language-game even when the tool no longer exists, and the sign 'N' to have meaning even when its bearer ceases to exist. (§41)

However, the defender of the view that names must stand for simples will reply that this is just shadow boxing: if we imagine a case where a word has meaning when the bearer ceases to exist, then that just goes to show that the word wasn't really a name after all. A real name signifies something that is not composite, something absolutely simple.

In §518, Wittgenstein quotes a closely related passage from the *Theaetetus* in which Socrates argues that imagination must be a matter of imagining something. As it provides an example of how one might begin to argue for the view that words must be about something really real, something that must exist, it can provide us with an introduction to the concerns that motivate Wittgenstein's discussion of simples in §§39–64:

518*. Socrates to Theaetetus: And if you imagine mustn't you imagine *something*? – Th.: Necessarily. – Soc.: And if you imagine something, mustn't it be something real? – Th.: It seems so.[50]

Socrates gets Theaetetus to agree with him that if I imagine something, then there is some thing I imagine. But what is that thing? It can't just be my idea of what I imagine, for I can also imagine things that are real. But then what are we to say about the case where I imagine something that doesn't exist? The *Tractatus*, like Socrates at this point in the *Theaetetus*, aims at a systematic explanation of what must be the case in order for true and false statements to be

---

[50] *Theaetetus* 189a. For further discussion of this passage see Stern 1995, 54–5.

possible. The Tractarian 'solution' is that we can't really talk or think about nonexistent objects: when we say something doesn't exist, or imagine something unreal, closer analysis must show we are talking or thinking about certain simpler objects which do exist, and denying that they are arranged in a specific way. In order to avoid a regress, one is forced to conclude that there must be some primary elements, which cannot be further analysed, that refer to things that must exist. The meanings of these directly referring terms just are the objects they refer to. For Russell, these terms were demonstratives, which picked out the contents of immediate experience; for the early Wittgenstein, they were the names that referred to simple objects. These simples cannot come into existence or cease to be, for they are the unchanging ground that makes change possible.

In §518, the quotation from Plato is followed by a couple of cryptic and leading questions that amount to a compressed outline of the familiar three-stage argument:

> And mustn't someone who is painting be painting something – and someone who is painting something be painting something real? – Well, what is the object of the painting: the person in the picture (e.g.), or the person that the picture represents? (§518b*)

The first sentence, a recasting of Socrates' questions in Wittgenstein's words, also does the work of Wittgenstein's Stage 1 formulation of the problem: we are asked to consider the case of a painting, say a painting of a person, as a good example of what Socrates has in mind. Wittgenstein will often propose that we examine a claim about imagining, or another mental state, by asking us to consider a parallel case that involves a picture, or some other public object. He does not deny that we imagine, or have mental lives, but thinks that we are often tempted to accept incoherent theories about the mind because we attribute mysterious powers to the mind, and that the incoherence only becomes clear when we consider an illustration of the account in question on the public stage.[51]

The last sentence of §518 gives us a choice between two different construals of the phrase 'the object of the painting'. The first gives us a way of understanding Socrates' argument on which he is making a

---

[51] See the discussion of §1d at the end of 4.1 for another example of this strategy.

simple and uncontroversial point: if we look at a picture of a man, we may say that the object of the picture is the person contained within the picture, the person depicted there; in this sense, the object of the picture certainly exists, even if the picture is the product of the artist's imagination. This is Stage 2: if we take the object of the picture to be the person in the picture, then any painting of a person must be a painting of someone, and in a similar way we can make sense of the claim that if I imagine, I imagine something, for the talk of imagining something is just another way of talking about my act of imagination. On the other hand, it is easy to see how a Stage 3 reading is possible: if we take the picture to be the person represented by the picture, the living (or dead) person that the picture represents, then there is no guarantee that the picture must be a picture of someone, for it is entirely possible to paint a picture that has no object in this sense. The point is spelled out quite explicitly a few remarks later, in §§522–3:

522.* If we compare a proposition to a picture, we must think whether we are comparing it to a portrait (a historical representation) or to a genre-picture. And both comparisons make sense.

When I look at a genre-picture, it 'tells' me something, even though I don't believe (imagine) for a moment that the people I see in it really exist, or that there have really been people in that situation. But suppose I ask: '*What* does it really tell me?'

523.* 'What the picture tells me is "itself"' – I should like to say. That is, its telling me something consists in its own structure, in *its* forms and colours.

Thus in §§518–23, Wittgenstein leads us to a way of looking at pictures, imagination, and other forms of representation on which Socrates' problem about imagining something real is dissolved. Paraphrasing the *Blue Book* on knowledge, we could say, 'There is no one exact usage of the word "picture" or "imagine"; but we can make up several such usages, which will more or less agree with the ways the word is actually used.'[52]

Wittgenstein's narrator's main line of response to Socrates' concerns about simples in §§46–64 is very similar. For the notion of simplicity is always relative to a context: what counts as simple depends on

---

[52] See above, p. 14, and *Blue Book*, 27.

what we identify as the constituents or components of the complex in question. In §§46–8, Wittgenstein's initial response to the view that real names refer to primary elements, he proposes that we yield to the temptation and see where it leads. In Stage 1, a quotation of Socrates' statement of the view that names really stand for primary elements plays the role taken by Augustine's description of learning to speak in §1:

46.* Now what about this matter of names really standing for something simple? –

Socrates says in the *Theaetetus*: 'If I make no mistake, I have heard some people say this: there is no explanation of the *primary elements* – so to speak – out of which we and everything else are composed; for everything that exists in its own right can only be *named*, no other determination is possible, neither that it *is* nor that it *is not* . . . But what exists in its own right has to be . . . named without any other determination. Consequently, it is impossible to talk of any primary element by way of an explanation; it, after all, admits of nothing but mere naming; its name is all it has. But just as what consists of these primary elements is itself composite, indeed is an interwoven structure, so its [the structure's] names become explanatory speech through this kind of interweaving, for the essence of speech is an interweaving of names.'[53]

Both Russell's 'individuals' and my 'objects' (*Tractatus Logico-Philosophicus*) were such primary elements.

Anscombe's translation of the opening sentence of §46 – 'What lies behind the idea that names really signify simples?' – is misleading, if it suggests that Wittgenstein thinks something does lie behind this idea, and he is about to tell us what it is. Wittgenstein, looking over Rhees' convoluted but fairly literal translation – 'What is the position with regard to whether names really stand in for what is simple?' – wrote instead: 'Now what about this matter of names really standing for something simple?'[54] This way of speaking, like the German, indicates that a topic is being picked up, rather than a position taken.

Immediately afterwards, §47 tries to show us that the idea in question, that a name ought really to signify a simple, makes no sense at all. For 'simple', if it means anything at all, surely means 'not composite',

---

[53] *Theaetetus* 202a–b. Like Anscombe's translation, this is not a direct translation of the Greek, but of the German translation (by Preisendanz) that Wittgenstein used. See p. xii for further information on the translations of the *Philosophical Investigations* in this book.

[54] Wittgenstein, TS 226, p. 31.

not made up of smaller parts. The philosopher of the simple is looking for something absolutely, contextlessly, simple, but 'composite' is itself a context-dependent term. Section 47 both gives a number of striking examples of different cases in which 'composite' can be understood in different ways, and sums up Wittgenstein's response to the philosophical question about the nature of the simple:

If I tell someone without any further explanation: 'What I see before me now is composite', he will have the right to ask: 'What do you mean by "composite"? For there are all sorts of things that that may mean!' – The question 'Is what you see composite?' makes good sense if it is already established what kind of complexity – that is, which particular use of the word – is in question . . .
We use the word 'composite' (and therefore the word 'simple') in an enormous number of different and differently related ways . . .
To the *philosophical* question: 'Is the visual image of this tree composite, and what are its component parts?' the correct answer is: 'That depends on what you understand by "composite".' (And that is of course not an answer but a rejection of the question.) (§47c, §47e, §47f)

As in §1d, the nub of Wittgenstein's way of rejecting the view under discussion is set out before the method of §2 is invoked. In §48, the barrage of objections we found in §47 is distilled into a language-game that plays the role of Stage 2, a language-game that is clearly proposed by the voice of correctness, the voice that aims to make what sense it can of the idea of real simples:

48. Let us apply the method of §2 to the account in the *Theaetetus*. Let us consider a language-game for which this account is really valid. The language serves to describe combinations of coloured squares on a surface. The squares form a complex like a chessboard. There are red, green, white and black squares. The words of the language are (correspondingly) 'R', 'G', 'W', 'B', and a sentence is a series of these words. They describe an arrangement of squares in the order:

1	2	3
4	5	6
7	8	9

And so for instance the sentence 'RRBGGGRWW' describes an arrangement of this sort:

R	R	B
G	G	G
R	W	W

Here the sentence is a complex of names, to which corresponds a complex of elements. The primary elements are the coloured squares.[55]

At this point, an interlocutory voice asks, 'But are these simple?' to which the voice of correctness replies, 'I do not know what else you would have me call "the simples", what would be more natural in this language-game.' But this immediately leads to Stage 3: however natural the proposed interpretation seems, a change of context can make another interpretation more natural.

But under other circumstances I should call a monochrome square 'composite', consisting perhaps of two rectangles, or of the elements colour and shape. But the concept of compositeness might also be extended in such a way that a smaller area was said to be 'composed' of a greater area and another one subtracted from it. (§48a*)

Of course, the idea proposed here is counter-intuitive at first sight, but as Wittgenstein points out, there are precedents for it: we do think of a plane's speed flying into a headwind as the result of subtracting the headwind from the plane's cruising speed, for instance. As usual, the point of the Stage 3 argument here is not that another construal is more natural, but that another construal is possible, given different circumstances, circumstances that may be quite far-fetched.

Wittgenstein's narrator goes on to offer a diagnostic explanation for the Socratic (and Tractarian) desire to say that simples must exist, that they can only be named, and that their existence is a condition of significant discourse. He suggests that this conviction arises out of a misunderstanding of the role of paradigmatic examples (such as colour samples) or rules (such as a table correlating colours and

[55] Readers of the 2001 3rd edition of the *Philosophical Investigations* should be warned that the use of seven black squares and two white ones in the second diagram in §48 is an error. In fact, none of the revised graphics incorporated in the reissued 2nd edition (1997) are taken up in the 2001 edition. Presumably, the text of the 2001 edition is based on a photocopy of a pre-1997 printing of the 2nd edition; this would explain why black ones replaced the coloured blocks, used in most printings of the text prior to 1997. For further discussion of the use of letters here, rather than colours, see Stern, forthcoming a.

their names) in our use of language. In §50, he offers the example of the standard metre in Paris – the specially constructed measuring rod that was once used as the standard for the construction of all other measures of length in the metric system. This rod, he claims, is the one thing of which one can neither say that it is, nor it isn't, one metre long. Not because its length is ineffable, but because these words (namely, 'The standard metre is one metre long') make no sense; to say that the standard metre is one metre long is comparable to saying 'But I know how tall I am!' and putting my hand on top of my head to prove it (§279), or maintaining that 'This is here', said pointing at something right in front of me, always makes sense (§117b). The words 'The standard metre is one metre long' have the sound of a logical truth, but the 'truth' is nonsense, precisely because we are no longer making use of the standard metre as a paradigm in order to measure something else, but rather turning it back on itself. If we take into account the circumstances in which we use these words, we see that what we are trying to do in such uses of words is to step outside the usual circumstances in which we locate and measure things, with the aim of stating something more profound and fundamental. Of course, we can imagine unusual circumstances in which 'The standard metre is one metre long' could make sense – perhaps in talking to someone who has no idea what a 'standard metre' is, or in which 'This is here' might do some work – perhaps pointing out a familiar pattern that had so far gone unnoticed; but the point of such philosophical 'truths', as the philosopher wants to use them, is that they are supposed to be stating something that must be true, not drawing our attention to something unexpected. Here we are inclined to misunderstand the role assigned to the object in the language-game as though it were a mysterious feature of the object itself, and the doctrine of simples is an ontological crystallization of this methodological role.[56]

---

[56] See Diamond in McCarthy and Stidd 2001 for further discussion of the standard metre.

CHAPTER 5

The critique of rule-based theories of meaning and the paradox of explanation: §§65–133

5.1 THE GENERAL FORM OF THE PROPOSITION AND THE PARADOX OF EXPLANATION: §§65–88

Almost without exception, commentators agree that §65 marks an important turning point, or change of focus, in the *Philosophical Investigations*. However, the precise character of this turn is more elusive than it seems at first.

Sections 60 to 64 clearly continue the discussion of simples that begins with §39, and §64 explicitly refers back to the language-game of §48, offering yet another problematic language-game for the defender of analysis into ultimate simples. In §64, we are asked to imagine people who have no names for monochrome blocks, but do have names for distinctive combinations of colours, such as the French tricolour. While most people see these flag-like blocks as composed of several colours, Wittgenstein's narrator suggests that those who are used to the alternate system of representation would see things differently. The conviction that we can analyse their blocks into what we regard as the simpler components used in the game of §48 is, he proposes, the product of our taking a familiar way of speaking for granted. 'We think: If you have only the unanalysed form you miss the analysis; but if you know the analysed form that gives you everything. – But may I not say that an aspect of the matter is lost on you in the *latter* case as well as the former?' (§63).[1]

---

[1] Readers familiar with Goodman's discussion of 'grue' – objects that are grue are green if examined before time t and red if examined after t, where t is a time shortly in the future – will see some analogies with the language-game of §64. Given that all the evidence we have for emeralds being green is also evidence for their being grue, Goodman challenges us to say why we expect emeralds to be green after t, rather than grue.

With §65, this discussion of objections to the notion of simples comes to an abrupt end, as the narrator directs our attention to the 'question that lies behind all these considerations'. He does so by bringing up an objection to the whole train of thought that has led up to this point:

– For someone might object against me: 'You take the easy way out! You talk about all sorts of language-games, but have nowhere said what the essence of a language-game, and hence of language, is: what is common to all these activities, and what makes them into language or parts of language. So you let yourself off the very part of the investigation that once gave you yourself most headache, the part about the *general form of propositions* and of language.' (§65a)

Wittgenstein's narrator responds as follows:

And this is true. – Instead of producing something common to all that we call language, I am saying that these phenomena have no one thing in common which makes us use the same word for all, – but that they are *related* to one another in many different ways. And it is because of this relationship, or these relationships, that we call them all 'languages'. I will try to explain this. (§65b*)

66.* Consider for example the performances that we call 'games'. I mean board-games, card-games, ball-games, Olympic games, and so on. What is common to them all? – Don't say: 'There *must* be something common, or they wouldn't be called "games" ' – but *look and see* whether there is anything common to all. – For if you look at them you will not see something that is common to *all*, but similarities, relationships, and a whole series of them at that. To repeat: don't think, but look! . . .

And the result of this examination is: we see a complicated network of similarities overlapping and criss-crossing: sometimes overall similarities, sometimes similarities of detail. (§66b*)

At first sight, it looks as if the narrator straightforwardly agrees with the objection he imagines being raised against him in §65a. But when he says 'And this is true', what, precisely, is he agreeing to, and what has he rejected? The objector's principal complaint is that Wittgenstein has given up on what he had once regarded as a central philosophical problem: saying what the essence of language consists in, or what all linguistic phenomena have in common. In the *Tractatus*, this had taken the form of specifying the 'general form

of the proposition'. The *Tractatus* begins by telling us that the world
is all that is the case, the totality of facts, not of things (1–1.1). Such
a world is perfectly suited to the Tractarian conception of language,
for one of the main aims of that book is to provide 'a description of
any sign-language *whatsoever* . . . what is essential to the most general
propositional form' (4.5).[2] This general form of the proposition is
specified as 'This is how things stand.' The rationale for this way of
conceiving of language is that any significant statement must make
some factual claim about the world, that this is how things stand,
that such and such is the case.

So, minimally, Wittgenstein's narrator is now agreeing that he
rejects this Tractarian way of conceiving of language. It is also clear
that he is rejecting a Socratic approach to language and concepts, on
which it is always legitimate to ask questions such as 'What is language?' or 'What is a game?' and to look for an answer that provides
a definition in terms of necessary and sufficient conditions. There is
a clear contrast in the German, not always preserved in Anscombe's
translation, between such a definition (*Definition*) and an explanation
(*Erklärung*), a broader term that covers the much wider variety of ways
in which we answer questions, questions not only about the meaning
of words, but also about why things happen as they do. Depending
on the context, Wittgenstein's use of 'explanation' covers not only
everyday explanations of meaning – the sorts of things one says when
asked the meaning of a particular word, such as 'game', 'language',
'chair', or 'Moses' – but also the explanations a scientist would give of
natural processes. In the sense of the term in which science provides
explanations, Wittgenstein is opposed to any place for explanation
in philosophy (§126). On the other hand, many expositors take §66
and the sections immediately following to amount to a sketch of the
place that explanations of meaning have in Wittgenstein's positive
philosophy.

We have seen that one of the leading themes of the opening sections
of the *Philosophical Investigations* is an attack on the idea that ostensive
definition provides the point of departure for an understanding of the
relationship between words and the world. For such devices only work
when most of our language is already in place: any successful definition

---

[2] This translation is from Wittgenstein 1961b.

of a word that depends on pointing to what it names presupposes a great deal of prior 'stage-setting'.[3] In the remarks that follow §65, Wittgenstein attacks the idea that we can rescue the project of a systematic philosophical understanding of the nature of language if we focus, not on ostensive links between words and non-linguistic items, but on analysing relationships between words. His initial target is the notion that we can provide such an analysis by means of verbal definition, a definition that specifies the meaning of words by stating necessary and sufficient conditions for their use.

However, one might reject these Socratic and Tractarian views about the nature of language, and still maintain that language has a nature, only one considerably more complex than Socrates, or the author of the *Tractatus*, had expected. For all the narrator actually says he has given up at this point is the idea that there is something common to everything that falls under the rubric of language. He now holds that 'these phenomena have no one thing in common which makes us use the same word for all' (§65b), and instead proposes that we think of them as related to each other in many different ways. There is no single essence, but only a criss-crossing pattern of similarities and dissimilarities, as in a family or in the case of games. It is not immediately clear whether this amounts to a more sophisticated statement of what is essential to language, or a Pyrrhonian rejection of the question. At this point, all that one can safely say is that Wittgenstein's narrator has given up certain rather extreme views about language and definition.

This, of course, leaves room for many less extreme views about the essence of language, and these have frequently been attributed to Wittgenstein, often on the basis of an interpretation of the sections immediately following §65. Indeed, whether an interpreter reads these sections as setting out a positive non-Pyrrhonian view about the nature of language, and if so, what form the view takes, provides a good indication of the extent to which he or she reads Wittgenstein as espousing a positive philosophy of language. It has seemed to many commentators as though Wittgenstein aims to replace definitional analysis by something looser but nevertheless rule-governed or systematic. Thus it is often taken for granted that Wittgenstein is

---

[3] See 4.3 and 7.2 for further discussion of this issue.

offering a 'family resemblance' analysis of concepts as a substitute for definition, or that 'explanations of meaning' really do enable us to specify the rules for the use of the words in question. On this non-Pyrrhonian way of reading Wittgenstein, he is replacing the *Tractatus* account of the '*general form of propositions* and of language' (§65a) with a new conception of 'the essence of a language-game, and hence of language' (§65a).

A classic early exposition of such a non-Pyrrhonian reading is Renford Bambrough's 'Universals and Family Resemblances'. He claims there that Wittgenstein 'solved the problem of universals . . . his remarks can be paraphrased into a doctrine which can be set out in general terms and can be related to the traditional theories, and which can be shown to deserve to supersede the traditional theories'.[4] Unfortunately, on Bambrough's reading, the traditional theories look suspiciously like straw men: the realist about universals holds that games have something in common other than that they are called games, while the nominalist holds that games have nothing in common except that they are called games. His Wittgenstein finds the middle position that takes what is best from each of these doctrines: he holds, with the realist, that there is an objective justification for applying the word 'game' to games, but agrees with the nominalist that there is no element that is in common to all games.

And he is able to do this because he denies the joint claim of the nominalist and the realist that there cannot be an objective justification for the application of the word 'game' to games unless there is an element that is common to all games . . . or a common relation that all games bear to something that is not a game.[5]

This, then, is the basis for a doctrine of 'family resemblances' as providing the underlying justification for the use of terms which do not pick out a group of things that all share a common feature: rather, the term applies because the things in question form a family, interconnected by a number of properties, each of which is shared by some of them. On Bambrough's reading, the point of Wittgenstein's discussion of games can be summed up as follows:

[4] Bambrough 1966, 198.   [5] Bambrough 1966, 199.

We may classify a set of objects by reference to the presence or absence of features ABCDE. It may well happen that five objects *edcba* are such that each of them has four of these properties and lacks the fifth, and that the missing feature is different in each of the five cases. A simple diagram will illustrate this situation:

$$e \quad\quad d \quad\quad c \quad\quad b \quad\quad a$$
$$ABCD \quad ABCE \quad ABDE \quad ACDE \quad BCDE^6$$

However, while this approach may at first sight seem to capture what Wittgenstein is saying in §65b and turn it to good use, it is deeply misleading. For what the narrator asserts about explaining the meanings of words, and how they can be compared to family resemblances, is supposed to be an obvious objection to a simple-minded theory, much in the spirit of the observation in §2 that some words do not name objects. The narrator's point is not that we can get a better theory of meaning by refining the overly simple account he begins with. Rather, like any Stage 2 objection to a proto-philosophical theory, this is an opening move in a longer discussion. While the broader aim is to get us to see how misguided it is to look for a theory of meaning or a systematic explanation of meaning, Wittgenstein was well aware that any self-respecting philosopher will regard the discussion so far as an invitation to provide a better analysis. Glock frames the issue along just these lines. On his reading, the claim that there is no analytic definition of 'game' is only argued for by

counter-examples to some plausible definitions. [Wittgenstein] is therefore open to the charge that, with persistence, game can be analytically defined, for example, as a rule-guided activity with fixed objectives that are of little or no importance to the participants outside the context of the game.[7]

But the issues raised by the discussion of games in the part of §66 not quoted above are much more far-reaching than the conclusions Bambrough and Glock find there. Wittgenstein's narrator is not only offering simple counter-examples to simple definitions; he is also addressing larger questions about the place of rules in an explanation of meaning. In particular, he is attacking the idea that for a concept

---

[6] Bambrough 1966, 189.
[7] Glock 1996, 120. Note, however, that there are games without fixed objectives, and many games are of great significance to the participants in a broader context.

to be usable, it must be precisely determined by a system of rules, that understanding a word or a sentence involves commitment to definite rules for its use. The problem is not only that certain specific predicates – psychological predicates, ordinary terms like 'game', or philosophical terms like 'language' – don't lend themselves to definition, but that *any* rule can be variously interpreted, including the rules we use when giving a definition of a term such as 'number' (§68). The point is not the vagueness, fuzziness, or open texture of our concepts, for we can certainly give rigorous definitions of number, but rather whether any definition can determine how a term is used, for any definition of number is only a definition of a particular kind of number:

I *may* give the concept 'number' rigid limits in this way, that is, use the word 'number' for a rigidly limited concept, but I may also use it so that the extension of the concept is *not* closed by a frontier. And this is how we do use the word 'game'. (§68a*)

Insofar as Wittgenstein's narrator does have something positive to offer in this section and the text immediately following, it is in the form of a reminder as to how we ordinarily answer questions such as 'What is a game?'[8] – namely, by giving examples. Thus, according to Baker and Hacker, Wittgenstein is offering an overview of our explanatory practices, helping us to see clearly how we do provide such explanations. But their account teeters on the line that separates the platitudinous Pyrrhonian – reminders of what we ordinarily say when answering requests for explanation – and the doctrinal non-Pyrrhonian – a systematic account of the rules that supposedly govern our explanatory practices, something not so very different from the doctrine of family resemblance that Bambrough finds in this passage. Baker and Hacker begin their essay on 'Explanation' by stressing the platitudinous:

The meaning of an expression is not something deeper and more theoretical than what is patent in the accepted practice of explaining this expression; and this practice, like any normative practice, must be familiar to its participants, open to inspection, and surveyable. (1980b, 30)

---

[8] And similar questions, such as 'What is a leaf?' (§§73–4) or 'Who was Moses?' (§79).

However, this soon slips over into a suspiciously systematic doctrine concerning the place of explanation in a system of linguistic rules:

> Giving an explanation consists in displaying some of the connections in the grammatical reticulation of rules. Explanations are rules, but, of course, not always or even usually application rules. Their normativity consists in the fact that a rule given by an acceptable explanation provides a standard to judge correct uses of an expression. This may be by way of *grounds* of application, legitimacy of *substitution*, or *criteria of understanding*. (1980b, 36–7)

'Reticulation' is a sublimely botanical-sounding word for a network; thus the 'grammatical reticulation of rules' is the network of rules concerning how our words are used that we take for granted when we provide explanations of meaning. The basic idea here is that an explanation provides us with a rule with which we can judge whether words are used correctly.

The principal issue at stake is whether explanation in particular, and language in general, is best understood as a set of rule-governed, systematic procedures; or whether it is better understood if we are equally attentive to the ways in which it is ad hoc and dependent on a particular circumstance and context. It is this Pyrrhonian aspect of the text that Cavell places at the centre of his interpretation:

> That everyday language does not, in fact or in essence, depend on . . . a structure and conception of rules, and yet the absence of such a structure in no way impairs its functioning, is what the picture of language drawn in the later philosophy is all about.[9]

On this reading, the underlying 'common factor' that Wittgenstein's narrator is rejecting is not only the analytic definitions that are the target of §66, but the very idea of a 'grammatical reticulation of rules'. As §69 and §71 stress, we frequently explain the meaning of words by offering paradigmatic examples. These examples need not be given in such a way that they are protected against all possibilities of misunderstanding; it is enough that they usually work, and it is part of how they work that they have no exact boundaries.

---

[9] Cavell 1966, 156.

69. How should we explain to someone what a game is? I imagine that we should describe *games* to him, and we might add: 'This *and similar things* are called "games".' And do we know any more about it ourselves? Is it only other people whom we cannot tell exactly what a game is? – But this is not ignorance. We do not know the boundaries because none have been drawn.

This is just how one might explain to someone what a game is. One gives examples and intends them to be taken in a particular way. – I do not, however, mean by this that he is supposed to see in those examples that common thing which I – for some reason – was unable to express; but that he is now to *employ* those examples in a particular way. Here giving examples is not an *indirect* means of explaining – in default of a better. For any general explanation can be misunderstood too. The point is that *this* is how we play the game. (I mean the language-game with the word 'game'.) (§71b*)

Wittgenstein's narrator is denying that if one understands a word, such as 'game' (or 'language', or for that matter, any arbitrary predicate, F), one must be able to formulate a rule that enables us to say whether any chosen item is an F. More generally, he opposes the idea that there is something lying behind my use of my words that justifies me in what I say, something over and above our use of the words, which can be used to provide a philosophical legitimation for it. Wittgenstein's narrator insists that the postulated entities, be they ideas in the mind, processes in the brain, or the grammatical reticulation of rules, are a philosophical fiction that do no work, like a wheel that appears to be connected to the rest of a mechanism, but actually is idling. One way of making this point is to imagine these entities in plain view, and see how ineffective they are; another is to point out that whatever work they do, they do within a particular context and setting. Instead, he points our attention to what is in plain view – the various relationships we attend to, and the examples and explanations we give when asked to explain a word's meaning.

The narrator's response to Socratic demands for an analysis of what words mean in terms of rules for their use culminates in the formulation of a paradox about explanation: any explanation hangs in the air unless supported by another one. The paradox is introduced in §86. We are asked to imagine a language-game like the builder's game in §2, but with the addition of a table of instructions. In it, the builders use a table to link written signs with pictures of building stones:

The signs given to B by A are now written ones. B has a table; in the first column are the signs used in the game, in the second pictures of building stones. A shows B such a written sign; B looks it up in the table, looks at the picture opposite, and so on. So the table is a rule which he follows in executing orders. – One learns to look the picture up in the table by receiving a training, and part of this training consists perhaps in the pupil's learning to pass with his finger horizontally from left to right; and so, as it were, to draw a series of horizontal lines on the table.

Suppose different ways of reading a table were now introduced; one time, as above, according to the diagram:

another time like this:

or in some other way. – Such a diagram is supplied with the table as the rule for its use.

Can we not now imagine further rules to explain *this* one? And, on the other hand, was that first table incomplete without the diagram of arrows? And are other tables incomplete without their diagrams? (§86a–c*)

The discussion of the language-game of §2 sets out some of the problems facing the philosopher attracted to the idea that the meaning of a word can be explained by pointing to the object it stands for. In a closely analogous way, the language-game of §86 takes aim at the idea that the meaning of a word can be explained by pointing to another sign.[10] For the explanation of words in terms of signs presupposes that a customary way of responding to words and signs is already in place, just as our ordinary practice of ostension presupposes that we follow the line formed by the speaker's pointing finger, not her forearm.

---

[10] However, while §2 is part of the opening of the discussion of ostension, §86 reformulates concerns about explanation that have already been raised in the preceding discussion.

The **paradox of ostension** – 'an ostensive definition can be variously interpreted in *every* case' (§28) – arises because we can always imagine a situation in which an ostensive definition misfires, or is misunderstood, because some aspect of the taken-for-granted context or circumstances is abnormal. Similarly, the **paradox of explanation** – 'an explanation can be variously interpreted in *every* case' – arises because we can always imagine a situation in which an explanation misfires because a further explanation is needed. Once we imagine an explicit explanatory table, of the kind pictured above, showing how words and signs are connected, we can also, of course, 'imagine further rules to explain *this* one' (§86c). Nevertheless, we surely want to reply to the closing questions in §86, that a table need not be incomplete without further diagrams; for if it is, a vicious regress threatens, in which every table requires a further table in turn before it can be understood. Wittgenstein's narrator has anticipated this issue, for the discussion of the analogy between a rule and a signpost in §85 raises just the kind of sceptical doubts he had earlier raised about ostensive definition, and leads to a closely parallel conclusion:

85. A rule stands there like a sign-post. – Does the sign-post leave no doubt open about the way I have to go? Does it show which direction I aim to take when I have passed it; whether along the road or the footpath or cross-country? But where is it said which way I am to follow it; whether in the direction of its finger or (e.g.) in the opposite one? – And if there were, not a single sign-post, but a chain of adjacent ones or of chalk marks on the ground – is there only *one* way of interpreting them? – So I may say, the sign-post does after all leave no room for doubt. Or rather: it sometimes leaves room for doubt and sometimes not. And now this is no longer a philosophical proposition, but an empirical one.

Whether or not a given rule or sign-post gives rise to doubts about what it means will depend both on its context and on our interpretation of that context. If a doubt does arise, then it will be appropriate to ask a question. What Wittgenstein denies is that every possible question must be answered for the sign to be any use. We do not need to explain how a potential ambiguity is to be resolved unless it actually arises. That explanation may, in turn, call for further explanations, but once again, only if it is necessary to prevent a misunderstanding.

Section 87 draws out some of the further consequences of this train of thought by exploring the implications of the worry that we need some way of replying to the question: what is to stop us thinking that every word we use in an explanation may itself stand in need of explanation? An interlocutory voice exclaims:

—— 'But then how does an explanation help me to understand, if after all it is not the final one? In that case the explanation is never completed; so I still don't understand what he means, and never shall!' (§87a)

Wittgenstein's narrator responds along lines very similar to his extended response to the paradox of ostension in §§29–32:

– As though an explanation as it were hung in the air unless supported by another one. Whereas an explanation may indeed rest on another one that has been given, but none stands in need of another – unless *we* require it to prevent a misunderstanding. One might say: an explanation serves to remove or to avert a misunderstanding —— one, that is, that would occur but for the explanation; not every one that I can imagine.

It may easily look as if every doubt merely *revealed* an existing gap in the foundations; so that secure understanding is only possible if we first doubt everything that *can* be doubted, and then remove all these doubts.

The sign-post is in order – if, under normal circumstances, it fulfils its purpose. (§87a–c)

However, the flat rejection here of the philosophical demand that we must be able to answer every possible doubt is itself only part of an intricate and complex dialogue with that demand. Both ostensive definition – explaining the meaning of a word by pointing to an object – and the explanatory diagrams discussed in §86 – are ways of specifying the meaning of words by providing a rule, and the problem that arises in each case is that it can seem as if nothing can guarantee that the rule will be understood correctly. In other words, the paradox of ostension and the paradox of explanation are both instances of a more general sceptical paradox about rules, which we can call the **rule-following paradox**, a theme that plays a leading role in much of the subsequent discussion. Making use of the format of §28 one more time, we can formulate it as follows: 'a rule can be variously interpreted in *every* case'. The philosophical response is that *something* must guarantee that the rule is correctly applied, just as something must guarantee that the name refers to its object, or an intention determines its conditions of satisfaction.

However, it is characteristic of Wittgenstein's way of proceeding in the *Philosophical Investigations* that the sceptical paradox is pursued by means of a close discussion of specific instances; indeed, the most explicit discussion of the paradox does not occur until §§198–202, by which time it plays the role of a recapitulation of the extensive discussion that has already taken place. In fact, while sceptical paradoxes about rule-following return to centre stage in §139 and the remarks that follow, they drop into the background in the remarks that immediately follow §87.

We can better appreciate Wittgenstein's reasons for postponing the further discussion of the rule-following paradoxes for another fifty remarks if we review the parallels with the course of the discussion that follows the formulation of the paradox of ostensive definition. As we saw in 4.4, the paradox of ostensive definition leads up to an extended consideration of 'sublime names', names that have a metaphysically guaranteed connection with simple objects. A leading motivation for this peculiar conception of names and objects is that they cannot be prised apart; it is an essential part of this conception of simple names and simple objects that they are constructed in such a way that each requires the other. In other words, this notion of simple names, the naming relation, and the object named is just what the philosopher needs to ensure that sceptical doubts about ostensive definition could not succeed. The problem, of course, is precisely that this fit between names and objects is too good to be true: the story about simple names is not based on close examination of what we say about names, but is instead a matter of responding to worries about what names must be like if the paradox of ostensive definition is to be overcome. Because such names and objects do not appear to be part of our everyday life and language, we are driven to postulate that they are somehow hidden, lying behind or beneath the familiar things we say and discuss.

A very similar dialectic motivates the remarks that follow §87. Just as the paradox of ostensive definition leads to a demand for names that must pick out the right object, the paradox of explanation leads to a demand for an analysis of our ordinary language in order to arrive at rules that guarantee their correct application – a sublime logic.

Despite Wittgenstein's narrator's insistence that examples and inexact explanations are often just what we need (§§70–1, 76–7, 88) and that a rule is in order 'if, under normal circumstances, it fulfils its purpose' (§87c), he is well aware that this will not dispel the attractiveness of the requirement that there must be something hidden behind the surface of our ordinary language, 'the *essence* of language, of propositions, of thought' (§92a). For it can seem as if 'a proposition must achieve a very extraordinary feat, in fact, a unique feat' (§93b*): somehow it must contain whatever is needed to overcome the sceptical paradoxes and connect words and the world. The very intractability of philosophical problems – the fact that they are not immediately dispelled by what the narrator has to say – is a central concern in §§89–133.

5.2 SUBLIMING LOGIC: §§89–133

89. These considerations bring us up to the problem: In what sense is logic something sublime?

Section 89 is a prominent point of transition in the text. The first sentence is clearly concerned with orienting the reader by connecting where we have come from ('these considerations') and where we are going ('the problem'). However, it is not entirely clear, at this point, where we have come from, and where we are going. Like the signposts in §85 and §87, what is said in §89 can be interpreted as pointing in a number of directions. We shall see that the next paragraph, §89b, is an exchange between different voices that lends itself to a number of very different readings.[11] Much depends on how one answers the following questions:

(1) What, precisely, is the problem of the sublimity of logic?
(2) To what extent is the problem of the sublimity of logic a new topic, and to what extent is it a development of a previous discussion?

Anscombe's translation leaves open the reading that the issues that have been discussed previously lead up to a further, related problem about the sublimity of logic. However, the German is not ambiguous in this way, nor was the translation Wittgenstein and Rhees wrote:

89. With these considerations, we find ourselves facing the problem: is logic, in some way, sublime?

---

[11] See the discussion of §89, §133, and §§89–133 on pp. 129–32.

Wittgenstein's choice of words makes it clear that he is taking up a problem we already face and must now attend to; they also make it clear that he is not asserting that there is a sense in which logic is sublime, but drawing our attention to a problem, or a question, about the 'sublimity' of logic.[12] The principal significance of these linguistic clues is that in answering our first question, we need not only to look forward to what is said in the rest of §89 and the following sections, but also to look back to the preceding text, and to attend to how the problem mooted in §89 arose there. But this brings us back to our first question: which considerations are the relevant ones, and what is the problem of the sublimity of logic?

Baker and Hacker interpret the talk of the 'sublimity of logic' as the beginning of a discussion of philosophical method. They take 'logic' here to be another way of talking of the 'logical investigations' referred to in §89b: philosophical investigation of language guided by the spirit of formal logic. They draw a close connection with §81 and §88, which criticize the idea that logic can appear 'better, more perfect, than our everyday language' and so provide the basis for thinking of philosophy as laying out the essence of what any world must be like, as a study of the structure of what is possible.[13] On this reading, the use of 'sublime' here is a way of indicating the overly elevated status given to formal logic in philosophical analysis; there is also an affinity with the Kantian conception of the sublime as an aesthetic category, a term for something unreachably deep or profoundly awe-inspiring. To sum up: to sublime logic is for a philosopher to aim at an illusory precision, and in doing so, to turn the logico-philosophical investigation of our language into spurious profundities. This is an account of the relationship between the everyday use of words and their metaphysical use whose centre of gravity is a quite particular conception of the everyday use of words, namely a non-Pyrrhonian philosophy of ordinary language; to sublime logic is to put forward illegitimate philosophical doctrines, theories that can be shown to break the rules of ordinary language.

---

[12] Rhees provided a very literal translation of the German turn of phrase: 'With these considerations we are at the place where the problem is: . . .', which Wittgenstein changed to 'With these considerations, we find ourselves facing the problem: . . .' As von Savigny puts it, the part of §89a prior to the colon 'means that by considerations which preceded §89 we already got involved in the problem' (1991, 309).

[13] Baker and Hacker 1980a, 195; see also 190. See also the discussion of Baker and Hacker on §89 and §133 on pp. 129–32, and the discussion of 'subliming' in 4.3–4.4.

One can object to the methodological reading that it fails to take seriously that 'logic' here simply means rules for the use of words. In that case, to sublime logic is not to pursue an inappropriately exacting method of doing philosophy that leads to mistaken theories; rather, it amounts to a systematic misrepresentation of how we ordinarily act and speak that leads to nonsense, by turning that usage into something nebulous that appears to solve our philosophical problems about the nature of language. This is an account of the relationship between the everyday use of words and their metaphysical use whose centre of gravity is a quite particular conception of the metaphysical use of words, namely a Pyrrhonian critique of philosophical language. On this reading, the talk of subliming logic is closely aligned with the 'tendency to sublime the logic of our language' of §38, where the term is clearly used to sum up objections to cutting off our actual use of language from the activities in which they are embedded. Section 89, then, brings us back to critical reflection on the idea that there are philosophical rules that govern the meaning of words, rules that are independent of the words' practical application. This is emphasized in the passage that wraps up the initial discussion of the topic in §§89–90:

Our investigation is therefore a grammatical one. And this investigation sheds light on our problem by clearing away misunderstandings. Misunderstandings concerning the use of words of our language, brought about among other things by certain analogies between different forms of expression. (§90b*)

On a Pyrrhonian reading, 'grammar' is not a matter of using the rules of ordinary language to police the bounds of sense, but rather consists in 'clearing away misunderstandings': 'The problems are solved, not by reporting any new experience, but by arranging what we have always known' (§109).

There is a more general point to be made here about the relationship between the book and the source materials. Baker, Hacker, Hilmy, and Glock attach a great deal of significance to the fact that some of the most striking passages in §§89–133 were among the first passages in the book to be written, and see this swatch of text as a condensation of the methodology already set out in the Big Typescript's 'Philosophy' chapter. But the connections between the two texts are considerably more complex. A rather small proportion of the

'Philosophy' chapter makes up a relatively small part of §§89–133; and it is far from obvious that the *Philosophical Investigations* is to be read as carrying out the programme set out in the Big Typescript. In fact, one of the greatest dangers in turning to Wittgenstein's writings from the first half of the 1930s, and especially the best-known materials, such as the 'Philosophy' chapter of the Big Typescript, the *Blue Book*, and the *Brown Book*, is that while they are in many ways quite similar to the *Philosophical Investigations*, they are often much more systematic and dogmatic.

Sections 89–133 are often spoken of as 'the chapter on philosophy'. The almost universally accepted reading of this part of our text is that §§89–133 set out Wittgenstein's metaphilosophy, his view of the nature of philosophy.[14] One strand of the standard metaphilosophical reading approaches these paragraphs as a positive statement of his 'philosophical method';[15] another emphasizes the way in which his later conception of philosophy arises out of, and is contrasted with, his earlier work.[16] In either case, it is usually taken for granted that the content of this 'chapter' is a compressed statement of a positive view about the right and the wrong way to do philosophy, a summary of Wittgenstein's objections to traditional ways of doing philosophy that contrasts them with his own non-Pyrrhonian views about the primacy of ordinary language and the autonomy of grammar.

The view that §§89–133 constitute the 'chapter on philosophy' – the place in the *Philosophical Investigations* where Wittgenstein summarizes his non-Pyrrhonian philosophical method and his ordinary language philosophy – looks, at first sight, as if it is strongly supported by an examination of previous versions of this material. For some of the most striking passages on philosophy and ordinary

---

[14] Von Savigny begins a paper challenging this consensus as follows: 'There is universal agreement in the literature – I have, in fact, not met with even one exception – that in section 89 to 133 . . . Wittgenstein is expounding his view of philosophy: of what it can and cannot achieve, of how it ought and how it ought not to be done. These passages are taken to express his metaphilosophy, in short' (von Savigny 1991, 307). Another exception is Fogelin's Pyrrhonian reading of §§89–133, which stresses that 'Wittgenstein's problems are philosophical rather than *meta*-philosophical . . . For Wittgenstein, philosophical problems are not genuine problems: they present nothing to be solved . . . A philosophical investigation should respond directly to a philosophical problem by exposing its roots and removing it' (Fogelin 1987, 142; cf. 1976, 127).

[15] McGinn 1997, 73.   [16] Baker and Hacker 1980b, ch. 13.

language, including the ones quoted above, can be dated to 1930 or shortly afterwards, and so are some of the first passages in the book to have been written.[17] Furthermore, those passages are included in a chapter on 'Philosophy' in the Big Typescript, assembled in 1932–3. Baker and Hacker summarize the situation as follows:

> The manuscript sources of [§§89–133] date *primarily* from two periods: 1930–1 and 1937... It is noteworthy that the general conception of philosophy that dominates Wittgenstein's later work emerged so early, namely in 1930–1. (The 1937 reflections are largely concerned with criticizing the idealization of logic and language that characterized *Tractatus*; these dominate PI §89–§108.)[18]

In view of the extensive use of material from the Big Typescript on topics such as meaning, naming, intention, and rule-following in the *Philosophical Investigations*, the conclusion can easily be generalized: not only Wittgenstein's later philosophical method, but also his characteristic approach to central issues, had already been worked out by 1933 at the latest. On this reading of the evidence:

> The Big Typescript . . . marks the end of the transition period, since it already contains his mature conception of meaning, intentionality and philosophy.[19]

However, to extract a 'general conception of philosophy' from a selected handful of striking passages is to beg any number of questions,

---

[17] *Philosophical Investigations* §§116, 119–20, 123–4, 126–9, 132; also parts of §§87, 88, 108, 111, 118, 122, and 133. Sources and dates for the material quoted above: §116a: MS 109, p. 246, 23 Nov. 1930; §116b: MS 110, p. 34, 4 Feb. 1931; §122: MS 110, p. 257, 2 July 1931; §126a1: MS 110, p. 217, 24 June 1931; §126a2–3: MS 110, p. 90, 18 Feb. 1931; §126b: MS 108, p. 160, 13 May 1930.

[18] Baker and Hacker 1980a, 188. Hilmy also sees the emergence of Wittgenstein's later conception of philosophy in this light:

> One needs only a quick glance at the content of the relevant passages in *Philosophical Investigations* to see that they are key expressions of Wittgenstein's 'later' approach to philosophy . . . the vast majority of these remarks were originally written between 1930 and 1932. [The Big Typescript] served as a significant source of remarks expressing his 'new' approach to philosophy – remarks he included unaltered in his master work.

(Hilmy 1987, 34). Hilmy's claim that 'the vast majority of these remarks were originally written between 1930 and 1932' is misleading, at best. Less than half of §§87–133 (seventeen remarks out of forty-six) contain any material drafted during 1930–2. Counting on a line-by-line basis, well over two-thirds of this swatch of text originates in material from 1936–7.

[19] Glock 2001, 15.

and to presuppose that Wittgenstein's 'approach to philosophy' is the same in the 1930–1 manuscripts, the 'Philosophy' chapter of the Big Typescript, and the *Philosophical Investigations*. Given the stress on the close examination of our use of words in these very passages, we need to attend to the specific methods pursued in the surrounding discussion of particular philosophical problems. For the kind of 'ordinary language philosophy' that is usually attributed to the *Philosophical Investigations*, in which appeals to 'what we would say' are used to show that 'the philosopher misuses ordinary language', does seem to have attracted Wittgenstein in the early 1930s. However, while the 'voice of correctness' may have the upper hand in the Big Typescript and *Blue Book*, this hardly settles the question of its place in the *Philosophical Investigations*.

Certainly, §§89–133 do contain some striking passages that can indeed be read as setting out, or summing up, a positive, non-Pyrrhonian, philosophical method. The crucial question here is whether Wittgenstein's narrator's appeals to what is 'in plain view' and 'ordinary language' are to be read as advocacy for ordinary language philosophy, or Pyrrhonian objections to any philosophical use of language. Consider the following leading examples of such passages:

116. When philosophers use a word – 'knowledge', 'being', 'object', 'I', 'proposition', 'name' – and try to grasp the *essence* of the thing, one must always ask oneself: is the word ever actually used in this way in the language which is its original home? –

What *we* do is to bring words back from their metaphysical to their everyday use.

122.* A main source of our failure to understand is that we do not *survey* the use of our words. – Our grammar is lacking in this sort of surveyability. ———— A surveyable representation produces just that understanding which consists in 'seeing connections'. Hence the importance of finding and inventing *intermediate cases*.

The concept of a surveyable representation is of fundamental significance for us. It signifies our form of representation, our way of looking at things.

126. Philosophy simply puts everything before us, and neither explains nor deduces anything. – Since everything lies open to view there is nothing to explain. For what is hidden, for example, is of no interest to us.

One might also give the name 'philosophy' to what is possible *before* all new discoveries and inventions.

On the non-Pyrrhonian reading, these passages advocate a methodology – an investigation of our use of words, clarifying the nature of our ordinary language, and so bringing words back from their metaphysical to their everyday use; and a metaphilosophy – the view that bad philosophy consists in metaphysical misuse of ordinary language, good philosophy takes ordinary language to be the privileged philosophical language and provides a clear view of it, a 'surveyable representation'. Taking the everyday use of words as its privileged point of departure, it aims to make clear standards of usage, criteria for the correct application of words. These criteria are presupposed by our ordinary use of language and allow us to show that the traditional philosopher's use of words is incorrect. Clarifying and disentangling the rules of the game in question enables us to gain what Wittgenstein calls an *Übersicht*, a key term that Anscombe variously translates as a 'clear view', a 'survey', or a 'perspicuous representation'.[20] The word literally means 'overview', but connotes a more thorough and intimate understanding than the English words suggest; I have adopted the policy of consistently translating it as 'survey' in quoted passages.

On the Pyrrhonian reading, Wittgenstein's narrator is attacking any positive philosophy that accords certain concepts, principles, or uses of language, 'ordinary' or 'metaphysical', a foundational or privileged status and exempts them from criticism. The appeals to the everyday are not appeals to ordinary language as a dogmatic point of departure, but rather a source of examples of alternatives to the traditional philosopher's dogmatic pronouncements that language must work in certain ways. These appeals also sum up his objections to any view about how things *must* be, namely that the philosopher's attempts to state the essence of language, to formulate metaphysical necessities and impossibilities, are internally incoherent. This does not presuppose that everyday use provides a standard by which to reject philosophical uses of words. In other words, the disagreement between the non-Pyrrhonian and Pyrrhonian interpretations of these passages is ultimately a disagreement over whether they are advocating

---

[20] The motto from Hertz's *Principles of Mechanics* in the typescript of the *Philosophical Investigations* which Wittgenstein replaced by the Nestroy quotation is a good summary of this 'rule-clarifying' strand: 'When these painful contradictions are removed, the question as to the nature of force will not have been answered; but our minds, no longer vexed, will cease to ask illegitimate questions.' (See Wittgenstein 2001, 741 n. 2; translation taken from Hertz 1956, x.)

a general philosophical method, emphasizing the aspect of bringing 'words back . . . to their everyday use' (§116); or whether they sum up the narrator's objections to particular philosophical misuses of words, emphasizing the aspect of bringing 'words back from their metaphysical . . . use' (§116).

After Baker's collaboration with Hacker on their analytical commentary came to an end, Baker came to have serious doubts about the methods they had attributed to Wittgenstein. In an article on different ways of understanding the contrast between 'everyday' and 'metaphysical' uses of words in the *Philosophical Investigations*, he argued that the very textual sources that once seemed to establish the 'ordinary language' interpretation should be read quite differently. Baker summed up the prevalent reading as one on which 'in the contrast "metaphysical"/"everyday", the term "everyday" wears the trousers. We are assumed to understand what counts as "everyday use" and how to establish what this is from case to case.' In other words, this non-Pyrrhonian reading takes 'everyday use' as its privileged and unproblematic point of departure:

This phrase is taken to signify the standard speech-patterns of the English-speaking peoples. Describing everyday use is a matter of establishing facts about a public normative practice, and it is presumed to be relatively uncontentious (objective?) what these facts are.[21]

'Metaphysical use' is then construed as a matter of transgressing against these rules, misusing ordinary language by breaking its grammatical rules. Glock provides the following convenient summary of this received wisdom:

Wittgenstein's ambitious claim is that it is constitutive of metaphysical theories and questions that their employment of terms is at odds with their explanations and that they use deviant rules along with the ordinary ones.[22]

Baker responded that a closer examination of Wittgenstein's use of the term 'metaphysical' makes it clear that he is not invoking 'what we ordinarily do' as underwriting a rulebook summing up publicly accepted criteria of correct usage, but rather as summing up Wittgenstein's opposition to quite specific problems, problems that have to do with the internal incoherence of particular philosophical strategies. In the spirit of the *Blue Book*'s criticism of 'tendencies connected with

---

[21] Baker 2002, 290–1.   [22] Glock 1996, 261–2. Cited, in part, by Baker 2002, 291.

particular philosophical confusions' that fuel our 'craving for generality',[23] Baker listed the following points of criticism: (1) Wittgenstein's attack on claims about what must or can't be the case by providing examples of alternatives, such as his objections to the view that every sentence must be composite in the opening remarks of the *Philosophical Investigations*. (2) Wittgenstein's attack on the use of words without antitheses, such as 'when we say "Every word in language signifies something" we have so far said *nothing whatsoever*; unless we have explained exactly *what* distinction we wish to make' (§13); his objection here is that *no* usage has been established. (3) Wittgenstein's critique of pseudo-scientific questions in philosophy, especially Socratic questions such as Augustine's 'what, then, is time' (§89c): 'We ask: "*What is* language?", "*What is* a proposition?" ' (§92). (4) Wittgenstein's objections to attempts to ground statements about how words are used by means of explanations grounded in the nature, or essence of things.[24]

This critique of the privileging of 'everyday use' is a valuable corrective to the one-sided orthodoxy he had previously articulated with Hacker. However, it leaves unanswered the question why that reading has proven so attractive to many of Wittgenstein's best interpreters, including the early Baker. It will hardly do to simply say that such readings are mistaken; it would be closer to the truth to say that such readings exemplify the very craving for generality they profess to overcome. Both early and late, Baker and Hacker have no hesitation about attributing sides and identifying positions taken in the text, even when Wittgenstein's words are far from unambiguous. Consider, as a case in point, the text of §89 and §133, and some very different answers to the question: who speaks? Most readings of §89 and §133 take it for granted that there is little difficulty in identifying which lines belong to the interlocutor, and which to the implicit author.[25] The first two paragraphs of §89 can be translated as follows:

89.* With these considerations, we find ourselves facing the problem: is logic, in some way, sublime?
     For it seemed as though a special depth – a universal significance – belonged to logic. As though logic lay at the foundation of all the sciences. –

---

[23] *Blue Book*, 17; see also 17–20.   [24] Baker 2002, 295–8.
[25] See Baker and Hacker 1980a, Glock 1991, Jolley 1993, von Savigny 1994–6, vol. I, McManus 1995, Read 1995. More equivocal readings can be found in Cavell 1996a and Glendinning 2001.

For the logical investigation investigates the essence of all things. It wants to get at the root of things and ought not to trouble about whether things actually happen this way or that way. — The logical investigation does not arise from an interest in the facts of nature nor from the urge to understand causal connections. But from our trying to understand the foundation, or essence, of all that's experiential. Not, however, as though in order to do this we should search for new facts: on the contrary, it is essential to our investigation that we don't want to learn anything *new* by it. We want to *understand* something that is already in plain view. For it's *this* that, in some sense, we don't seem to understand.

Baker and Hacker construe the first half of the paragraph, the four sentences prior to the longer, double dash, to echo the *Tractatus* in giving 'reasons for this apparent sublimity' while 'the rest of [§89b] is W.'s response'.[26] They summarize the non-Pyrrhonian view they find there as follows:

It is true that logic is not concerned with contingent facts or causal connections, but with the 'essence' or 'nature' of everything empirical. This search for the 'essence' of reality, *properly understood*, is not chimerical, nor absurd (cf. §92). But to grasp the essence of reality, thus understood, requires no new facts or discoveries. What we want to understand is already *in plain view*.[27]

In dividing §89 up into four sentences setting out the errors of the *Tractatus* and followed by five sentences setting out Wittgenstein's response, they focus our attention on the confrontation between a Tractarian interlocutor and a post-Tractarian narrator. But in so doing, they miss the extent to which the sentences immediately before and after the double dash in the middle of that paragraph can be read both as 'fighting the fantasy' that logic explores the essence of all things, 'or granting it'.[28] If §89b begins with a Tractarian vision of logic and 'winds up sounding like a self-description of the *Investigations*',[29] it proceeds by way of sentences that can be turned in either direction. 'This double reference, both forward and backward to the *Tractatus*, confers a peculiar ambiguity on the whole paragraph.'[30] In other words, the relationship between the *Tractatus* and the *Philosophical Investigations* is both closer and more complicated than Baker and Hacker's account suggests. Their focus on the particular kind of impossibly precise logical analysis the *Tractatus* promised, and on the

---

[26] Baker and Hacker 1980a, 195.   [27] Ibid.
[28] Cavell 1996a, 378.   [29] Ibid.   [30] Hallett 1977, 170.

a priori study of the essence of language and world, as Wittgenstein's particular targets in §89, is overly narrow. In a wonderful line-by-line reading of §89b, Cavell construes its ambiguities as providing a way of 'seeing his turn from the thoughts of the *Tractatus* to those of the *Investigations*',[31] where this is not a matter of a once-and-for-all break, a clear demarcation of temptation and correctness, but a way of turning the Tractarian fantasy of a final solution into something practical. Because this is a movement Wittgenstein is compelled to repeatedly return to in the course of the *Philosophical Investigations*, it should not be surprising that Cavell's reading of §89b is uncannily applicable to §133c–d. Like the first sentence of §89b, §133c1* – 'The real discovery is the one that makes me capable of breaking off doing philosophy when I want to' – can both be read as an expression of an earlier vision of the end of philosophy – the idea that there is a Real Discovery to be made – and the later rejection of that idea.

And then appears one of those dashes between sentences in this text, which often mark a moment at which a fantasy is allowed to spell itself out. It continues:

> The one that gives philosophy peace, so that it is no longer tormented by questions which bring *itself* in question. – Instead, a method is shown by examples; and the series of examples can be broken off.' (§133c)

Is Wittgenstein fighting the fantasy or granting it? Then a larger dash, and following it:

> 'Problems are solved (difficulties eliminated), not a *single* problem.' (§133c)

But again, is this good or bad, illusory or practical? Then finally:

> 'There is not *a* philosophical method, though there are indeed methods, like different therapies.' (§133d)

So something in this philosophical fantasizing turns out to be practical after all, and something that winds up sounding like a self-description of the *Investigations*.[32]

---

[31] Cavell 1996b, 378, on §89. Section 133c–d, the conclusion of Wittgenstein's discussion of subliming logic (§§89–133), is very similar in structure to the opening remark, §89b, which also lends itself to equally one-sidedly serious and satirical readings. The application to §133 is my responsibility throughout.

[32] Cavell 1996a, 378. Cavell's words, quoted here, are part of a close reading of §89, and the three quotations from Wittgenstein he gives are all from the second paragraph of §89 (§89b3–4, §89b5, and §89b6–8); the replacement by quotations from §133 is entirely my responsibility.

To sum up: on close inspection, each passage invites both Pyrrhonian and non-Pyrrhonian readings, rather like those ambiguous images that Wittgenstein repeatedly discusses, such as a drawing of a cube, or the duck-rabbit.

5.3 METAPHYSICAL AND EVERYDAY USE AND THE PARADOX OF INTENTIONALITY: §§89–133 AND §§428–36

Sections 90–120 contain a number of telegraphic discussions of misunderstandings that can lead us to approach language as governed by hidden rules. Among them are the focus on Socratic 'what is...?' questions (§89c, §92a) and a search for hidden essences that provide an a priori ground for our use of language (§§91–2, §97). Wittgenstein's narrator takes on the role of the voice of correctness and engages in an extended dialogue with the voice of temptation, both criticizing the moves that the voice of temptation finds attractive and providing therapeutic redescription of those temptations. However, the form of this dialogue is rather different from the two main kinds of dialogue that occur in §§1–88. The first is a straightforward confrontation between two opposed and clearly marked voices; examples of this kind of direct discourse include §1d, §§27–8, §§47–8, and §80. The second is the narrator's description of what he imagines or expects the interlocutor will say. This usually takes the form of direct discourse, typically introduced by a phrase such as 'Suppose, however, someone were to object...' (§33), 'But suppose someone said...' (§34), or 'For someone might object against me...' (§65); or indirect discourse, a report in the speaker's words of what the other says, typically introduced by phrases such as 'One thinks that...' (§26) or 'But if you say that...' (§81). It is characteristic of both of these forms of dialogue that they maintain a sharp distinction between the standpoint of the narrator and interlocutor.

Much of the dialogue in §§90–120, on the other hand, is in the form of free indirect discourse. As in indirect discourse, the narrator describes what the interlocutor says, or would say, in the narrator's words, but what makes it 'free' is that the narrator also introduces elements of his own viewpoint and perspective into that description. The increasing use of this form of discourse in novels from the late nineteenth and early twentieth century is closely connected with the decline of the omniscient narrator, for this form of report lends itself to blurring the boundaries between narrator and interlocutor. So, for instance, the narrator tells us what we want to say when tempted by philosophical illusions, but tells us in terms that are the narrator's, not the interlocutor's, terms which incorporate criticism of the temptation in question:

101.* We want to say that there can't be any vagueness in logic. Now it is natural for us to believe in the idea that the ideal *'must'* lie in reality. At the same time, we don't yet see *how* it has come to lie there, nor do we understand the nature of this 'must'. We believe it must lie in the real world; for we believe we see it there already.

The final paragraph of §89 begins with a short quotation taken from Augustine's *Confessions*, XI.14.

What *is* this time? If no one asks me, I know; if I want to explain it to a questioner, I do not know.[33]

The quotation in §1 is from the first chapter of the *Confessions*, which tells the story of Augustine's childhood and youth; the eleventh chapter, the source of this passage, concerns God and time, in which Augustine develops his answer to the question 'What was God doing before He made heaven and earth?'[34]

In the *Confessions*, the passage leads in to a discussion of philosophical difficulties raised by the idea that time flows from the past into the future; Augustine is particularly exercised by the question how it is possible to measure the passage of time. Although Wittgenstein had previously discussed Augustine's view of the nature of time in some detail, as an example of philosophical perplexity, the *Philosophical Investigations* does not set out the particulars of Augustine's question about the nature of time, nor offer diagnostic criticism of his solution.[35] Part of the significance of the words Wittgenstein quotes from Augustine in §89c is that they return us to the questions about the nature of philosophy raised by the Augustine quotation in §1. In particular, they are balanced on a knife-edge between expressing a

[33] Augustine 1993, 219.   [34] Augustine 1993, 218.
[35] This critique of Augustinian views about time is summarized in the *Blue Book*, 26–7 and the *Brown Book*, 107–8; the approach to time in the *Tractatus* (see 2.0121, 2.0251, 6.3611, 6.4311, 6.4312) is closer to Augustine's. There is an extensive discussion of changes in Wittgenstein's treatment of time in Stern 1995, 140–72.

Socratic philosophical problem about the nature of time ('if I want to explain it to a questioner, I do not know') and a Pyrrhonian dissolution of the problem ('if no one asks me, I know').

The principal problem that Wittgenstein does discuss in the remarks following §89 takes on a very similar form to the two construals of Augustine just proposed: a philosophical perplexity about the nature of language in general, and the proposition in particular. Indeed, in §§89c–90a Wittgenstein's narrator turns away from Augustine's question about the nature of time to a much more general point: that Augustine's problem, like any philosophical problem, is not a scientific problem that calls for empirical research, but rather is a problem about understanding what we ordinarily say; and that it is everyday statements 'about the duration of events, about events past, present or future' (§90a*), not philosophical ones, that Augustine calls to mind. Indeed, it is just the question of the relationship between philosophy and ordinary language that connects the quotation from Augustine in §89 with the final quotation from the *Confessions* in §436, even though both passages come from the same part of Augustine's discussion of time in chapter 11 of that book. In the latter passage Augustine provides the following examples of what we ordinarily say about time:

We are forever talking of time and times. 'How long did he speak', 'How long did it take him do that', 'For how long a time did I fail to see this', 'This syllable is double the length of that.' So we speak and so we hear others speak, and others understand us, and we them. They are the most evident and everyday of words, yet again they are very much hidden and their discovery comes as something new.[36]

It is the final sentence of this passage that is quoted in §436b, where it forms a final, parenthetical paragraph.[37] In the *Confessions*, Augustine's 'They' refers back not only to the topic of the previous sentence, namely what we say when we speak and understand each other, but also to the simple utterances he has listed just before. In

[36] Augustine 1993, XI. 22, p. 224; changes in the translation of the final sentence are by Thomas Williams.

[37] In English translations prior to the 2001 edition, it is mistakenly incorporated into the previous paragraph, which can give the appearance that it is a translation of the previous sentence.

§436, the sentence is presumably intended as a comment on §436a, which is about the philosophical illusion that our everyday words are too crude to capture the fine structure of our immediate experience, in which case 'they' would refer to the words of our ordinary language we use to describe everyday phenomena. Here, as in §89 and the remarks that follow, what Wittgenstein takes from Augustine is not so much the particular question about time, but rather an illustration of a recurrent them in the *Philosophical Investigations*: the way philosophers flip-flop between regarding language as something extremely familiar and unproblematic, and something deeply mysterious and paradoxical. In the remarks following §89, the principal topic is the misunderstanding of the logic of language that leads us to move back and forth in this way, to move from taking language for granted to searching for a hidden '*essence* of language, of the sentence, of thought' (§92), to thinking that 'a sentence[38] *does* something strange' (§93b):

93.* One person might say: 'A sentence, that's the most everyday thing in the world'; and another: 'A sentence is something peculiar – very extraordinary!' —— And that person is unable simply to look and see how sentences really work. After all, the forms we use concerning sentences and thought stand in his way.

What, then, is the source of the '*misunderstanding*' (§93b) that contains 'in germ the subliming of our whole account' (§94*) and can lead us to think that a sentence is something 'queer', 'extraordinary', 'strange', or 'remarkable'?[39] The misunderstanding is one we have already met in the paradoxes of ostension and explanation. In the case under discussion here, it takes the form of a wonder, an amazement, at the fact that language does succeed as a means of communication, that sentences and words reach their objects. At the level of

---

[38] 'Sentence' here translates the German word *Satz*, rather than 'proposition', the word used in both the Rhees and Anscombe translations. While *Satz* can ordinarily be translated as 'proposition', 'statement', or 'sentence', the current philosophical usage of 'proposition' is to talk about the meaning of a sentence, just the kind of thing that can't be variously interpreted – a regress-stopper, rather than the raw material for a regress of interpretations.

[39] These are all translations that Wittgenstein considered for *merkwürdig* in §93 and §94, which could more literally be translated as 'strange', 'odd', or 'peculiar'.

the sentence, it finds expression in a paradoxical truism such as the following:

> If we say, and *mean*, that such and such is the case, then we, and our meaning, don't stop anywhere short of the fact; but we mean: *this – is – so*. (§95*)

At the level of the word, the corresponding truism is the one that motivates the discussion of simple names: that when we say and mean a name, the word refers to the very thing that is named. For these truisms become paradoxical once we concentrate our attention on the signs we use and attend to the fact that we can always come up with alternative interpretations of those signs, and so find ourselves searching for the thing which is responsible for the intentional relation between sentence and fact, name and object, that which enables those signs to represent.

Section 428, the opening of the final chapter of Part 1 of *Philosophical Investigations*, gives expression to a train of thought very similar to §93, but is rather more specific about the character of the philosophical disorientation in question, namely an astonishment at the fact that language, or thought, can reach out to its objects.

> 428.* 'Thought – what a peculiar thing' – but it doesn't strike us as peculiar when we're thinking. Thought doesn't strike us as mysterious while we're thinking, but only when we say, as it were retrospectively: 'How was that possible?' How was it possible for thought to be about this very object *itself*? It seems to us as if by its means we had captured reality.

Sections 429–34 further develop the interlocutor's conviction that nothing merely physical, such as acoustic blasts or ink marks, or even words and gestures – 'signs' of one kind or another – can possibly communicate thought. For such tokens taken by themselves are 'dead', and can only be animated, have life breathed into them, by something inner, such as an act of understanding. This is simultaneously contrasted with the narrator's alternative account: that the life of the sign consists in its use. As with previous paradoxes, the formulation of the paradox is immediately preceded by an intimation of the proposed dissolution – a reminder that the life of the sign is not something inner, but rather is a product of context and circumstance:

> 432.* Every sign, *on its own*, seems dead. *What* gives life to it? It lives *in use*. Does it have living breath in itself? Or is the *use* its breath?

Like the previous conflicts over scepticism about ostension, explanation, and rule-following, it leads up to a formulation of what we can call the **paradox of intentionality** (§433): that 'a sign can be variously interpreted in *every* case'.

433.* When we give an order, it may look as if the ultimate thing sought by the order had to remain unexpressed, as there is always a chasm between an order and its execution. Say I want someone to make a particular movement, say to raise his arm. To make it quite clear, I do the movement. This picture seems unambiguous till we ask: how does he know that *he is to make that movement?* – How does he know at all what use he is to make of the signs I give him, whatever they are? – Perhaps I shall now try to supplement the order by means of further signs, by pointing from myself to him, making encouraging gestures, etc. Here it looks as if the order were beginning to stammer.

As in the previous paradoxes, the answer follows almost immediately, if rather cryptically – we already understand the words, and the problem lies rather in what has led us to think there's a problem, to think that our words, or our experience, easily elude us, and that the task of grasping them amounts to a problem that calls for a sublime solution:

435.* If one asks: 'How does a sentence do it, how does it represent?' – the answer might be: 'Don't you know? You do see it, when you use it.' After all, nothing is concealed.

How does a sentence do it? – Don't you know? After all, nothing is hidden.

But given this answer: 'You know, don't you, how a sentence does it, for nothing is concealed' one would like to retort 'Yes, but it all flows by so quickly, and I should like to see it as it were laid out in more detail.'

436.* Here it is easy to get into that dead-end in philosophy, where one believes that the difficulty of the task consists in our having to describe phenomena that are hard to catch, the quickly escaping present experience, or something like that. Where ordinary language seems too rough to us, and it looks as if we had to do, not with the phenomena that are spoken about everyday, but with ones that 'easily elude us, and, in their coming to be and passing away, produce those others proximately'.

(Augustine: They are the most evident and everyday of words, yet again they are very much hidden and their discovery comes as something new.)

What's 'quickly escaping' in §436a1 is not only the experience of the present experience, as it is understood by the interlocutor, continually slipping from our grasp, but also the non-philosophical statements that Wittgenstein and Augustine begin with, 'the *kind of statement* that we make about phenomena' (§90a).[40]

The aim of §§89–133 is to redirect our attention towards our everyday use of words, off the 'slippery ice' of philosophical theorizing about thought, world, and language and 'back to the rough ground' (§107). That aim 'gets its light, that is to say its purpose, from the philosophical problems' (§109), but it does not take them on their own terms. Close attention to quite particular philosophical arguments is complemented by the repeated insistence that after all, nothing is hidden, nothing concealed, that philosophical paradoxes must be dissolved, not solved. In §§89–133, Wittgenstein concentrates our attention on some of the ways we may be tempted to sublime logic, without the detailed attention to particular philosophical problems characteristic of the opening remarks and the remarks that follow §133. Wittgenstein's method is often clearer in his discussion of his chosen examples than the very general remarks about rules and philosophy in this part of the book. For this reason, I have drawn out some of the close connections with the concerns of §§428–36, which make clearer just what is at stake here. In the case of the debate over how words succeed in conveying a meaning, how they perform the extraordinary feat of reaching out to their objects, the narrator's answer is that nothing else, beyond their ordinary use, is necessary – both hearer and speaker understand an order by means of the words that are spoken.

503.* If I give someone an order then it's *quite enough* for me to give him signs. And I would never say: after all, that's only words, and I have got to get behind the words. Equally, if I've asked someone something and he gives me a reply (and hence a sign) I am satisfied – that was the sort of thing I expected – and don't object: Look here – that's merely a reply!

504.* But if someone says: 'How am I to know what he means, after all, I see only his signs?' then I say: 'How is *he* to know what he means, for he has nothing but signs either?'

---

[40] See von Savigny 1994–6, II.130.

CHAPTER 6

The critique of rule-based theories of meaning and the paradoxes of rule-following: §§134–242

6.1 THE PARADOXES OF RULE-FOLLOWING

Sections 134–7 link the concerns of §§65–133 with those of §§138–242 by returning once more to the Tractarian claim that the general form of the proposition, the essential feature that every significant statement must possess, is that it must tell us 'This is how things are.' This part of the text begins with a review of the anti-Socratic strategy of §§65–71: the voice of correctness tells us that we have a concept of what a proposition is, 'just as we also have a concept of what we mean by "game". Asked what a proposition is – whether it is another person or ourselves that we have to answer – we shall give examples . . . *This* is the kind of way in which we have such a concept as "proposition"' (§135).[1] The voice of temptation responds that we can give a sharp definition of a proposition, namely that it is whatever can be true or false. In reply, the narrator points out that if this is to cast light on the nature of the proposition, we will need an independent grasp of the concept of truth and falsity 'which we could use to determine what is and what is not a proposition' (§136c). In that case, there would be a 'fit' between the concept of truth and the concept of a proposition, much as two cogwheels in a machine may engage with each other and produce movement. We would then be in a position to first evaluate whether or not a given form of words was capable of being true or false, and so say if it passed the proposed test for being a proposition. The problem with this account, however, is that the concepts in question – being a proposition, and being a truth-bearer – are not independent, but rather are like two sides of

---

[1] See the discussion of the role of examples in 5.1 on §69 and §71. Here the translation of *Satz* as 'proposition' is appropriate, as the topic under discussion is the nature of the proposition.

one cogwheel – they 'belong' to each other as a matter of logic. To say that they 'fit' each other would be just as misleading as to say that a coloured patch exactly 'fits' its immediate surroundings.[2] To draw a link between being a proposition and being a truth-bearer is to move in a tight logical circle: to say that p is true is to assert that p is the case, and so talk of truth and falsity does not provide us with any further purchase on the nature of the proposition. For the same reason, talk of doing 'the same thing' does not provide an independent point of departure for determining what does, and doesn't, fit a rule: 'The use of the word "rule" and the use of the word "same" are interwoven. (As are the use of "proposition" and the use of "true")' (§225).

The principal trains of argument in §§138–242 closely parallel those we have met in the previous remarks: as before, the voice of temptation begins to sketch a number of philosophical theories, and the voice of correctness replies that 'it ain't necessarily so'; as before, the voice of temptation is repeatedly criticized for turning a striking but quite particular example into a general philosophical principle, overlooking the exceptions to the proposed rule; as before, the voice of temptation's views lead to unacceptable paradoxes. Indeed, §140, §142, and §144 not only provide an unusually clear and explicit summary of what has just been done in §138, §139, §141, and §143; they also amount to a review of some of the main argumentative strategies that have been pursued from the very beginning of the book. However, the focus of the discussion has changed from naming and explanation to understanding and rule-following, and the character of the discussion rapidly becomes considerably more intricate and complex. In the remarks that precede §138, each interlocutory proposal receives an immediate answer; indeed, we saw that §1d and §47 actually anticipate, in some detail, the narrator's reply to the problems raised in §2 and §48. When a particular problem does receive further development in §§1–137, this usually takes the form of the interlocutor coming up with a somewhat different version of the view under discussion, which leads the narrator to respond with a somewhat different answer, such as the further discussion of ostension in §§33–7, or simples in §§53–64.

---

[2] This analogy, from §216, is discussed in more detail below.

Unlike the compressed and sequential discussion of the particular topics raised by the three-stage argument in §§1–133, the discussion of the paradoxes in §§133–242 is more extended and interwoven. Like a series of Russian dolls, opening the first problem leads to the next, which in turn leads us to see another one within it. Only after a whole series of related problems have been opened up in this way does the narrator provide his considered response to each of them.

For instance, consider the place of the opening questions about how to understand talk of a word's meaning 'fitting' into a sentence that are first raised in §§136–8. They are next discussed in §182; that remark raises a series of questions about our use of the words 'to fit', 'to be able', and 'to understand', with the aim of getting us to see that the notion of 'fitting' is considerably more complicated than it seems at first sight. The narrator goes on to claim that this failure to take heed of the complexity of the circumstances in which words are used – their 'role' in our language – is characteristic of philosophical paradoxes:

their employment in the linguistic intercourse, that is carried on by their means, is more involved – the role of these words in our language other – than we are tempted to think.

(This role is what we need to understand in order to dissolve philosophical paradoxes. And hence a definition usually won't be sufficient; and even less so will a remark to the effect that a word is 'indefinable'.) (§182b–c*)

This warning comes just after an extended discussion of the place of 'circumstances' and context in a dissolution of paradoxes about rule-following, and just as the narrator is returning to the paradoxes concerning sudden understanding and rule-following that were raised previously in §138, §143, and §151. However, it is only much later, in §216, that the narrator addresses the vacuity of subliming the notion of fit into a 'super-concept':

216.* 'A thing is identical with itself.' – There is no finer example of a useless sentence, which yet is connected with a certain play of the imagination. It is as if in imagination we put a thing into its own mould and saw that it fitted.

We might also say: 'Every thing fits into itself.' Or again: 'Every thing fits into its own mould.' At the same time one looks at a thing and imagines that there was a space left for it, and that now it fits into it exactly.

Does this spot ♣ *'fit'* into its white surrounding? – *But that is just how it would look* if there had at first been a hole in its place and it then fitted into the hole. But when we say 'it fits' we are not simply describing this picture; not simply this *situation*.

'Every coloured patch fits exactly into its surrounding' is a rather specialized form of the law of identity.

In §138, Wittgenstein's interlocutor proposes another source for a notion of 'fitting' that could be used to support the thesis that there is a 'fit' between the concepts of truth and proposition: the phenomenon of suddenly having the meaning of a word come to mind, and seeing that it fits the sense of a sentence. The principal examples of such a 'fit' that are discussed later on are being able to continue a series of numbers, and seeing the formula that governs the series. Beginning with the voice of temptation's initial proposal that we conceive of the meaning of a word as something immediately present to consciousness, something we can 'grasp *in a flash*' (§139), the discussion moves on to consider a number of other ways of conceiving of what animates, or underlies, our meaning and understanding the words we use. This, in turn, is connected with issues that arise out of turning the paradoxes raised in earlier sections to the question of what is involved in grasping the meaning of a word, or following a rule.

The discussion takes the form of a dialogue between the voice of correctness, who holds the decidedly un-Pyrrhonian view that 'the meaning [of a word] is the *use* we make of the word' (§138) and is consistently critical of attempts to sublime the use of language, and the voice of temptation, who is repeatedly drawn towards articulating theories about meaning and understanding that are incompatible with a conception of word-meaning as use. These include Cartesian theories of mental processes as animating meaning, finalist theories on which meaning ultimately consists in underlying rules, and mechanist theories on which the connection is ultimately causal.

The **paradox of rule-following** – 'a rule can be variously interpreted in every case' – is a central concern in what I have been calling the third chapter of the *Philosophical Investigations*, namely §§134–242. Like my statement of the other paradoxes, this wording is based on the last sentence of §28.[3] While a discussion of particular instances

---

[3] See 4.3 and the closing pages of 5.1.

of the paradox takes up most of §§138–85, the most general and explicit statements of the paradox form part of a later recapitulation of the overall trajectory of this train of argument in §§198–202:

198. 'But how can a rule show me what I have to do at *this* point? Whatever I do is, on some interpretation, in accord with the rule.'

201. This was our paradox: no course of action could be determined by a rule, because any course of action can be made out to accord with the rule.

Pursuing these issues in §138 and the remarks that follow, Wittgenstein frequently returns to the question of what it is to understand a word in a flash, to suddenly understand how to use a word. For the experience of understanding a word in a flash can easily look as though it provides a decisive counter-example to any conception of meaning that insists on the primacy of context and circumstance. Thus, in §§139–41, the rule-following paradox is spelled out at some length for the case of the idea that understanding the word 'cube' consists in bringing a picture of a cube to mind.

Certainly we have all had the experience of understanding a word all of a sudden, but the danger here lies in thinking that this gives us an insight into the essence of understanding. For the narrator argues that 'what is essential' (§140c) is that the same image, picture, or representation can mean different things in different contexts or circumstances. A change in the context of application can yield a change in meaning, and therefore meaning cannot be identified with anything independent of the context of meaning.

Sections 139 and 141 provide us with no less than three instances of the familiar argument scheme, each picking up where the previous one leaves off:

Stage 1.

What really comes before our mind when we *understand* a word? – Isn't it something like a picture? Can't it *be* a picture? (§139c)

Stage 2.

Well, suppose that a picture does come before your mind when you hear the word 'cube', say the drawing of a cube. In what sense can this picture fit or fail to fit a use of the word 'cube'? – Perhaps you say: 'It's quite simple; – if that picture occurs to me and I point to a triangular prism for instance, and say it is a cube, then this use of the word doesn't fit the picture.' (§139d)

Stage 3.

– But doesn't it fit? I have purposely so chosen the example that it is quite easy to imagine a *method of projection* according to which the picture does fit after all.

The picture of the cube did indeed *suggest* a certain use to us, but it was possible for me to use it differently. (§139d–e)

The figure of the cube seems at first sight a natural example of a case in which an image comes to mind when one hears the word; but there is nothing to stop us from using a prism to stand for a cube.[4] The narrator's target in this passage is restricted to the idea that it is mental images that are intrinsically meaningful. In the discussion that follows, he raises the same objections against those theories that invoke philosophical entities or activities to fill the gap in the mental image account, such as an associated mental act, the grasping of a sense, or a method of projection.

Stage 1.

141. Suppose, however, that not merely the picture of the cube, but also the method of projection comes before our mind?

Stage 2.

—— How am I to imagine this? – Perhaps I see before me a diagram showing the method of projection: say a picture of two cubes connected by lines of projection. (§141a*)

Stage 3.

– But does this really get me any further? Can't I now imagine different applications of this diagram too? (§141a*)

The interlocutor finds this just as unsatisfying as the first three-stage argument, and this forces the narrator to further specify the options available:

Stage 1.

—— Well, yes, but then mayn't an *application come before my mind?* (§141a)

---

[4] Compare the discussion of different ways of interpreting the drawing of a cube in *Tractatus* 5.5423 and *Investigations* II. xi, 193/165.

Stage 2.

– It may: only we need to get clearer about our application of *this* expression. Suppose I explain various methods of projection to someone so that he may go on to apply them; let us ask ourselves when we should say that *the* method that I intend comes before his mind.

Now clearly we accept two different kinds of criteria for this: on the one hand the picture (of whatever kind) that at some time or other comes before his mind; on the other, the application which – in the course of time – he makes of what he imagines. (And can't it be clearly seen here that it is absolutely inessential for the picture to exist in his imagination rather than as a drawing or model in front of him; or again as something that he himself constructs as a model?) (§141a–b)

Stage 3.

Can picture and application clash? Well, they can clash in the sense that a picture may lead us to expect a different use, for in general people apply *that* sort of picture *that* way. (§141c*)

According to the narrator, understanding a sentence consists in being able to use those words correctly, which, in turn, is a matter of applying them 'in the course of time' (§141b). He does not deny that people do sometimes understand a word or the meaning of a sentence in a flash, when it 'comes before our mind in an instant' (§139b). However, he does maintain that the phenomenon of sudden understanding is a dangerously limited basis for any insight into the essence of understanding. 'Application' is a slippery word here, precisely because it can be used to run together what comes before my mind and my later use of the words in question. For the same image, method of projection, or other item that comes before my mind can mean different things in different contexts:

What is essential is to see that the same thing may come before our minds when we hear the word and the application still be different. Has it the *same* meaning both times? I think we shall say not. (§140c)

The narrator argues that we cannot identify understanding with being in any particular mental state, for the criteria for understanding involve success in application and are quite independent of being in any mental state.

What was the effect of my argument? It called our attention to (reminded us of) the fact that there are other processes, besides the one we originally thought of, which we should sometimes be prepared to call 'applying the picture of a cube'. So our 'belief that the picture forced a particular application on us' consisted in this, that only the one case and no other occurred to us. 'There is another solution as well' means: there is something else that I am also prepared to call a 'solution'; to which I am prepared to apply such-and-such a picture, such-and-such an analogy, etc. (§140b*)

Once we acknowledge that it is always possible to imagine a situation in which the words we utter in giving an explanation can be misunderstood, it is only a small step further to apply the same sceptical strategy to the images and mental acts that accompany our words, for they are equally susceptible to this. No occurrent act of meaning or intending can give a rule the power to determine our future actions, because there is always the question of how that act is to be interpreted. As a result, the idea that a rule, taken in isolation, can determine all its future applications turns out to be misguided. We ignore the context and think that some isolated act or event can have a determinate meaning regardless of its context.

Nothing taken in isolation from its context can determine how we go on, as all determination is dependent on our proceeding in the usual way:

142. It is only in normal cases that the use of a word is clearly prescribed; we know, are in no doubt, what to say in this or that case. The more abnormal the case, the more doubtful it becomes what we are to say ... What we have to mention in order to explain the significance, I mean the importance, of a concept, are often extremely general facts of nature: such facts as are hardly ever mentioned because of their great generality.[5]

In order to focus our attention on a convenient and pointed example of how it is only in normal cases that the use of a word is prescribed, and of the role of 'facts of nature' in rule-following, Wittgenstein's narrator turns to the example of teaching a person to continue a mathematical series, say the series 2, 4, 6, 8, . . . The narrator provides a number of examples of how communication with a child learning the series might break down. The aim of these examples is to get us to see that 'the pupil's capacity to learn *may* come to an end here' (§144,

---

[5] The final sentence, printed on p. 56/48, was marked for insertion prior to the final sentence of §142 in TS 227b; see Wittgenstein 2001, 826.

referring to §143), if only because so much taken-for-granted 'stage-setting' has to be in place in order for one person to get another to follow a rule. He is not arguing that such sceptical doubts are ordinarily legitimate, or that a refutation of every conceivable doubt is necessary, for in practice the normal background of training and exhibiting correct behaviour is sufficient. Instead, the narrator's aim is to draw our attention to the importance of context and circumstance as a precondition for grasping the rule, a point that is explicitly flagged in the previous remark, which stresses that it is 'only in normal cases that the use of a word is clearly prescribed' (§142).

What we are supposed to see here is that there can be no guarantee that the next case will not be abnormal – that the child will not respond in the usual way to the statement of a rule (or a table of the kind used in §86, or a signpost or pointing finger (§85, §87, §185d)). The point of this, however, is not the one offered by the voice of correctness, an ordinary language philosopher's instruction in the grammar of what we ordinarily say. Rather, it is a Pyrrhonian reminder that there can be no philosophical proof that the world will conform to our expectations. Wittgenstein's way of proceeding is set out particularly clearly here; both §140 and §144 explicitly pause to ask what the effect of the argument just offered is supposed to be, and both provide an unusually insistent statement of the point of the exercise in question. Thus in §144, Wittgenstein's narrator explains the intended effect of the story he has just told about someone who is learning the natural numbers:

144.* What do I mean when I say 'the pupil's capacity to learn *may* come to an end here'? Do I say this from my own experience? Of course not. (Even if I have had such experience.) Then what am I doing with that sentence? Well, I should like you to say: 'Yes, it's true, that's conceivable too, that might happen too!' — But was I trying to draw someone's attention to the fact that he is capable of imagining that? —— I wanted to put that picture before him, and his *acceptance* of the picture consists in his now being inclined to regard a given case differently: that is, to compare it with *this* rather than *that* series of pictures. I have changed his *way of looking at things*. (Indian mathematicians: 'Look at this.')[6]

---

[6] In the Early Investigations, Wittgenstein explains the parenthetical allusion: 'I once read somewhere that a geometrical figure, with the words "Look at this", serves as a proof for Indian mathematicians. This looking too effects an alteration in one's way of seeing.' Wittgenstein 2001, 301. See also *Zettel*, §461.

It is characteristic of Wittgenstein's Socratic style of argument that from time to time the voice of correctness continues the discussion on behalf of the voice of temptation. Sometimes this is clearly signalled by a phrase such as 'Perhaps you say . . .' (§139d; see also §146a, §147b), 'Thus you were inclined to use such expressions as . . .' (§188b) or 'I understand you. You want to look about you and say . . .' (§398a). In other cases, we have to infer that the voice of correctness is speaking for the voice of temptation from the way that the passage uses the first person to dismiss or ridicule views that have attracted the voice of temptation. For instance, §153, which is entirely in the first person, begins by summarizing the voice of temptation's views, but goes on to belittle them. Occasionally, we also hear from a third voice, that of a Pyrrhonian commentator, stepping back from the fray and taking up a position much like one of Nestroy's leading characters during a solo scene, sometimes directly addressing the reader, sometimes reflecting on what we can learn from the preceding exchange (§142 and the text at the bottom of that page; §§142d3–144; §203).

In other words, §§138–242 amount to an extended critique of those views about meaning, understanding, and rule-following that attract the voice of temptation. These tempting accounts begin with familiar phenomena, such as associating the image of a cube with the word 'cube' (§140), continuing a series of numbers (§143), reading a newspaper (§156), or being guided (§172), but in each of these cases, the narrator argues that the characteristic experiences the voice of temptation fastens onto are neither a necessary nor a sufficient condition for successfully carrying out the task in question. Thus, the voice of correctness repeatedly makes use of the sceptical strategy, familiar from the preceding remarks, of pointing out that we can easily imagine circumstances in which the experiences that seem to embody our understanding, or knowing how to go on, do occur, but we do not actually understand, or know how to go on, and that there are cases in which we do know how to go on but do not have the supposedly characteristic experiences. Just as an act of ostension or an explanation can be variously interpreted in every case (§28, §§85–7, §163), so can an image (§139), a method of projection (§141), a series of numbers (§143, §185), or our saying 'Now I understand!' (§151, §179, §183). The explicit cross-references in this part of the book, to the paradox of explanation in §86 in §163, to the paradox of rule-following in

§143 in §185, and to §151 on sudden understanding in §179 and §185, highlight the central role of these and related paradoxes.

Three central examples of the paradoxes of rule-following form the leading themes of this chapter of the *Philosophical Investigations*.

(1) §§138–42: repeated application of the three-stage argument scheme to the voice of temptation's construal of the case of understanding a word 'in a flash'. We return to this most directly in §§191–7, with a critique of sublime 'solutions' to the paradox of sudden understanding. The discussions of suddenly knowing how to continue a series in §§151–5 and §§179–84, and of the experience of 'being guided' in §§169–78, are also closely connected with this strand of the material.

(2) §§143–50: the case of teaching the rule for adding two. The paradox of rule-following comes up again in §§185–90 and §§198–202. As in (1), the opening passage contains a three-stage dissolution of the interlocutor's attempts to formulate a theory of rule-following, while §§185–90 are focused on the emptiness of retreating to sublime super-solutions.

(3) §§156–68: 'reading', where this is understood as correctly reproducing in speech the sounds that are associated with the words on a page of text.

In §155, the narrator asserts that it is the circumstances in which the experiences occur, not the experience itself, to which we should look if we want to get at what justifies someone in saying that he knows how to go on or understands a system. Sections 154–5 are an interim summary of the argument so far that highlights the place of context and circumstance, and tells us that the role of circumstances will be made clearer by §156 and the remarks that follow. There, narrator and interlocutor explore the case of a person who is a 'reading machine'. We are asked to imagine someone trained to produce the right sounds on seeing the written signs, whether or not the reader understands those signs. 'Reading' here covers not only reading out loud, but also 'writing from dictation, writing out something printed, playing from a score, and so on' (§156a). This scenario is less complicated than the case of teaching someone how to continue a series, precisely because here understanding is not an issue. It is an instance of the method of §2, in that it gives both behaviourist and mentalist what they say they want. For the behaviourist, it gives us a case of rule-following where mental processes are ruled out of court. For the mentalist, it gives us a way of acting out in the material world the very processes that supposedly go on in the mind, just as the grocer does at the end of §1. The discussion that follows aims to show that neither theory can do justice to the role of context and circumstance, for both analyses are overly simple, even in a case that appears to be most favourable.

The overall trajectory of the dialectical discussion of each of these topics is the one outlined at the beginning of 1.2 and discussed in detail in chapters 4 and 5: we begin with Socratic questioning, which leads to the repeated formulation of a paradox and its dissolution, followed by a critique of sublime 'solutions' to the philosophical problems in question. As before, the three-stage argument scheme is used again and again.

The sceptical train of thought that runs through the paradoxes concerning sudden understanding, adding two, and their relatives – that none of the familiar objects one might turn to provide a philosophical justification for these phenomena – ultimately drives the voice of temptation to search for, or to postulate, quite unfamiliar items that cannot, as a matter of logic, be misinterpreted, misunderstood, or taken out of context. These rules, lying behind what we ordinarily say, are composed of sublime regress-stoppers of one kind or another: '*super*-concepts' (§97b) or '*super*-expressions' (§192) or an image that is a 'super-likeness' (§389). Wittgenstein introduces this superlative turn of phrase in the context of his commentator's Pyrrhonian rejection of the idea that there are privileged philosophical concepts that can be exempted from criticism:

We are under the illusion that what is peculiar, profound, essential, in our investigation, resides in its trying to grasp the incomparable essence of language. That is, the order existing between the concepts of proposition, word, proof, truth, experience, and so on. This order is a *super*-order between – so to speak – *super*-concepts. Whereas, of course, if the words 'language', 'experience', 'world', have a use, it must be as humble a one as that of the words 'table', 'lamp', 'door'. (§97b)

Throughout the rule-following chapter, the voice of temptation struggles to find the right words for the particularly tight 'fit' between a rule and its application, the 'compulsion of a rule' (§231). This finds a particularly striking 'symbolic expression' (§221*) in the sublime image of the beginning of a series as 'a visible section of rails invisibly laid to infinity' (§218), and the accompanying conviction that the rule 'traces the lines along which it is to be followed through the whole of space' (§219a).[7] In the case of scepticism about rule-following, super-concepts and their like hold out the promise of decisively solving the paradoxes by establishing an unbreakable link between rule and application, image and object, or the act of intention and its conditions of satisfaction – something that ensures that we, and our meaning, do not stop short of the very fact that we and they aim at. That is why the 'unique relation' between the sublime super-likeness and its object is

'closer than that of a picture to its subject'; for it can be doubted whether a picture is the picture of this thing or that. (§194b)

On the other hand, it is essential to the super-likeness that it *must* be a picture of its object:

389.* 'The image must be more like its object than any picture. For, however like I make the picture to what it is supposed to represent, it may still be the picture of something else as well. But it is intrinsic to the image that it is the image of *this* and of nothing else.' Thus one might come to regard the image as a super-likeness.

In this way, super-concepts seem to force a particular use or a particular application on us as a matter of logical compulsion (§140a), and so guarantee a 'super-strong connexion . . . between the act of intending and the thing intended' (§197). In 'some *unique* way' they appear to predetermine the steps involved in applying a formula in advance (§188) or to provide us with an image that 'is the image of *this* and of nothing else' (§389). These candidate solutions usually take the form of hidden processes of one kind or another, such as an image in the mind (§§139–42), whatever it is that justifies me in saying 'Now I understand!' (§151), 'a process occurring behind or side by side with that of saying the formula' (§154), the connections set up in the brain when we learn a word (§158), or an unspecified 'insight' or 'intuition' (§186).

---

7 We return to this image at the end of the chapter.

6.2 SUBLIMING RULES

Most commentators have read *Philosophical Investigations* §§134–242 very differently. They have taken Wittgenstein's narrator to be setting out his own, non-Pyrrhonian philosophical position on the topic of rule-following, and have seen their task as a matter of extracting and refining his philosophical theory from the admittedly unconventional exposition he provides. While the decidedly un-Pyrrhonian idea that Wittgenstein's sceptical questions about how rule-following is possible led Saul Kripke to a theory of practice can already be found in Winch (1958) and Fogelin (1976, 1987), his *Wittgenstein on Rules and Private Language*, first presented as a lecture in 1976, rapidly became the standard point of reference in discussions of this issue. Kripke reads Wittgenstein as raising, and attempting to answer, a form of scepticism about rule-following, that is, as replying to someone who holds that we cannot satisfactorily answer the question about what it is to follow a rule. Kripke argues that Wittgenstein put forward a scepticism about meaning on which it is always possible that one's explanations of what one means by one's words may be misunderstood. Consequently, there is never any fact of the matter about whether one has followed a rule correctly, because one can always come up with a reading of the rule on which another action is the right one. Because Kripke explicitly avoids committing himself to the view that the argument is Wittgenstein's, or endorsing it himself, it is convenient to put questions of authorship to one side again, by speaking of the sceptical view as 'Kripke's Wittgenstein'.

Kripke's exposition turns on Wittgenstein's summary of 'our paradox' in §201, namely that 'no course of action could be determined by a rule, because any course of action can be made out to accord with the rule'.[8]

Like Wittgenstein in §143 and §185, Kripke uses a simple mathematical example to explain how his paradox arises. He introduces 'quaddition', a deviant relative of addition. Quaddition is defined in such a way that every calculation I have done so far is a case of both addition and quaddition. The two functions diverge, however, for

---

[8] Kripke does briefly discuss §1 and §§28–34, but only as partial anticipations of the sceptical paradox, subsuming the main concern of those passages into his own.

certain calculations I have not yet considered. Kripke asks us to consider two numbers that he has not yet added, say 68 and 57, and that the sceptic asks him why he should think that they yield 125 rather than 5. Kripke's sceptic asks:

(Q1) Is there any fact that he meant plus, not quus, in the past? and
(Q2) Does he have good reason to be so confident that he should answer '125' rather than '5'?

Kripke further maintains that both questions must be answered successfully if we are to have a reply to the sceptic. That is, we need both

(A1) 'an account of what fact it is (about my mental state) that constitutes my meaning plus, not quus' and
(A2) to 'show how I am justified in giving the answer "125" to "68+57"'.[9]

Kripke responds that no such response is possible, because my previous calculations are equally compatible with the hypothesis that I used plus or quus, and anything I may have said about the nature of the rule is wide open to a further deviant interpretation. Any more basic rule we appeal to as a regress-stopper only invites a repetition of the initial sceptical move.[10]

Kripke's Wittgenstein maintains there is no 'straight solution' to the sceptical problem, one that would show the sceptic to be wrong. There are no such facts about meaning, and I am unjustified in using one form of words rather than another. Kripke takes Wittgenstein to accept the 'sceptical conclusion' and so maintain both

(KW1) that there is no fact about me as to whether I meant plus or quus, and
(KW2) that I have no justification for one response rather than another.

So Kripke's Wittgenstein gives a 'sceptical solution': he concedes that the sceptic is right. Despite this, he still maintains that our ordinary practice is, in a sense, justified, for it does not require the kind of justification the sceptic has shown to be untenable.[11]

On Kripke's reading of Wittgenstein, following a rule consists in doing as one's community does, and that is not something one can do by oneself. 'Ultimately we reach a level where we act without any

---

[9] Kripke 1982, 11.   [10] Kripke 1982, 16ff.   [11] Kripke 1982, 66.

reason in terms of which we can justify our action. We act unhesitatingly but *blindly*.'[12] This makes Wittgenstein's view of rule-following turn on accepting a paradoxical view of the matter: when it comes right down to it, we can't give any reason for following a rule as we do, yet we blindly go ahead in the same way, and as our agreement is the most we can hope for, we are entitled to call it a justification. The text that is usually taken to settle the case for this reading is §219:

> When I obey a rule, I do not choose.
> I obey the rule *blindly*. (§219c–d)

Kripke's Wittgenstein holds that what justifies these actions, when they are justified, is not any fact about me, but is determined by the public checks on my conformity to the rule that are provided by my linguistic community. These basic considerations about meaning are consistent with the sceptical conclusion about meaning, considered individualistically: my linguistic community always determines the meaning of my words. On the 'community view' of meaning, it is impossible for someone to give a word meaning in isolation from the practices of a community of language users; words only have meaning in the context of the practices of a particular linguistic community.

This is also how Fogelin reads §219d: as the prime example of a place where Wittgenstein turns our ordinary concepts of acting and doing into super-concepts. Under the pressure of responding to his sceptical paradoxes, he is supposedly led to 'philosophical hyperbole' and to saying something 'blatantly false' about the case in which I don't even have to think about what to do because the rule is so familiar, or so unquestioned:

> Here Wittgenstein seems to have hatched a gratuitous paradox, for to say that someone does something blindly, in the ordinary way of understanding this metaphor, is to say that the action is performed without rule – rhyme or reason. And Wittgenstein's contrast between following a rule as a matter of choice and doing this blindly is similarly peculiar. Sometimes when I follow a rule, I am very careful to watch my step. It seems, then, that even in the *Philosophical Investigations* Wittgenstein shows some tendencies to turn 'doing' and 'acting' into philosophical superlatives – into superconcepts.[13]

---

[12] Kripke 1982, 87.　　[13] Fogelin 1994, 219–20.

But this turns on a misreading of 'blind' in §219d: Wittgenstein's talk of obeying 'blindly' specifies the particular kind of obedience under discussion, and is not incompatible with watching my step. In such a case, I am blind to distractions, not to what is relevant to doing the right thing. On Fogelin and Kripke's reading of Wittgenstein on following a familiar and straightforward rule, following the rule 'blindly' involves ignoring reasons, and trusting in blind Fate. Indeed, this passage is often read along such lines, as evidence of Wittgenstein's relativism or irrationalism. But the relevant metaphor here is the blindfold usually associated with Justice, a blindness to whatever is irrelevant. That does not stand in the way of doing the right thing, for the right reasons.[14]

Despite insisting that our everyday practices are justified, there is a sense in which Kripke takes Wittgenstein's arguments to lead to scepticism, for he argues that the solution he attributes to Wittgenstein doesn't work, and Kripke does nothing to show that a better answer is possible. A few interpreters have actually read Wittgenstein as such a sceptic himself. Michael Dummett described Wittgenstein as a 'full-blooded' conventionalist who held that every single case of rule-following involves an element of decision, and so it is never necessary to follow a rule one way rather than another.[15] Henry Staten's reading of the rule-following discussion in the *Philosophical Investigations* also stressed the role of decision, interpreting Wittgenstein as a sceptic and proto-deconstructionist.[16] On this Derridean reading of Wittgenstein, there is an unbridgeable gap between a rule and its application, an abyss that makes any positive theory about what it is to follow a rule an impossibility.

While Kripke's way of understanding scepticism about rule-following has few supporters, it has become the point of departure and disagreement for the standard approaches to rule-following. Most readers agree with Kripke that Wittgenstein is replying to scepticism about rule-following, but disagree over what kind of answer he gave, and whether or not it is successful. The two main camps are known as 'individualists' and 'communitarians'. 'Individualists', such as Baker and Hacker, Robert Fogelin, Colin McGinn, and Simon Blackburn,

---

[14] See Baker and Hacker 1985, 215; von Savigny 1994–6, 1.266, 267.
[15] Dummett 1959.   [16] Staten 1984, ch. 2.

maintain that a single individual could, at least in principle, provide the resources for a solution.[17] In other words, the practices involved in following a rule may be the practices of an isolated individual, often referred to as a 'Robinson Crusoe'. This is, however, misleading, as Crusoe grew up in the normal way, and was only isolated while on a desert island. 'Communitarians' such as Peter Winch, Norman Malcolm, and David Bloor, hold that answering the sceptical problem is only possible if one is a member of a community – a group of a certain kind – and so the practices in question must be social, if not community-wide.[18] Before the publication of Kripke's book, it was usually taken for granted that Wittgenstein was offering a communitarian solution. While Kripke himself endorses this reading, he drew attention to the importance of the distinction between individualists and communitarians, and the differences between them became a leading issue in the resulting controversy.[19]

As a counterpoint to Kripke on Wittgenstein on rule-following, it will be helpful to consider Peter Winch's exposition in *The Idea of a Social Science and its Relation to Philosophy*, one of the principal sources of the predominant approach to the topic in the 1960s and 1970s. Winch's book aimed to redirect positivistic social scientists towards an interpretive approach to social science. However, the principal legacy of Winch's interpretation of Wittgenstein was that it provided a point of departure for the subsequent controversy in philosophy and the social sciences about how best to understand the place of rules,

---

[17] See Fogelin 1984 (1976), Baker and Hacker 1984, McGinn 1984, and Blackburn 1984a, 1984b.

[18] See Winch 1990 (1958), Malcolm 1986, and Bloor 1983, 1997.

[19] For instance, Bloor's first book on Wittgenstein, published in 1983, takes it for granted that he was a communitarian, and argues for a sociological construal of 'community' and 'practice'; his second (1997) is an extended defence of communitarianism. Kripke and Bloor agree that Wittgenstein begins by arguing that meaning is underdetermined by the available evidence and then provides a community-based solution – meaning is determined by the community's social practices, or 'form of life'. But Kripke argues that this is only a second-best, 'sceptical' solution, one which does not meet the standards set by the sceptical problem about meaning, while Bloor maintains that appealing to a community is a 'straight' solution, one that really does solve the sceptical problem. In other words, Bloor accepts Kripke's starting point, an argument that there is a gap between a rule and its application, but holds that social practices, the forms of human activity studied by the sociologist, provide the answers. While very few philosophers have had any sympathy for such attempts to turn Wittgenstein into a forerunner of a social or cultural theory of knowledge, this way of reading Wittgenstein has been very attractive to anti-foundationalist social scientists. For further discussion, see Stern 2002.

and facilitated the transformation of Wittgenstein's ideas about rule-following into a new sociology of knowledge. Winch's exposition of Wittgenstein's ideas about language and practice is particularly important because this is how Wittgenstein entered the 'rationality debates' of the 1960s and 1970s: as the proponent of a relativistic challenge to universal standards of rationality in philosophy and social science.[20] Despite the fact that this reading turns some of Wittgenstein's and Winch's most interesting ideas into a very bad theory, more Frankenstein than Wittgenstein, it is well worth discussing, not only because so many philosophers still take this undead theory for granted, but because it is a good example of how Wittgenstein has been systematically misunderstood. For this reason, it will be helpful to approach the variety of conceptions of practice by looking at the fate of Winch's interpretation. In order to put to one side questions about whether this is a fair reading of Winch, or Wittgenstein, I will speak of the holder of this view, whoever it may be, as 'Winchgenstein'.

One of the main aims of Winch's very short and programmatic book was to argue against the view that the method of the social sciences should be the method of the natural sciences, as conceived of by logical positivist and empiricist philosophy of science. It also argued for an interpretive approach to social science that begins from what its subjects take for granted:

> I do not wish to maintain that we must stop at the unreflective kind of understanding . . . But I do want to say that any more reflective understanding must necessarily presuppose, if it is to count as genuine understanding at all, the participant's unreflective understanding.[21]

Winch maintains that language and action – what people say and do – cannot be understood in isolation from their broader practical and cultural context, the 'forms of life' of the people in question. Because of the way in which what we say and do is embedded within this broader context, language and world are inextricably intertwined. One consequence that Winch draws is that the realist's conviction that reality is prior to thought, that the world is independent of our ways of representing it, is incoherent:

[20] See Winch 1990 (1958), 1964, and also Wilson 1970, Dallmayr and McCarthy 1977, Hollis and Lukes 1982, and Hiley, Bohman, and Shusterman 1991.
[21] Winch 1990 (1958), 89.

Our idea of what belongs to the realm of reality is given for us in the language that we use. The concepts we have settle for us the form of the experience we have of the world . . . The world *is* for us what is presented through those concepts.[22]

Because social institutions embody ideas of what is real and how it is to be understood, Winch holds that causal methods will prove utterly inadequate for the task of understanding our social world: 'the central concepts which belong to our understanding of social life are incompatible with concepts central to the activity of scientific prediction'.[23] Winch is not merely making the familiar claim that the methods of the natural sciences will prove unsuccessful when applied to social questions, but that the very attempt to do so is logically flawed, and strictly speaking, nonsense.

   Winch's principal argument for these far-reaching conclusions is contained in his exposition of Wittgenstein on rule-following.[24] Winch begins by pointing out that words do not have meaning in isolation from other words. We may explain what a word means by giving a definition, but then we still have to explain what is involved in following a definition, in using the word in the same way as that laid down in the definition. For in different contexts, 'the same' may be understood in different ways: 'It is only in terms of a given *rule* that we can attach a specific sense to the words "the same".'[25] But of course the same question can be raised about a rule, too: how are we to know what is to count as following the rule in the same way? Given sufficient ingenuity, it is always possible to think up new and unexpected ways of applying a rule. However, in practice we all do, for the most part, conform:

given a certain sort of training everybody does, as a matter of course, continue to use these words in the same way as would everybody else. It is this that makes it possible for us to attach a sense to the expression 'the same' in a given context.[26]

   An essential part of the concept of following a rule, Winch contends, is the notion of making a mistake, for if someone is really following a rule, rather than simply acting on whim, for instance, we must be able to distinguish between getting it right and getting

---

[22] Winch 1990 (1958), 15.   [23] Winch 1990 (1958), 94.
[24] Winch 1990 (1958), 24–39.   [25] Winch 1990 (1958), 27.   [26] Winch 1990 (1958), 31.

it wrong. Making a mistake is to go against something that 'is *established* as correct; as such, it must be *recognizable* as such a contravention . . . Establishing a standard is not an activity which it makes sense to ascribe to any individual in complete isolation from other individuals.'[27] Rule-following presupposes standards, and standards presuppose a community of rule-followers.[28]

In a section on the relations between philosophy and sociology, where Winch sums up the results of this argument, he describes it as a contribution to 'epistemology'. Winch makes it clear that epistemology, as he uses the term, has little to do with traditional theories of knowledge, but is instead his preferred name for first philosophy, that part of philosophy which is the basis for all others. For epistemology, as Winch understands it, deals with 'the general conditions under which it is possible to speak of understanding' and so aims at elucidating 'what is involved in the notion of a form of life as such'.[29] Thus, on Winch's reading, 'Wittgenstein's analysis of the concept of following a rule and his account of the peculiar kind of interpersonal agreement which this involves is a contribution to that epistemological elucidation.'[30]

Winch's argument concerning the need for a community if one is to follow rules is extremely compressed, and a full defence or critique would require examining many of the now-familiar difficulties that have been rehearsed so often in the interim. For instance, the connection Winch drew between rule-following, community standards, and a community's being able to verify that a rule has been followed has proven highly controversial, for it appears to depend on an implausibly strong verificationism. Furthermore, the notion of 'community' his argument called for is extremely problematic, in that it presupposed we can draw a sharp line between members and non-members in such a way that outsiders are disqualified from criticizing insiders. However, for our purposes the most important point is the *use* Winch made of this argument. His contemporaries took the main force of such Wittgenstein-inspired arguments about rule-following to be the negative consequences for traditional approaches to epistemology

---

[27] Winch 1990 (1958), 32.
[28] For further discussion of the question whether an individual's following a rule presupposes a community of rule-followers, see pp. 155–6.
[29] Winch 1990 (1958), 40–1.   [30] Winch 1990 (1958), 41.

such as Cartesian dualism, scepticism, and phenomenalism. Winch, on the other hand, used it to argue for a new conception of epistemology, as the result of following through the implications of his Wittgensteinian grammatical analysis. That epistemology could be positively applied to questions about the nature of society, questions that had previously been regarded as empirical questions for the sociologist:

> the central problem of sociology, that of giving an account of the nature of social phenomena in general, itself belongs to philosophy. In fact, not to put too fine a point on it, this part of sociology is really misbegotten epistemology. I say 'misbegotten' because its problems have been largely misconstrued, and therefore mishandled, as a species of scientific problem.[31]

To sum up: Winch puts forward a quite general philosophical argument that neither formal logic nor empirical hypotheses are appropriate methods for the study of society. Instead, one must aim at an interpretive investigation of that society's ideas and forms of life, a philosophical investigation that will make clear the kind of work that is appropriate within the social sciences. As a result, the methods of natural science are unsuited not only to central questions about the nature of social phenomena, but also to the detailed understanding of particular aspects of our lives; the only successful strategy is to use those particularistic, interpretive methods recommended by Winch's epistemology of forms of life.

The Winchgensteinian approach gives centre stage to everyday action, understood on the model of following rules. It takes for granted that those rules are usually implicit but can, if the need arises, be stated explicitly, either by the rule-users themselves, or by a sympathetic investigator such as a philosopher or an anthropologist. However, it is crucial to this approach that those rules only make the sense they do within a given form of life that, in turn, consists of certain shared practices. Winch argues that Wittgenstein's treatment of rule-following shows that we must start in philosophy and social science with 'forms of life', the social practices of human groups. This turn to forms of life, understood as culture-specific practices,

---

[31] Winch 1990 (1958), 43. For further discussion of this passage and its reception, see Stern 2002.

is one way of supplanting the central role occupied by representation in traditional theory of knowledge and philosophy of science – 'knowledge that' – with skills or abilities – 'know-how'. However, a great deal turns on just how one conceives of this embedding of knowledge in social practice, in 'forms of life'. How, precisely, are the practices in question to be understood? Can they be made fully explicit, or do they consist of patterns that can never be precisely and finally demarcated? One possibility is that they are patterns of activity, patterns that include action, equipment, and sites of activity. A second possibility is that the appropriate notion of practice is rather that of what must be in place for the language-game to go on. This complementary conception of practices is as 'background': as whatever must be in place for the rules to operate.

While Winchgensteinians frequently invoke the notion of a 'form of life' here, there are barely a handful of uses of this term in the *Investigations*, and it has been understood in the most diverse ways: transcendentally (e.g. as necessary condition for the possibility of communication); biologically (e.g. an evolutionary account of how practice is possible); and culturally (e.g. a sociological or anthropological account of what members of a particular social group have in common).[32] However, in the 1950s and 1960s, practices were usually understood in terms of a set of rules, rules that govern use of the language in question, tacitly accepted by participants but only codified by researchers. The activities included under this conception of rule-governed language use were extremely diverse. At one end of the spectrum, there were particular, ordinarily small-scale patterns of action, such as cooking a meal, making a promise, playing a game, praying, or carrying out an experiment. At the other end, there were patterns of patterns of action, which might include such matters as a regional cuisine, a legal system, the Olympic tradition, religion, or Newtonian physics.

Although Wittgenstein and Winch stress the ways in which 'the common behaviour of mankind' (§206) enables us to make sense of strangers and foreigners, most Winchgensteinians have primarily conceived of these taken-for-granted ways of behaving as specific to

---

[32] The term 'form of life' is used five times in the *Philosophical Investigations*: §19, §23, §241, pp. 174/148, 226/192.

a given community. Even though he later came to regret it, Winch did provide a clear and controversial statement of how a relativism of standards can arise out of differences in background:

[C]riteria of logic are not a direct gift of God, but arise out of, and are only intelligible in the context of, ways of living or modes of life. It follows that one cannot apply criteria of logic to modes of social life as such. For instance, science is one such mode and religion is another; and each has criteria of intelligibility peculiar to itself. So within science or religion actions can be logical or illogical . . . But we cannot sensibly say that either the practice of science or that of religion is either illogical or logical; both are non-logical.[33]

Because the practice turn provides a way of conceiving of scientific theorizing as a social product, the most heated controversy has been around the application of the practice turn to knowledge, and especially scientific knowledge. Initially, Winchgensteinian ideas received most attention in the philosophy of anthropology, thanks to 'Understanding a Primitive Society'.[34] But they soon found a particularly fertile home in post-positivist philosophy of science and the sociology of scientific knowledge, a constructionist sociology of science that analyses the content of scientific knowledge by means of sociological methods.[35]

While Winchgensteinian approaches directed attention to a conception of practice as a system of rules, and forms of life as the bedrock of such an account, topics that generated great philosophical debate in the 1960s and 1970s, by the end of the 1970s most philosophers had lost interest in these controversies, partly because they became convinced that Winchgensteinian arguments depended on verificationist premises that had little to recommend them, and partly because scientifically inspired approaches to the philosophy of mind and language gained prestige and interest. Kripke refocused philosophers' attention on Wittgenstein's treatment of rule-following by showing that one could extract a provocative and intriguing sceptical argument that could be considered on its own merits, without having to pay further attention to those aspects of a Winchgensteinian approach that had proved unattractive or problematic.

---

[33] Winch 1990 (1958), 100–1.   [34] Winch 1964.   [35] For further discussion, see Stern 2002.

Another way of raising the problems we find ourselves facing here is to pose the Socratic question: What is it to follow a rule correctly? Taken by itself, the verbal formulation of a rule does not determine its next application, for it is always possible that it will be misunderstood, and any attempt to drag in more rules to determine how to apply the original rule only leads to a vicious regress. However, a great deal depends on how one frames and approaches the problems about rule-following that I have just sketched so quickly. Considered in abstraction from its context, a rule, like an ostensive definition, can be made to conform to every course of action. In such a case, 'we give one interpretation after another; as if each one contented us at least for a moment, until we thought of yet another standing behind it' (§201). It is only when we return to the 'rough ground' (§107) and consider the background of practices to which a rule belongs that the rule takes on a determinate form. This turn to context and circumstance makes Wittgenstein a holist about rule-following: rules can only be understood aright if we appreciate their place in a larger whole. But what sort of holism, and what sort of conception of practice is he advocating?

Hubert Dreyfus draws a helpful distinction between two kinds of holism about meaning and interpretation.[36] **Theoretical holism** holds that all understanding is a matter of interpreting, in the sense of applying a familiar theory, a 'home language', to an unfamiliar one, the 'target language'. On this Quinean model, we always have to start from our understanding of our own language, an understanding that consists in a system of rules and representations. In short, for the theoretical holist, the 'whole' in question is a theory, a theory that can, at least in principle, be fully and explicitly formulated. This view has close affinities with the conception of language learning Wittgenstein attributes to Augustine:

> Augustine describes the learning of human language as if the child came into a strange country and did not understand the language of the country; that is, as if it already had a language, only not this one. (§32b)

On this approach, a theory of language is prior to practical linguistic skills.

---

[36] Dreyfus 1980.

Practical holism, which Dreyfus attributes to both Wittgenstein and Heidegger, is the view that while understanding 'involves explicit beliefs and hypotheses, these can only be meaningful in specific contexts and against a background of shared practices'.[37] The practical holist agrees with the theoretical holist that we are always already within the 'hermeneutic circle' – we have no alternative to starting with our current understanding – but argues that theoretical holism mistakenly conceives of understanding a language on the model of formulating a theory, or mapping an unfamiliar landscape. This leaves out the background practices, equipment, locations, and broader horizons that are not specific presuppositions or assumptions, yet are part and parcel of our ability to engage in conversation or find our way about.[38]

The theoretical holist will reply to the practical holist that if such a background is necessary, it must be analysable in terms of further rules, intentions, or a tacit belief system. In turn, the practical holist will respond that it is a mistake to postulate tacit belief whenever explicit beliefs cannot be found, and to fail to do justice to the contextual, embodied, and improvisational character of practice. Rules are not self-interpreting, and their application depends on skill: 'rules leave loop-holes open, and the practice has to speak for itself'.[39]

In *Being-in-the-World*, Dreyfus argues that for both Wittgenstein and Heidegger, conformity to publicly established norms is woven into the fabric of our lives, that 'the source of the intelligibility of the world is the average public practices through which alone there can be any understanding at all'.[40] The norms that are constitutive of these practices should not be understood in terms of sharing explicitly stated or statable beliefs or values, or in terms of conscious intentions – although these will certainly play a part from time to time – but rather as a matter of unreflectively acting in the same way as others, of doing what 'one' does. Good examples are the way in which one typically conforms to local patterns of pronunciation and comportment:

If I pronounce a word or name incorrectly others will pronounce the word correctly with a subtle stress on what I have mispronounced, and

---

[37] Dreyfus 1980, 7.
[38] 'A philosophical problem has the form: "I don't know my way about."' (§123)
[39] Wittgenstein 1969b, §139.   [40] Dreyfus 1991, 155.

often I shape up without even noticing. (We certainly do not notice how we are shaped into standing the distance from others one is supposed to stand.)[41]

The 'averageness' of these practices is not primarily statistical or causal: it is the result of the way conformity shapes what we do and what we are. Dreyfus reads Heidegger and Wittgenstein as replacing a view on which communication is made possible by our knowledge of objects by a view on which knowledge of objects is made possible by a shared language and background practices: 'We have *the same thing* in view, because it is in *the same* averageness that we have a common understanding of what is said.'[42] Another way of putting this point is to say that 'our social practices embody an ontology'.[43]

In defending the Heideggerian thesis that conformity is the source of intelligibility, Dreyfus cites a much-quoted passage from Wittgenstein's *Investigations* (§241) and provides a parenthetical translation:

Wittgenstein answers an objector's question just as Heidegger would:

> 'So you are saying that human agreement decides what is true and what is false?' – It is what human beings *say* that is true and false; and they agree in the *language* they use. That is not agreement in opinions [intentional states] but in form of life [background practices].[44]

We can sum up this practical holist reading as follows: unless we shared a language, where a language is understood to include background practices, we could not say anything, true or false. However, the places where Wittgenstein comes closest to endorsing practical holism, such as *Investigations* §241 or §§198–202, are places where the narrator is responding to aggressive questions, and should not be read as a definitive formulation of dogmatic theses. The text of the *Investigations* is best read, I believe, as a Pyrrhonian dialogue that includes both a voice that is tempted by theoretical holism and a narrator who corrects the first voice by advocating a form of practical holism, rather than as unequivocally endorsing either of these views.

Critics of practical holism usually take talk of practices or forms of life to be another way of talking about a more familiar category,

---

[41] Dreyfus 1991, 152. [42] Heidegger 1962, §35, p. 212.
[43] Dreyfus 1991, 16. [44] Dreyfus 1991, 155.

such as the causes of behaviour, observable regularities in behaviour, or systems of belief, material that can be used as a starting point for a theory of practice. But practices are neither simply intentional states nor behaviour, and theories of practice that attempt to account for practices in those terms alone fail to do them justice. At the very least, a practice is something people do, not just once, but on a regular basis. But it is more than just a disposition to behave in a certain way: the identity of a practice depends not only on what people do, but also on the significance of those actions and the surroundings in which they occur. This is only to begin to answer the question how we are to understand 'what people do' when they are engaged in a practice, or just what a practice amounts to. For there are enormous differences among philosophers and social theorists on just this point, and the differences are far-reaching. Discussions of practice make use of several overlapping clusters of loosely connected and ambiguous terms, terms that suggest connections that lead in a number of different directions. These include: activity, praxis, performance, use, language-game, customs, habit, skill, know-how, equipment, habitus, tacit knowledge, presupposition, rule, norm, institution, paradigm, framework, tradition, conceptual scheme, world view, background, and world picture. One way of classifying such theories is by looking at which terms are central to competing conceptions of practice. For instance, one could contrast individualistic with social conceptions, local with global, normative with descriptive, or implicit with explicit. But this would reintroduce at the very beginning the very dichotomies that are so philosophically problematic, and it would not do justice to the fact that many of the terms in question are just as disputed as practice itself.

While Dreyfus stresses the parallels between his reading of Heidegger and the later Wittgenstein's insistence on the primacy of practice, he does not lose sight of the principal disanalogy between the early Heidegger and the later Wittgenstein. Heidegger's 'existential analytic', his elaborate account of the structure of the background of everyday activity, is a systematic theory of practice, while Wittgenstein 'is convinced that the practices that make up the human form of life are a hopeless tangle . . . and warns against any attempt to systematize this hurly-burly'.[45] But Wittgenstein's description of this 'hurly-burly'

---

[45] Dreyfus 1991, 7.

is only a 'hopeless tangle' from the perspective of an inveterate systematizer. For those looking for an approach to practice that starts from particular cases, for a way of investigating practices without doing practice theory, Wittgenstein's unsystematic approach holds out the hope of doing justice to the indefinite and multicoloured filigree of everyday life:

624. We judge an action according to its background within human life, and this background is not monochrome, but we might picture it as a very complicated filigree pattern, which, to be sure, we can't copy, but which we can recognize from the general impression it makes.

625. The background is the bustle of life.

629. How could human behaviour be described? Surely only by showing the actions of a variety of humans, as they are all mixed together. Not what *one* man is doing *now*, but the whole hurly-burly, is the background against which we see an action, and it determines our judgment, our concepts, and our reactions.[46]

In these passages, Wittgenstein provides a particularly clear statement of an approach to practice that insists on staying on the surface, by attending to the detail and complexity of the complicated patterns that make up our lives. Much of his post-1945 writing on the philosophy of psychology is an exploration of this theme. Part II of the *Philosophical Investigations* consists of carefully selected excerpts from this work, originally gathered as readings for Norman Malcolm and his students when visiting Cornell in 1948.

However, to anyone attracted to the idea that the philosopher or social scientist must go beyond simply describing the detail of our everyday lives, such an approach is akin to a naive empiricism or extreme subjectivism, a misguided attempt to give up all theorizing in favour of a first-person perspective on social life. To such a critic, Wittgensteinian description is so atheoretical that it no longer holds out the hope of a theory of practice: by discarding the goals of system and rigour, it avoids the problems involved in trying to formulate a theory of practice, but no longer has the explanatory power of the original, admittedly problematic, notion of a theory of practice.

---

[46] Wittgenstein, *Remarks on the Philosophy of Psychology*, vol. II, §§624–5, §629.

The point of such a theory of practice would be to provide a philosophical justification of our talk of meaning and understanding. This usually takes the form of an account that provides a ground for such talk, locating it either within the space of causes – a scientific account of its causal basis – or within the space of reasons – a normative account of the reason why we are justified in speaking as we do. Pierre Bourdieu calls this antinomy the 'dilemma of mechanism or finalism'.[47] 'Mechanists' offer a non-intentional or non-normative theory of practice, by placing it in a broader context of human behaviour that can be described in naturalistic and causal terms.[48] 'Finalists' give an intentional or normative theory of practice, by placing it in a broader context of human behaviour that can best be described in terms of justification or reason-giving.[49] On the other hand, Wittgenstein would reply that these attempts to discern a systematic pattern behind the phenomena go too far in the opposite direction, substituting a mechanistic theory of fictitious causal forces or a finalistic theory of rule-governed action for close observation of what actually goes on in our lives.

But the debates between supporters of mechanism or finalism, or defenders of theoretical holism or practical holism, miss Wittgenstein's Pyrrhonian point, which is that there is no philosophical problem about rule-following, no 'gap' between rules and their application of the kind that concerns both sceptic and anti-sceptics. For instance, in §§187–8, the narrator criticizes his interlocutor's conviction that an act of meaning or intending is what connects his grasp of a formula, on the one hand, and his readiness to apply it to particular steps in the process of calculation, on the other. This provokes the following exchange:

[Interlocutor:] 'But *are* the steps then *not* determined by the algebraic formula?'
[Narrator:] – The question contains a mistake. (§189a)

The narrator explains this response by considering a mechanistic construal of the use of the expression 'The steps are determined by the formula . . .' in §189b, in which it refers to the fact that people are trained to use a formula in a certain way, and a finalistic construal in §189c, on which it refers to a grammatical norm.

---

[47] Bourdieu 1977, 22.   [48] See e.g. Bloor 1983, 1997, and 2001.
[49] See e.g. Brandom 1994.

The anti-theoretical reading I have been outlining here is often known as 'quietism', for its denial that Wittgenstein has anything to say on the subject of grand philosophical theories about the relation between language and world. According to the quietist, Wittgenstein's invocation of forms of life is not the beginning of a positive theory of practice, or a pragmatist theory of meaning, but rather is meant to help his readers get over their addiction to theorizing about mind and world, language and reality. Hilary Putnam, Cora Diamond, and John McDowell are among the leading advocates of this approach.[50] McDowell observes that Wittgenstein's readers often take his talk of 'customs, practices, institutions', and 'forms of life' as the first steps towards a positive philosophy. The point of the positive views would be to give a non-intentional, or non-normative, justification of our talk of meaning and understanding, by placing it in a broader context of human interaction, interaction that can be described in non-intentional terms.

But there is no reason to credit Wittgenstein with any sympathy for this style of philosophy. When he says 'What has to be accepted, the given, is – so one could say – *forms of life*' [PI ii.xi, 226/192] his point is not to adumbrate a philosophical response, on such lines, to supposedly good questions about the possibility of meaning and understanding, or intentionality generally, but to remind us of something we can take in the proper way only after we are equipped to see that such questions are based on a mistake. His point is to remind us that the natural phenomenon that is normal human life is itself already shaped by meaning and understanding.[51]

On this reading, the task of these sections of the *Philosophical Investigations*, then, is to help us see that such questions are based on a mistake, and so dissolve those problems. But a great deal turns on the terms in which we understand that mistake. Critics of quietism reply that the quietest faces an unattractive dilemma: either the quietest provides philosophical arguments that convince us that the questions are mistaken, in which case the quietest has not given up philosophical argument at all, or the quietist really does forgo philosophical argument, in which case she or he has nothing philosophically convincing to offer.

---

[50] See Diamond 1991a and McDowell 1981, 1993, 1994; Diamond, McDowell, and Putnam in Crary and Read 2000; Schulte 2002.
[51] McDowell 1993, 50–1.

In the conclusion to *Pyrrhonian Reflections on Knowledge and Justification*, Fogelin construes the *Philosophical Investigations* as an unresolved conflict between what he calls its Pyrrhonian and non-Pyrrhonian strands, presenting a Wittgenstein who failed to clearly distinguish these strands.[52] Similarly, many Wittgenstein interpreters identify a conflict in the *Philosophical Investigations* between its characterization of the philosophy practised there as a dissolution of philosophical problems, a 'struggle against the bewitchment of our understanding' (§109*), and the narrator's apparent endorsement of quite specific solutions to particular philosophical problems. As Crispin Wright puts it, 'it is difficult to reconcile Wittgenstein's pronouncements about the kind of thing which he thinks he ought to be doing with what he actually seems to do'.[53] But what looks to Fogelin, Wright, and many other readers like an author who's not entirely in control of his material, oscillating between global statements of a Pyrrhonian method and endorsing particular non-Pyrrhonian philosophical views, is better understood as a matter of different voices within the dialogue setting out opposing philosophical views, within an argument that is in service of a Pyrrhonism about philosophy. The non-Pyrrhonian positions advocated by the principal voice(s) in its dialogue – 'Wittgenstein's narrator' or the 'voice of correctness' – are only one voice within an argumentative dialogue that serves its author's Pyrrhonian convictions. Rather than construing the author of the *Philosophical Investigations* as genuinely conflicted between quietism and substantive philosophical views (unless, of course, that comes down to no more than saying that he was well aware of just how attractive both of those views can be), it would be closer to the truth to approach him as a quietist who sees that any attempt to explicitly articulate quietism will lead to dogmatism of one kind or another, and that therefore the best way to advocate quietism is to write a genuinely conflicted dialogue in which non-Pyrrhonian participants play the leading roles. This is, after all, the classically Pyrrhonian way out of the dilemma presented by the anti-Pyrrhonian philosopher: the text really does contain philosophical argument, but the author regards the argument as a ladder that we should throw away after we have drawn the Pyrrhonian moral.

[52] Fogelin 1994, 205–22.   [53] Wright 1980, 262.

CHAPTER 7

The critique of a private language and the paradox of private ostension: §§243–68

7.1 ON THE VERY IDEA OF A PRIVATE LANGUAGE: §§243–55

Sections 243–55 introduce the idea of a private language; §§256–315 contain an extended attack on the very idea of a private language, interwoven with a host of related issues. In the opening remarks, Wittgenstein's narrator attends not only to the question of the kind of privacy that is under discussion, but also to the more general issue of the relationship of first- and third-person statements about sensation.

This part of the text has struck many interpreters as a place where Wittgenstein is at his most un-Pyrrhonian. For he appears to proceed in a highly dogmatic fashion. Three examples stand out in the opening remarks of this chapter of the *Philosophical Investigations*. He is widely taken to be maintaining the following controversial philosophical views. (1) In §244, he appears to summarize his 'expressive theory of meaning' for first-person psychological discourse. On the 'expressive theory' of pain, first-person talk about one's current pain is not a report on an inner state, but rather has the role of a learned replacement for instinctive pain-behaviour – in other words, saying 'I am in pain' is to be construed as akin to saying 'Ouch!', which in turn takes the place of the cries of a child that has not yet learned to speak.[1] (2) In §246, he maintains that it is a grammatical error to say 'I know I am in pain' rather than 'I am in pain.' (3) Sections 249–50 appear to deny that a dog or a baby can pretend or play-act.

Before turning to the narrator's attack on the very idea of a private language, let us briefly consider the first two examples of

---

[1] See Tugendhat 1989 for a review of the literature on this topic.

non-Pyrrhonian dogma mentioned above, views that are often attributed to Wittgenstein in order to show that he is, in practice, inconsistent in his claim that he is not advancing a theory.[2] While the 'expressive theory of meaning' is never actually formulated in the *Philosophical Investigations*, it is routinely attributed to Wittgenstein on the basis of what is said in §244 and related passages. Section 244 begins with the interlocutor's asking: 'How do words *refer* to sensations?' He thus draws our attention to the question of the nature of the connection between words and sensations, the question that will be at the centre of discussion in §256 and the remarks that follow. The narrator first responds by saying: 'There doesn't seem to be any problem here; don't we talk about sensations every day, and give them names?' This leads the interlocutor to reformulate his initial question as a query about how words and what they stand for become linked: 'But how is the connexion between the name and the thing named set up?' The narrator begins his reply by saying that this amounts to asking how a human being learns the meaning of the names of sensations, such as the word 'pain', for example, and then says the following:

Here is one possibility: words are connected with the initial, the natural, expressions of the sensation and used in their place. A child has hurt himself and he cries; and then adults talk to him and teach him exclamations and, later, sentences. They teach the child new pain-behaviour.

'So you are saying that the word "pain" really means crying?' – On the contrary: the verbal expression of pain replaces crying and does not describe it. (§244a–b*)

The narrator aims to draw our attention to what he modestly calls a 'possibility', though it certainly is as applicable to our use of pain-vocabulary as the interlocutor's focus on a direct link between words and sensations. What he provides is an alternative way of approaching the connection between words and sensations; as in §144, the narrator is offering us a different picture of our use of words, one that aims to change our 'way of looking at things'. Rather than asking 'How do words *refer* to sensations?' (§244), he suggests that we take a wider look around at how words for pain are taught and used. A similar

---

[2] For discussion of §249–50, see Stern 2004.

approach is at work in the other two controversial passages mentioned above.

The standard reading of §246 and other passages where the narrator attacks the interlocutor's conviction that 'only I can know whether I am really in pain; another person can only surmise it' (§246a) is that this is the consequence of Wittgenstein's commitment to a theory of the conditions for making a statement with a sense. The theory usually attributed to him is that in order to be entitled to claim that I know something, that claim must be made on the basis of evidence, evidence that is, at least in principle, open to doubt. For my sensations are not something I can find out about, in the way that I can find out about others' pains; rather, the point is that 'I *have them*', and have them in a way that makes it senseless to assert that I know I am in pain. Certainly, the narrator does say that 'It can't be said of me at all (except perhaps as a joke) that I *know* I am in pain. What is it supposed to mean – except perhaps that I *am* in pain?' (§246a). But this does not have to be interpreted as a commitment to the theory sketched above. Rather, we can construe it as a way of getting us to be suspicious of the philosophical use of the word 'know' in this way, as a way of motivating a picture of the mind on which only I have direct access to my inner states.

As in the case of the controversy over the book's opening remarks, this way of reading the text, on which the author supposedly sets out a theory of language of his own as the basis for a refutation of traditional philosophical approaches, is overhasty and misleading. None of the views in question are actually explicitly expressed by the narrator, and so must be inferred from the narrator's considerably more equivocal statements. Furthermore, the narrator's wording in these passages has the character of a reminder of what we would ordinarily say, rather than the articulation of a philosophical theory. In any case, we cannot simply assume that the author endorses everything that his narrator asserts or implies, let alone the detailed and sophisticated articulation of those views that has been developed in the secondary literature. However, philosophers have found it extremely attractive to construe this part of the text as providing the materials for a master argument that decisively undermines familiar philosophical theories, such as Cartesian dualism, a foundationalism that starts from inner experience, or the view that the mind depends on a 'language of thought'. Indeed, one of the reasons why this part of the *Philosophical Investigations* has attracted such philosophical attention is that it has struck expositors as the place where Wittgenstein sets out his own non-Pyrrhonian views about the nature of experience, engages directly with traditional philosophical theories, such as dualism or foundationalism, and attacks them head-on. However, because Wittgenstein's principal targets here are the trains of thought that lead us into thinking of our inner experiences as a privileged starting point for philosophy, and his ultimate aim is to get the reader to see that such theories of inner experience make no sense, the connection between the text of this part of the *Philosophical Investigations* and mainstream topics in the philosophy of mind is not as close as it might seem.

The discussion of private language begins by distinguishing between the ordinary sense of privacy in which my hidden diary, my secret code, or my concealed pain are private matters, and the sublime conception of privacy that is the focus of the interlocutor's interest. While a diary, a code, or a pain may well be private – that is, no one else knows about it – it is always possible, at least in principle, that others find out about such matters. The interlocutor, on the other hand, asks us to imagine a language that is necessarily private, one that no one else could possibly understand, because the words 'refer to what can only be known to the person speaking; to his immediate private sensations. So another person cannot understand the language' (§243). 'Super-private' is a convenient shorthand for this super-concept, a term that Wittgenstein coined when writing a paper for an English audience on the topic;[3] in the *Philosophical Investigations*, Wittgenstein sometimes makes it clear that he is talking about super-privacy, rather than ordinary privacy, by putting 'private' in scare-quotes (§202, §256, §653). In the remarks that follow, Wittgenstein's narrator raises problems for the very idea of such a language, a 'language which describes my inner experiences and which only I myself can understand' (§256), while his interlocutor takes on the role of the 'private linguist', the defender of the idea that there can be a private language in this specially introduced sense.

---

[3] See Wittgenstein, *Philosophical Occasions*, 447; Stern 1995, 6.3.

7.2 THE PARADOX OF PRIVATE OSTENSION: §§256–68

In §256, Wittgenstein's narrator draws our attention back to the idea of a private language, and the question of how, precisely, the words of that language are connected to their inner objects. First of all, he makes it clear that we could not, strictly speaking, make any ordinary sensation or experience the subject of a word in a private language. This qualification even applies to the main examples he goes on to discuss, namely being in pain and seeing red. For if there already is a public word for the sensation in question, or if it is one of those experiences that has characteristic 'natural expressions' – Wittgenstein's principal example here is pain, and the ways people typically respond to pain (§244) – then it will always be possible to tell another about them. In that case, the language cannot be private in the strong sense that the private linguist is looking for. This leads up to the core of the proposal as to how we are to imagine a private language: we are to think of a case where there is no natural expression for the sensation, and no pre-existing vocabulary that describes it. In this case, the usual links to bodily expression and linguistic classification do not stand in the way of super-privacy, 'and now I simply *associate* names with sensations and use these names in descriptions' (§256).

In effect, the strategy outlined at the end of §256 amounts to applying the 'method of §2' (§48) to the case of a private language: thinking of a situation which appears to give the interlocutor what he wants, and then pointing out its shortcomings. We have seen that in §2, §48, and most of the other examples of the method of §2 we have considered so far, it was relatively unproblematic to describe a language-game that fitted the bill; the disabling problem was that the description in question was only appropriate for a 'narrowly circumscribed region, not for the whole of what you were claiming to describe' (§3). However, the principal problem with the idea of a private language is not that it has limited applicability – the private linguist would be the first to acknowledge that – but that it is incoherent, and so has no applicability at all. In effect, Wittgenstein's narrator contends that the defender of a private language must choose between a pair of unacceptable alternatives. Either the concept of privacy involved is one we are already familiar with, in which case it will not support the philosophical use the private linguist wants to make of it; or it is a philosophical super-concept, custom-built to underwrite the philosopher's theory, but sublimely disconnected from the rest of our language: ' But what are these words to be used for now? The language-game in which they are to be applied is missing' (§96). However, this is much too fast for anyone who finds the notion of a private language attractive, which is why the discussion in §256 is immediately preceded by a critical discussion of 'what we are "tempted to say"' (§254) about privacy and super-privacy. It begins with relatively restrained statements of views that the interlocutor regards as important truths, and builds towards increasingly emphatic and insistent proclamations:

– Well, only I can know whether I am really in pain; another person can only surmise it. – (§246a)

'Only you can know if you had that intention.' (§247a)

'Sensations are private.' (§248)

'What would it be like, if it were otherwise?' (§251a)

'I can't imagine the opposite.' (§251b)

'Another person can't have my pains.' (§253a)

'But surely another person can't have THIS pain!' (§253c)

In each of these cases, the narrator's response is to try to show that what the interlocutor actually says is either an empty truism, or plainly false, or nonsensical. If the interlocutor's claims are given a carefully constructed context, the words in question turn out to either state a platitude, such as a reminder of how words are ordinarily used (§247a, §248), or a falsehood (the second half of §244a, §253a). However, the narrator will also argue that without such a context, which is the way in which such claims are usually made, the words make no sense at all. Consequently, what Wittgenstein's narrator does in §256 and the remarks that follow it is to describe a number of scenarios that come as close as possible to fulfilling the interlocutor's wishes and then go on to show how each of them fails to yield a private language. Two leading examples of such a strategy are pursued in §257 and §258.

Section 257 considers an imaginary case in which there is no customary way of expressing pain, and so no way of teaching pain-vocabulary: in this case, at least a 'private language' for pain is not ruled out, as it is for us, by the existence of pain-vocabulary and natural expressions of pain. This requires, of course, that the speaker of the supposed private language makes it up by himself, and cannot explain its meaning to anyone else. The remarks begin with the interlocutor asking us to imagine what a world would be like in which people never expressed their pains, to which the narrator responds that one couldn't, in that case, teach a child the use of a term for pain such as 'tooth-ache'. Given the extraordinarily limited resources available to the child, the narrator is left to exclaim that the child may still be smart enough to work out how to name the sensation for herself:

– Well, let's assume the child is a genius and himself invents a name for the sensation! (§257)

This leads the narrator to observe that the name couldn't be used to communicate with anyone else, and then to a barrage of questions about just what is supposed to be going on:

– So does he understand the name, without being able to explain its meaning to anyone? – But what does it mean to say that he has 'named his pain'? – How has he done this naming of pain?! And whatever he did, what was its purpose? (§257)

We saw in chapter 4 that Wittgenstein's narrator argues in the opening remarks of the *Philosophical Investigations* that ostensive definition is not as simple as it seems. For it can only be successful if one already grasps what kind of role the word is to play, how the other words are to be used, and the significance of the expectations, activities, and gestures that typically accompany the use of these words. More generally, one of the main themes of the *Philosophical Investigations* as a whole is that explicit linguistic acts such as giving an ostensive definition, providing a verbal explanation of a word's meaning, or interpreting a rule take place on the background of a great deal of practical ability, and that their significance depends both on the particular circumstances in which they take place, and the broader context provided by the 'weave of our life' (PI ii.i, 174/148). Ostension in particular, and language as a whole, always depend on a practical context. As a result, ostensive definition, whether it concerns inner or outer objects, always depends on a prior context of practices and institutions. In §257, Wittgenstein's narrator makes it clear that this previous point about ostensive definition is also true of inner ostension:

> – When one says 'He gave a name to his sensation' one forgets that a great deal of stage-setting in language is presupposed if the mere act of naming is to make sense. And when we speak of someone's giving a name to pain, what is presupposed is the grammar of the word 'pain'; it shows the post where the new word is stationed. (§257*)

The precise nature of the analogies and disanalogies between the cases of public ostensive definition and private ostensive definition deserves further attention. In response to the paradox of ostension (§28), Wittgenstein's narrator observes that the problem does not ordinarily arise, because 'the place is already prepared' (§31b) for the word that is to be defined. In other words, ostensive definition is usually a satisfactory way of explaining the meaning of a word because we do already speak the language in question, and only need to have the precise role of that word brought to our attention. No such response is available to the private linguist, precisely because a private language is supposed to be an autonomous system of representation that can only be understood by its speaker. Consequently the private linguist cannot help himself to the taken-for-granted framework of our ordinary use of language in replying to what we can call the **paradox of private ostension:** 'a private ostensive definition can be variously interpreted in *every* case'.

On the reading I am advocating, Wittgenstein's principal point is not that we could not go on to use a super-private definition consistently, nor that one would be unable to tell that one was using it correctly. Instead, it is much simpler: that nothing one could actually do would ever amount to setting up such a language, for the role of training and practice in ostension prevent a 'private linguist' from using a sign to mean anything at all, even once. In other words, the problem is ultimately the logical one highlighted in §257: the 'stage-setting' that it presupposes would not be in place.[4] The objection is not that the private sign won't work once it is given a meaning, but that it has not been given a meaning in the first place. For a particular way of using a word is a practice, a linguistically structured procedure that may be contingently private, in the sense that I may choose to

---

[4] See Fogelin 1987, 155–65 (1976, 138–52); Stroud 2000, 67–79 and 213–32.

keep it secret. But to conceive of it as necessarily private, as 'super-private', is to misunderstand our use of language. Merely *thinking* one is obeying a rule is not enough to establish that one is obeying a rule, just as *thinking* one is giving money is not enough to make it the case that one is doing so. In each case, my sincere conviction is insufficient (and unnecessary); what matters is that the circumstances and consequences must be right.

268. Why can't my right hand give my left hand money? – My right hand can put it into my left hand. My right hand can write a deed of gift and my left hand a receipt. – But the further practical consequences would not be those of a gift. When the left hand has taken the money from the right, etc., we shall ask: 'Well, and what of it?' And the same could be asked if a person had given himself a private definition of a word; I mean, if he has said the word to himself and at the same time has directed his attention to a sensation.

As it is hard to imagine a case in which anyone would be tempted to think that their right hand was giving money to their left hand, this is a case of what Wittgenstein calls 'obvious nonsense', and so the analogy with the private linguist is necessarily limited. However, we can easily think of parallel cases of non-obvious nonsense, such as someone under the age of consent signing a legal agreement, where the signer might well want to sign the contract, and believe that he or she had successfully entered into an agreement.

In the world of super-private language, where one had cut out everything that might provide a reason for judging that one was or was not following a rule, all that one would be left with would be 'thinking one was obeying a rule' (§202), and with acts every bit as bizarre as one's right hand giving one's left hand money, such as concentrating one's attention on a feeling and insisting: 'But I can (inwardly) undertake to call THIS "pain" in the future' (§263). In broad outline, then, the narrator's principal objection to the notion of a private language is that it is nonsense, a fantasy of inner naming that can never get off the ground: all we are left with is an empty ceremony, and the illusion that something significant has been done.

However, not only are other approaches to understanding Wittgenstein's objections to a private language extremely popular in the secondary literature, it is frequently taken for granted that they are the only ways of making sense of this part of the *Philosophical Investigations*. One way of approaching this issue, popularized by Kripke, is to maintain that the sections following §243 'deal with the *application* of the general conclusions about language drawn in §§138–242 to the problem of sensations'.[5] On Kripke's reading, the core of Wittgenstein's discussion of private language is already to be found in the preceding treatment of rule-following: a rule only has content insofar as the rule-follower can be considered to be acting as part of a wider community, for it is only the community that can underwrite the attribution of correct or incorrect rule-following. While this 'community view' is, as we have seen, a highly problematic interpretation, Kripke is surely right to stress the connections between the discussion of private language that begins with §243, and the previous material on rule-following and practice. In particular, Kripke stresses the fact that §202, which he takes to sum up the conclusion of the 'real private language argument', immediately follows the review of Wittgenstein's treatment of the paradoxes of rule-following in §§198–201:

202.* And so 'obeying a rule' is a practice. And *thinking* one is obeying a rule isn't obeying a rule. And that's why one can't obey a rule 'privately', for otherwise thinking one was obeying a rule would be the same thing as obeying it.[6]

Here we can see a programmatic outline of how the broader discussion of practice and rule-following will connect up with the later discussion of private language. Given that 'there can't have been just one occasion on which a person obeyed a rule' (§199*), that rule-following and the like are '*customs* (practices, institutions)' (§199*), it follows that super-private rule-following is an incoherent notion: not because Wittgenstein thinks he has proved language is necessarily

---

[5] Kripke 1982, 79; see also ch. 3 of that book for further articulation of this reading. For further discussion of Kripke on rule-following, see 6.2.

[6] In their response to Kripke, Baker and Hacker emphasize that §202 was originally part of a discussion of private language, and only inserted in its current place at a late stage in the composition of the *Philosophical Investigations* (Baker and Hacker 1984, 11–21; 1985, 152–3). However, unless one assumes that the best way of understanding a given remark in the *Philosophical Investigations* is to trace it back to its source, this hardly shows that the effect of this transposition is to 'transform a perspicuous back reference into an opaque anticipation' (1985, 153).

social (as Kripke maintains), but because Wittgenstein has reminded us that language is a practice, and a practice cannot be super-private. Much of the literature on the 'private language argument'[7] presupposes that the principal problem Wittgenstein's narrator is raising for the private linguist arises not at the point at which the private definition is first introduced, but occurs further down the road, when the privately defined word is to be used. According to the exponents of this construal, we are asked to imagine, for the sake of argument, that the private linguist does make the initial moves involved in setting up a private language, such as uttering the intended name of the sensation in question under the best possible circumstances. However, it is then argued that when the time comes to repeat the name on a second occasion, a necessary condition for use of the name cannot be met. On this way of understanding Wittgenstein, his main objection to a private language is that there can be no possibility of making use of such a definition, or no way of knowing that one has used such a term successfully. In outline, the objection is that a necessary condition for the use of the term in question cannot be satisfied. This is supposedly because one would have no reliable test, or no test at all, as to whether one was using the word in question correctly. For instance, it has often been argued that under these circumstances the private linguist lacks a 'criterion of correctness', an objective standard by which to tell whether the word has been used correctly, or that some other condition, such as being able to tell whether he has remembered the word correctly, is not satisfied. The precise nature of this condition, and the nature of Wittgenstein's supposed argument for it, has been the subject of an extraordinary amount of debate. Indeed, the question of how to state this is often taken to be the principal issue at stake in understanding and evaluating the 'private language argument'. As Canfield aptly puts it, it is usually taken for granted that 'the key to

---

[7] This is a term that never appears in the *Philosophical Investigations*, or anywhere else in Wittgenstein's papers. However, many of Wittgenstein's best-known expositors regard Wittgenstein's 'private language argument' as the 'centre-piece' (Pears 1988, 361) of the *Philosophical Investigations*, a tradition that has its roots in reviews of the book by Malcolm and Strawson. While this part of the *Philosophical Investigations* certainly does argue against the possibility of a private language, it is far from clear that it does contain the particular conception of the 'private language argument' that one finds in Malcolm, Strawson, and Pears, which remains the most commonly accepted interpretation of §§243–315.

understanding Wittgenstein's later thought is to grasp its centre point, some elusive and obscurely presented refutation of the possibility of a (metaphysically) private language'.[8]

This way of reading Wittgenstein becomes very attractive if one concentrates on identifying a free-standing argument on the basis of those sentences which look as if they contain the core of such a proof. Oddly, immediately after noting the dangers of such a strategy, precisely because of the way in which Wittgenstein's writing hangs together, David Pears proposes that the treatment of a private language amounts to an exception to this rule, quotes the very sentences that are the crux of the standard reading, and summarizes, in a very general way, its overall conclusion:

It would be simplistic to suppose that it is possible to take a late text of Wittgenstein's, cut along the dotted lines, and find that it falls into neatly separated arguments. The structure of his thought is too holistic for that kind of treatment. However, though this is generally true of his later work, his private language argument is something of an exception. It is brief, looks self-contained, and after it has been cut out of *Philosophical Investigations*, it proves to be memorable and eminently debatable:

> . . . But in the present case I have no criterion of correctness. One would like to say: whatever is going to seem right to me is right. And that only means that here we can't talk about 'right'.

The topic is the reidentification of sensation-types, and the argument is that a case can be described in which there would be no distinction between applying a word to a sensation-type correctly, and applying it incorrectly.[9]

Pears' final sentence is sufficiently broadly worded that it covers a wide range of different approaches to this text. Naturally, it is primarily applicable to the construal he explores with extraordinary determination and subtlety, namely that reidentification fails because the distinction between applying the word correctly and applying it incorrectly cannot be invoked because some quite specific condition for the successful use of a word is lacking. On Pears' reading, the argument turns on the idea that if the words of the private linguist's 'language' are to count as part of a language, then the use of those expressions must be governed by rules. But if those words are rule-governed,

---

[8] Canfield 2001, 377.   [9] Pears 1988, 328; the embedded quotation is from the end of §258.

there must be a distinction between applying the rules correctly and incorrectly. Yet if the only standard available to the private linguist is what seems right to him or her, then there is no standard at all, for any such standard must be independent of what seems right to the private linguist. Hence the 'language' and 'rules' are not really rules at all, and so the notion of a private language is incoherent. Only the practice of a community of language users provides the independent, public check on the correct use of words. Fogelin has called this the 'public check' argument, as it turns on the requirement that there be a public standard that is capable of providing a way of checking whether a speaker has used a word correctly.[10] Although this argument, in one form or another, has proven enormously popular as a reading of §258 in particular, and as the crux of §§243–315 as a whole, it is, in the end, a deeply problematic reading. First, one can object that if what really matters is whether or not there is a standard independent of what seems right to the private linguist, then in the situation just described, there is no reason why the private linguist could still have access to some standards, such as memory or a written record. These are capable of providing a way of checking whether what seems right to him or her is right. Although it would only be a private check, the publicity requirement has to do with the need for an independent check, and the point of the reply is that those resources could be provided without recourse to a check by others. Second, one can object that the same question can also be directed at the supposed solution: what independent standard can we turn to in this case, to assure that the community is correct? If the answer is only that no standard is needed here, because public language takes care of itself, then it looks as if the requirement for an independent standard has been applied in a question-begging way.

However, Pears' final sentence can also serve as a summary of the interpretation that I am advocating – that there is no distinction in 'the present case' between applying such a word correctly and applying it incorrectly, because there was never any identification of a sensation-type in the first place, and so there is only the illusion of a distinction and of reidentification, for no word is being used at all. Pears, like most other interpreters, regards §258 as providing

---

[10] Fogelin 1994, 213–15; see also 1987, 168–9 and 179–84.

some of the strongest evidence for the deeply un-Pyrrhonian public check argument, but there is no reason why it cannot equally well be read as supporting the Pyrrhonian reading on which the narrator is arguing that the story of the private linguist is nonsense. If we look at §258 as a whole, rather than plucking the final sentences out of context, it is striking that it is one of the few remarks in which the interlocutor has more words than the narrator, and that the narrator's words are a series of negative replies to the interlocutor's suggestions. Highlighting the interlocutor's words in bold, the passage reads as follows:

258.* **Let us imagine the following case. I want to keep a diary about the recurrence of a certain sensation. To this end I associate it with the sign 'S' and write this sign in a calendar for every day on which I have the sensation.** — I will observe first of all that a definition of the sign can't be formulated. – **But still I can give one to myself as a kind of ostensive definition!** – How? Can I point to the sensation? — **Not in the ordinary sense. But I speak, or write the sign down, and at the same time I concentrate my attention on the sensation – and so, as it were, point to it inwardly.** – But what is this ceremony for? For that is all it seems to be! A definition surely serves to establish the meaning of a sign. – **Well, that is done precisely by the concentrating of my attention; for in this way I impress on myself the connexion between the sign and the sensation.** – But 'I impress it on myself' can only mean: this process brings it about that I remember the connexion *right* in the future. But in the present case I don't have any criterion of correctness. Here, one would like to say: whatever is going to seem right to me is right. And that only means that here we can't talk about 'right'.

The passage begins with the interlocutor asking us to imagine a private language that is very different from the scenario described in §257: he imagines himself introducing a familiar sign – the letter 'S' – and a familiar category of object – a sensation. In §261, the narrator will point out that these assumptions are illegitimate, that if 'S' names a sensation, then it is a word intelligible to everyone who speaks our language. But in §257 he contents himself with pointing out that no definition can be formulated – for any such definition would unquestionably make 'S' a publicly teachable word. The interlocutor responds that an inner surrogate for ostensive definition is nevertheless possible, with the concentrating of my attention taking the place of pointing to the object in question. As before, the narrator insists that this is an empty charade, for no sign has thereby been given a definition. The interlocutor asserts that the concentrating of my attention amounts to an inner definition, for that is how I impress the connection on myself. In this context, the narrator's closing words are best read as providing a forceful restatement of the case for thinking that the interlocutor has done nothing that amounts to giving a word a meaning. Whatever is going to seem right to me is right, because no word has been defined, no rules have been set up. Interpreters have often read this passage as if Wittgenstein had arrived at a result concerning the lack of a criterion of correctness as the endpoint of a subtle train of reasoning, summed up in the final two sentences. But Wittgenstein's closing words are better read as a robust rejection of the very idea that I could possibly have such a criterion.

Conclusion

This book began by noting that while Wittgenstein is widely regarded as the most important philosopher of the twentieth century, there is almost no agreement on even the most basic questions about how to understand the *Philosophical Investigations*. Rather than simply adding one more interpretation to the already lengthy list of competing interpretations, each condemning – or ignoring – all the others, a principal aim of this introduction to the *Philosophical Investigations* has been to provide some insight into why such a wide variety of readers have hailed the book as the final solution to the problems of philosophy. We have seen that the *Philosophical Investigations'* wide-ranging appeal arises out of its unusual combination of an open-ended and conversational way of writing, which invites a multiplicity of interpretations, and its quite specific argumentative structure.

My principal proposal about understanding the relationship between the argument of the book and its style has been that readers are too ready to identify the author's viewpoint with whatever conclusions the reader attributes to Wittgenstein's narrator, and so fail to take account of the overall character of the book. At the very least, a careful reader must be aware that the author's use of certain arguments does not amount to an endorsement of them. However, for this very reason the secondary literature on the *Philosophical Investigations* has a particularly valuable role to play in helping a reader to come to understand the pitfalls involved in a close reading of that text. For there is no better way of appreciating the variety of possible readings of the *Philosophical Investigations* than to turn to that literature.

Recommended further reading

The following list is extremely selective; for further bibliographical information, consult the following book-length bibliographies.

BIBLIOGRAPHIES

Frongia, Guido 1989 *Wittgenstein: A Bibliographical Guide*. Oxford: Blackwell. Selective, but provides informative abstracts of many of the items listed.

Shanker, S. G. (ed.) 1986 *Ludwig Wittgenstein: Critical Assessments*, vol. v. London: Croom Helm.

EXCELLENT INTRODUCTIONS TO WITTGENSTEIN

Coope, C., P. T. Geach, T. Potts, and R. White 1970 *A Wittgenstein Workbook*. Berkeley: University of California Press. Helpful exercises on a range of topics in the *Tractatus* and *Philosophical Investigations*. Very useful for students looking for help in beginning research on specific topics.

Fogelin, Robert 1987 *Wittgenstein*. London: Routledge & Kegan Paul. Revised 2nd edn; 1st edn 1976. Critical but sympathetic interpretation of both *Tractatus* and *Philosophical Investigations*.

Glock, Hans-Johann 1996 *A Wittgenstein Dictionary*. Oxford: Blackwell. Encyclopedic and analytic coverage of dozens of key topics, in the form of short essays; copious references to key passages throughout the Wittgenstein papers. Hacker's approach to Wittgenstein is taken for granted; little attention given to other interpretations.

Kenny, Anthony 1973 *Wittgenstein*. Cambridge, MA: Harvard University Press. Provides an overview of the development of Wittgenstein's thought and many of his central concerns; elementary and accessible interpretation of key passages and their implications.

Kripke, Saul 1982 *Wittgenstein on Rules and Private Language*. Cambridge, MA: Harvard University Press. Short, clearly written, and extremely influential. A powerful reconstruction of a line of argument Kripke finds in Wittgenstein, but misunderstands Wittgenstein's use of that argument.

Malcolm, Norman 1994 *Wittgenstein: A Religious Point of View?* ed. with a response by Peter Winch. Ithaca, NY: Cornell University Press. Malcolm's short essay provides a very accessible introduction to his reading of Wittgenstein's philosophy as a whole; Winch's response is also very valuable.

McGinn, Marie 1997 *Wittgenstein and the 'Philosophical Investigations'.* London: Routledge. Lucid exposition of leading topics, with chapters on style and method, Wittgenstein's critique of Augustine, rule-following, private language, the inner and outer, and seeing aspects.

Pears, David 1986 *Ludwig Wittgenstein.* Cambridge, MA: Harvard University Press. 2nd edn with a new preface by the author; 1st edn 1969. Closely focused on a few key issues, yet succeeds in covering a lot of ground; emphasizes Wittgenstein's Kantianism. More demanding than most other short introductions, however.

Schulte, Joachim 1992 *Wittgenstein: An Introduction,* trans. William H. Brenner and John Foley. Albany, NY: SUNY Press. Elementary and accessible, but also sophisticated and judicious.

MORE CHALLENGING

Cavell, Stanley 1979 *The Claim of Reason.* Oxford: Oxford University Press. A classic and controversial book. Generates strong reactions, both for and against.

Diamond, Cora 1991 *The Realistic Spirit: Wittgenstein, Philosophy and the Mind.* Cambridge, MA: MIT Press. Difficult, but important and influential, especially on Wittgenstein's conception of nonsense and philosophical method.

Eldridge, Richard 1997 *Leading a Human Life: Wittgenstein, Intentionality, Romanticism.* Chicago: Chicago University Press. The second half of the book is a refreshingly accessible exposition of a Cavellian reading of the first half of Part 1 of *Philosophical Investigations*; the first half argues that the book should be seen as a development of themes in post-Kantian German idealism and romanticism.

Garver, Newton 1994 *This Complicated Form of Life: Essays on Wittgenstein.* Chicago: Open Court. Highlights the Kantian and Aristotelian aspects of Wittgenstein's work, and the relationship between grammar and metaphysics.

Hacker, P. M. S. 1986 *Insight and Illusion: Themes in the Philosophy of Wittgenstein.* Oxford: Clarendon Press. Revised 2nd edn; 1st edn 1972. Focuses on the development of Wittgenstein's views on philosophy and the mind. The interpretations in the two editions are very different; the first is strongly Kantian, but this is greatly modified in the second, which is an excellent introduction to Hacker's interpretation.

Hintikka, M. B. and J. Hintikka 1986 *Investigating Wittgenstein*. Oxford: Blackwell. Controversial and provocative reading of the early Wittgenstein as a phenomenalist and the later Wittgenstein as a physicalist.

Mulhall, Stephen 1990 *On Being in the World: Wittgenstein and Heidegger on Seeing Aspects*. London: Routledge. An insightful comparison of *Being and Time* and the *Philosophical Investigations*.

Pears, David 1987 *The False Prison*, vol. 1. Oxford: Clarendon Press. The first sixty pages provide an excellent introduction to Pears' approach to Wittgenstein's philosophy as a whole; the remainder is devoted to the *Tractatus*, with particular attention to solipsism and the picture theory.

Pears, David 1988 *The False Prison*, vol. ii. Oxford: Clarendon Press. Concentrates on the private language argument and rule-following; intricate but masterful.

Wilson, Brendan 1998 *Wittgenstein's 'Philosophical Investigations': A Guide*. Edinburgh: Edinburgh University Press. A concise discussion of some of the leading interpretations of the principal arguments in the book, with special attention to the private language argument.

ONLINE RESOURCES

A good starting point for exploring web-based materials is the Wittgenstein Archives at the University of Bergen's Wittgenstein portal: http://www.wittgenstein-portal.com/index.htm

The *Stanford Encyclopedia of Philosophy* contains helpful entries on Wittgenstein (by Anat Biletzki and Anat Matar) and on private language (by Stewart Candlish): http://plato.stanford.edu/entries/wittgenstein/ http://plato.stanford.edu/entries/private-language/

BIOGRAPHY AND HISTORICAL BACKGROUND

Biletzki, Anat 2003 *(Over) Interpreting Wittgenstein*. Dordrecht: Kluwer. A short history of Wittgenstein reception. The survey is wide-ranging and well chosen, nearly always focusing on the most significant figures. Helpful guide to the literature for beginners.

Flowers, F. A. (ed.) 1999 *Portraits of Wittgenstein*. 4 vols. Bristol: Thoemmes. A convenient and extensive anthology, mostly assembled from previously published material.

Hacker, P. M. S. 1996 *Wittgenstein's Place in Twentieth Century Analytic Philosophy*. Oxford: Blackwell. Magisterial, but one-sided.

Janik, Allan and Stephen Toulmin 1996 *Wittgenstein's Vienna*. Reprint, with minor corrections. Chicago: Ivan R. Dee. First published New York: Simon and Schuster, 1973. The first book-length account of the relationship between Wittgenstein's philosophy and the cultural and intellectual history of fin-de-siècle Vienna, and an excellent introduction to that milieu.

Klagge, James (ed.) 2001 *Wittgenstein: Biography and Philosophy*. Cambridge: Cambridge University Press.

Malcolm, Norman 1984 *Ludwig Wittgenstein: A Memoir*. Revised 2nd edn, with a biographical essay by G. H. von Wright and Wittgenstein's letters to Malcolm; 1st edn 1958. Oxford: Oxford University Press. The best short book-length biography.

McGuinness, Brian 1988 *Wittgenstein: A Life. Young Ludwig (1889–1921)*. London: Duckworth. More detailed discussion of the early philosophy and its intellectual background than Monk.

Monk, Ray 1990 *Ludwig Wittgenstein: The Duty of Genius*. New York: The Free Press. Very readable; an excellent philosophical biography.

Nedo, M. and M. Ranchetti 1983 *Wittgenstein: Sein Leben in Bildern und Texten*. Frankfurt: Suhrkamp. A beautifully illustrated and well-documented collection of memorabilia, both photographs and documents; despite the German title, the book is, for the most part, bilingual.

Passmore, J. 1996 *A Hundred Years of Philosophy*. London: Duckworth.

Rhees, R. (ed.) 1984 *Recollections of Wittgenstein*. New York: Oxford University Press. Revised edn; previously published in 1981 as *Ludwig Wittgenstein: Personal Recollections*. Oxford: Blackwell.

Skorupski, J. 1993 *English-Speaking Philosophy 1750–1945*. New York: Oxford University Press. Despite the title, Frege, Wittgenstein, and the Vienna Circle play as large a part as Mill and Russell in this history of 'analytic modernism'.

COMMENTARIES

Baker, Gordon and Peter Hacker 1980 *An Analytical Commentary on Wittgenstein's 'Philosophical Investigations'*. Chicago: University of Chicago Press. Both scholarly and argumentative, these commentaries provide a systematic and detailed interpretation of the text as a whole, as well as drawing extensive links with the source material. A 2nd edition is in preparation.

    1980 *Wittgenstein, Meaning and Understanding: Essays on the 'Philosophical Investigations'*. Chicago: University of Chicago Press.

1985 *Wittgenstein: Rules, Grammar and Necessity.* Chicago: University of Chicago Press.

Hacker, P. M. S. 1990 *Wittgenstein: Meaning and Mind. An Analytical Commentary on the 'Philosophical Investigations',* vol. III. Oxford: Blackwell.

1996 *Wittgenstein: Mind and Will. An Analytical Commentary on the 'Philosophical Investigations',* vol. IV. Oxford: Blackwell.

Hallett, Garth 1977 *A Companion to Wittgenstein's 'Philosophical Investigations'.* Ithaca, NY: Cornell University Press. An encyclopedic and informative resource, but the exposition is often uncritical and reproductive.

Lugg, Andrew 2000 *Wittgenstein's 'Investigations' 1–133: A Guide and Interpretation.* New York: Routledge.

ANTHOLOGIES

Arrington, R. and H. Glock (eds.) 1991 *Wittgenstein's 'Philosophical Investigations': Text and Context.* London: Routledge. Close readings of difficult passages.

Block, Irving 1981 *Perspectives on the Philosophy of Wittgenstein.* Oxford: Blackwell. A valuable collection.

Canfield, J. (ed.) 1986 *The Philosophy of Wittgenstein.* 15 vols. New York: Garland Publishing. A wide-ranging and comprehensive collection of essays; a convenient resource that provides quick access to several hundred carefully selected items from the secondary literature.

Crary, Alice and Rupert Read 2000 *The New Wittgenstein.* New York: Routledge. Some excellent papers, but the main ideas are not new, and the claims made for them in the introduction are over-ambitious.

Pitcher, George (ed.) 1966 *Wittgenstein: The 'Philosophical Investigations'.* Garden City, NY: Doubleday. The collection contains many of the reviews and essays written during the fifties and early sixties that set the agenda for subsequent discussion of key topics such as family resemblance, private language, and logic. Most are still standard reference points in the secondary literature. While the book is out of print, most of the essays are reprinted in Canfield 1986 and/or Shanker 1986.

Shanker, Stuart (ed.) 1986 *Ludwig Wittgenstein: Critical Assessments.* 4 vols. London: Croom Helm. Like Canfield, another wide-ranging collection of the most important essays on Wittgenstein up to the mid-1980s.

Shanker, Stuart and David Kilfoyle (eds.) 2002 *Ludwig Wittgenstein: Critical Assessments of Leading Philosophers, 2nd series.* 4 vols. London: Routledge. A sequel to the previous Shanker anthology, containing a wide range of work, with particular attention to interdisciplinary scholarship, from the mid-1980s to the late 1990s.

Sluga, Hans and David Stern (eds.) 1996 *The Cambridge Companion to Wittgenstein*. Cambridge: Cambridge University Press. A wide-ranging collection of newly commissioned essays on Wittgenstein.

FOR GERMAN READERS

Kaal, Hans and Alastair McKinnon 1975 *Concordance to Wittgenstein's 'Philosophische Untersuchungen'*. Leiden: E. J. Brill. While it has been superseded by the electronic edition, it remains the most convenient way of looking up Wittgenstein's uses of a term in the *Philosophical Investigations*.

Lange, Ernst Michael 1998 *Ludwig Wittgenstein, 'Philosophische Untersuchungen': Eine kommentierende Einführung*. Paderborn: Schöningh.

Pichler, Alois 1997 *Wittgensteins 'Philosophische Untersuchungen': Zur Textgenese von PU §§1–4*. [*Wittgenstein's 'Philosophical Investigations': On the Genesis of the Text of PI §§1–4*.] Working Papers from the Wittgenstein Archives at the University of Bergen 14. A 'polyphonic' reading of the text, with a close study of the genesis.

Raatzsch, Richard 2003 *Eigentlich Seltsames: Wittgensteins 'Philosophische Untersuchungen'*, vol. 1: *Einleitung und Kommentar PU 1–64*. Paderborn: Schöningh. The first volume of a new commentary on the *Philosophical Investigations*.

Von Savigny, Eike 1994, 1996 *Wittgenstein's 'Philosophische Untersuchungen': Ein Kommentar für Leser*. 2 vols. 2nd edn. Frankfurt am Main: Klostermann. Adopts a 'text-immanent' methodology: aims to interpret the text on its own terms, without appealing to other work by Wittgenstein. Close attention to details of German usage.

Von Savigny, Eike (ed.) 1998 *Ludwig Wittgenstein: 'Philosophische Untersuchungen'*. Berlin: Akademie Verlag. A collection of essays on leading topics.

WORKS BY WITTGENSTEIN

1922 *Tractatus Logico-Philosophicus*, trans. on facing pages by C. K. Ogden. London: Routledge and Kegan Paul. 2nd edn 1933.

1953 *Philosophical Investigations*, ed. G. E. M. Anscombe and R. Rhees, trans. on facing pages by G. E. M. Anscombe. Oxford: Blackwell. 2nd edn 1958, revised edn 2001.

1958 *The Blue and Brown Books: Preliminary Studies for the 'Philosophical Investigations'*. 2nd edn 1969. Oxford: Blackwell. While the subtitle is misleading, as these materials date from a somewhat earlier stage of Wittgenstein's thinking, they do provide an excellent introduction to many of the themes in the *Philosophical Investigations*.

1961 *Notebooks, 1914–1916*, ed. G. H. von Wright and G. E. M. Anscombe, trans. on facing pages by G. E. M. Anscombe. 2nd edn 1979. Source materials for the *Tractatus*.

1967 *Zettel*, ed. G. E. M. Anscombe and G. H. von Wright, trans. on facing pages by G. E. M. Anscombe. Oxford: Blackwell. 2nd edn 1981.

1969 *On Certainty*, ed. G. E. M. Anscombe and G. H. von Wright, trans. G. E. M. Anscombe and D. Paul. Oxford: Blackwell.

1980 *Culture and Value*. First published in 1977 as *Vermischte Bemerkungen* (German text only), ed. G. H. von Wright. 2nd edn, Oxford: Blackwell. Revised 3rd edn, with revised translation on facing pages by P. Winch, Oxford: Blackwell, 1998; not yet available in the USA. A collection of excerpts from Wittgenstein's writing that cast light on his outlook on a wide range of topics.

1993 *Philosophical Occasions, 1912–1951*, ed. James Klagge and Alfred Nordmann. Indianapolis, IN: Hackett. Gathers and reliably edits many of the most important shorter publications in a single volume.

1994 *A Wittgenstein Reader*, ed. Anthony Kenny. Oxford: Blackwell. A very convenient collection of important material, providing a one-volume survey of all of Wittgenstein's writing, but no substitute for the *Tractatus* and *Philosophical Investigations*.

2000 *Wittgenstein's Nachlass: The Bergen Electronic Edition*. Oxford: Oxford University Press. An invaluable resource, combining the capabilities of electronic text with transcriptions and copies of each page of Wittgenstein's philosophical papers. For further discussion, see Note on the Text, Stern (1996a), and Stern forthcoming a.

2001 *Philosophische Untersuchungen: Kritisch-genetische Edition* [*Philosophical Investigations: Critical-Genetic Edition*] ed. Joachim Schulte. Frankfurt am Main: Suhrkamp. A beautifully edited collection of the principal manuscripts and typescripts of the *Philosophical Investigations*, from the 'Early Investigations', written in 1936–7, to the sources of the published text. Enables the reader to trace Wittgenstein's principal revisions and rearrangements of the text. For further discussion, see Note on the Text.

2003 *Ludwig Wittgenstein: Public and Private Occasions*, ed. James Klagge and Alfred Nordmann. Lanham, MD: Rowman & Littlefield. Contains previously unavailable information on Wittgenstein's lectures and a translation of recently rediscovered personal diaries from the 1930s.

References

Anscombe, G. E. M. 1959 *An Introduction to Wittgenstein's 'Tractatus'*. London: Hutchinson. Revised 2nd edn 1963.

1981 'A Theory of Language'. In Irving Block (ed.) *Perspectives on the Philosophy of Wittgenstein*. Cambridge, MA: MIT Press.

Augustine 1992 *Confessions*, ed. James J. O'Donnell. Oxford: Clarendon Press.

1993 *Confessions*, trans. F. J. Sheed. Indianapolis: Hackett.

Baker, Gordon 2002 'Wittgenstein on Metaphysical/Everyday Use'. *Philosophical Quarterly* 52 (208): 289–302.

Baker, Gordon and Peter Hacker 1980a *An Analytical Commentary on Wittgenstein's 'Philosophical Investigations'*. Chicago: University of Chicago Press.

1980b *Wittgenstein, Meaning and Understanding: Essays on the 'Philosophical Investigations'*. Chicago: University of Chicago Press.

1984 *Scepticism, Rules and Language*. Oxford: Blackwell.

1985 *Wittgenstein: Rules, Grammar and Necessity*. Chicago: University of Chicago Press.

Bambrough, Renford 1966 'Universals and Family Resemblances'. In Pitcher 1966, 186–204. First published in *Proceedings of the Aristotelian Society* 61 (1960–1): 207–22.

Barker, Andrew W. 1985–6 'Nestroy and Wittgenstein: Some Thoughts on the Motto to the *Philosophical Investigations*'. *German Life and Letters* 39 (2): 161–7.

Bearn, Gordon 1997 *Waking to Wonder: Wittgenstein's Existential Investigations*. Albany, NY: SUNY Press.

Black, Max 1964 *A Companion to Wittgenstein's 'Tractatus'*. Ithaca, NY: Cornell University Press.

Blackburn, Simon 1984a 'The Individual Strikes Back'. *Synthese* 58: 281–303.

1984b *Spreading the Word*. Oxford: Oxford University Press.

Bloor, David 1983 *Wittgenstein: A Social Theory of Knowledge*. New York: Columbia University Press.

1997 *Wittgenstein, Rules and Institutions*. London: Routledge.

2001 'Wittgenstein and the Priority of Practice'. In Schatzki, Cetina, and von Savigny 2001.

Bourdieu, Pierre 1977 *Outline of a Theory of Practice*, trans. Richard Nice. Cambridge: Cambridge University Press. Originally published in French as *Esquisse d'une théorie de la pratique*, 1972.

Bouveresse, Jacques 1992 '"The Darkness of This Time": Wittgenstein and the Modern World'. In A. P. Griffiths (ed.) *Wittgenstein Centenary Essays*, 11–39. Cambridge: Cambridge University Press.

Brandom, Robert 1994 *Making it Explicit: Reasoning, Representing and Discursive Commitment*. Cambridge, MA: Harvard University Press.

Burnyeat, M. F. 1987 'Wittgenstein and Augustine "De Magistro"'. *Proceedings of the Aristotelian Society, Supplementary Volume* 61: 1–24.

Canfield, J. (ed.) 1986 *The Philosophy of Wittgenstein*. 15 vols. New York: Garland Publishing.

2001 'Private Language: The Diary Case'. *Australasian Journal of Philosophy* 79: 377–94.

Carroll, Lewis 1895 'What the Tortoise Said to Achilles'. *Mind* 4: 278–80.

1974 *The Annotated Alice*, ed. and annotated by Peter Heath. New York: St Martin's Press.

Carruthers, Peter 1984 'Critical Study: Baker and Hacker's Wittgenstein'. *Synthese* 58: 451–79.

Cavell, Stanley 1966 'The Availability of Wittgenstein's Later Philosophy'. In Pitcher 1966, 151–85. First published in *Philosophical Review* 71 (1962): 67–93.

1979 *The Claim of Reason*. Oxford: Oxford University Press.

1989 *This New yet Unapproachable America: Lectures after Emerson after Wittgenstein*. Albuquerque, NM: Living Batch Press.

1996a 'Notes and Afterthoughts on the Opening of Wittgenstein's *Investigations*'. In Sluga and Stern 1996, 261–95.

1996b 'The *Investigations*' Everyday Aesthetics of Itself'. In Stephen Mulhall (ed.) *The Cavell Reader*, 369–89. Cambridge, MA: Blackwell.

Conant, James 1989a 'Throwing Away the Top of the Ladder' *Yale Review* 79: 328–64.

1989b 'Must We Show What We Cannot Say?' In Richard Fleming and Michael Payne (eds.) *The Senses of Stanley Cavell*, 242–83. London: Associated University Presses.

1991 'The Search for Logically Alien Thought: Descartes, Kant, Frege and the *Tractatus*'. *Philosophical Topics* 20 (1): 115–80.

1995 'On Putting Two and Two Together: Kierkegaard, Wittgenstein and the Point of View for their Work as Authors'. In T. Tessin and M. von der Ruhr (eds.) *Philosophy and the Grammar of Religious Belief*, 248–331. London: Macmillan.

2002 'The Method of the *Tractatus*'. In E. H. Reck (ed.) *From Frege to Wittgenstein: Perspectives on Early Analytic Philosophy*, 374–462. Oxford: Oxford University Press.

Copi, Irving and R. W. Beard (eds.) 1966 *Essays on Wittgenstein's 'Tractatus'*. London: Routledge.

Crary, Alice and Rupert Read (eds.) 2000 *The New Wittgenstein*. New York: Routledge.

Dallmayr, Fred R. and Thomas A. McCarthy (eds.) 1977 *Understanding and Social Inquiry*. Notre Dame, IN: University of Notre Dame Press.

Diamond, Cora 1991a *The Realistic Spirit: Wittgenstein, Philosophy and the Mind*. Cambridge, MA: MIT Press.

1991b 'Ethics, Imagination, and the Method of Wittgenstein's *Tractatus*'. In Richard Heinrich and Helmuth Vetter (eds.) *Bilder der Philosophie*, 55–90. Vienna: Oldenbourg. Reprinted in Crary and Read 2000, 149–73.

1997 'Realism and Resolution: Reply to Warren Goldfarb and Sabina Lovibond'. *Journal of Philosophical Research* 22: 75–86.

Dreyfus, Hubert 1980 'Holism and Hermeneutics'. *Review of Metaphysics* 34: 3–24.

1991 *Being-in-the-World: A Commentary on Heidegger's 'Being and Time'*, Division I. Cambridge, MA: MIT Press.

Dummett, Michael 1959 'Wittgenstein's Philosophy of Mathematics'. *Philosophical Review* 68: 324–48. Reprinted in Pitcher 1966, 420–47, Shanker 1984, and Canfield 1986.

Drury, M. O'C. 1984 'Recollections of Wittgenstein'. In Rhees 1984.

Eagleton, Terry 1994 'My Wittgenstein'. *Common Knowledge* 3 (1): 152–7. Reprinted in Stephen Regan (ed.) *The Eagleton Reader*. Oxford: Blackwell, 1998, 336–41.

Engelmann, Paul 1967 *Letters from Ludwig Wittgenstein with a Memoir*, trans. L. Furtmüller, ed. B. F. McGuinness. Oxford: Blackwell.

Feyerabend, Paul 1955 'Wittgenstein's *Philosophical Investigations*'. *Philosophical Review* 64: 449–83. Reprinted in Pitcher 1966 and Canfield 1986.

Fogelin, Robert 1987 *Wittgenstein*. Revised 2nd edn. London: Routledge & Kegan Paul. 1st edn 1976.

1994 *Pyrrhonian Reflections on Knowledge and Justification*. Oxford: Oxford University Press.

Genette, Gérard 1997 *Paratexts: Thresholds of Interpretation*, trans. from the French by Jane E. Lewin. Cambridge: Cambridge University Press. First published 1987.

Glendinning, Simon 2002 'Wittgenstein's Apocalyptic Librarian'. In Rudolf Haller and Klaus Puhl (eds.) *Wittgenstein and the Future of Philosophy:*

A Reassessment after Fifty Years, 71–80. Proceedings of the 24th International Wittgenstein-Symposium. Vienna: Hölder-Pichler-Tempsky.

Glock, Hans-Johann 1990 '*Philosophical Investigations*: Principles of Interpretation'. In Rudolf Haller and Johannes Brandl (eds.) *Wittgenstein: Towards a Re-evaluation*, 152–62. Vienna: Hölder-Pichler-Tempsky.

1991 '*Philosophical Investigations* Section 128: "Theses in Philosophy" and Undogmatic Procedure'. In Robert L. Arrington and Hans-Johann Glock (eds.) *Wittgenstein's 'Philosophical Investigations': Text and Context*, 69–88. London: Routledge.

1992 'Critical Discussion: Eike von Savigny, *Wittgenstein's "Philosophische Untersuchungen", Ein Kommentar für Leser*'. *Erkenntnis* 36: 117–28.

1996 *A Wittgenstein Dictionary*. Oxford: Blackwell.

2001 'The Development of Wittgenstein's Philosophy'. In Hans-Johann Glock (ed.) *Wittgenstein: A Critical Reader*, 1–25. Oxford: Blackwell.

Goldfarb, Warren 1983 'I Want You to Bring Me a Slab: Remarks on the Opening Sections of the "*Philosophical Investigations*"'. *Synthese* 56: 265–82. Reprinted in Canfield 1986.

1997 'Metaphysics and Nonsense: On Cora Diamond's *The Realistic Spirit*'. *Journal of Philosophical Research* 22: 57–74.

2000 '*Das Überwinden*: Anti-Metaphysical Readings of the *Tractatus*'. Unpublished paper presented at a conference on 'The Analytic Tradition: A Tribute to Burton Dreben', Boston University, 26 October 2000.

Hacker, P. M. S. 1986 *Insight and Illusion: Themes in the Philosophy of Wittgenstein*. Revised 2nd edn. Oxford: Clarendon Press. 1st edn 1972.

2000 'Was He Trying to Whistle It?' In Crary and Read 2000.

Hallett, Garth 1977 *A Companion to Wittgenstein's 'Philosophical Investigations'*. Ithaca, NY: Cornell University Press.

Heal, Jane 1995 'Wittgenstein and Dialogue'. In Timothy Smiley (ed.) *Philosophical Dialogues: Plato, Hume, Wittgenstein*. Oxford: Oxford University Press.

Heidegger, Martin 1962 *Being and Time*, trans. from the German by John Macquarrie and James M. Robinson. New York: Harper & Row. Originally published as *Sein und Zeit*, 1927.

Hertz, Heinrich 1956 *The Principles of Mechanics in a New Form*, trans. from the German by D. E. Jones and J. T. Walley. New York: Dover.

Hiley, David R., James F. Bohman, and Richard Shusterman (eds.) 1991 *The Interpretive Turn: Philosophy, Science, Culture*. Ithaca, NY: Cornell University Press.

Hilmy, S. Stephen 1987 *The Later Wittgenstein: The Emergence of a New Philosophical Method*. Oxford: Blackwell.

1991 '"Tormenting questions" in *Philosophical Investigations* section 133'. In Robert L. Arrington and Hans-Johann Glock (eds.) *Wittgenstein's 'Philosophical Investigations': Text and Context,* 89–104. London: Routledge.

Hintikka, M. B. and J. Hintikka 1986 *Investigating Wittgenstein.* Oxford: Blackwell.

Hollis, Martin and Stephen Lukes (eds.) 1982 *Rationality and Relativism.* Cambridge, MA: MIT Press.

Janik, Allan and Stephen Toulmin 1996 *Wittgenstein's Vienna.* Reprint, with minor corrections. Chicago: Ivan R. Dee. First published New York: Simon and Schuster, 1973.

Jolley, Kelly Dean 1993 '*Philosophical Investigations* 133: Wittgenstein and the End of Philosophy?' *Philosophical Investigations* 16: 327–32.

Kenny, Anthony 1973 *Wittgenstein.* Cambridge, MA: Harvard University Press.

1984 *The Legacy of Wittgenstein.* Oxford: Blackwell.

King, Peter 1998 'Augustine on the Impossibility of Teaching'. *Metaphilosophy* 29 (3): 179–95.

Kirwan, Christopher 2001 'Augustine's Philosophy of Language'. In E. Stump and N. Kretzmann (eds.) *The Cambridge Companion to Augustine.* Cambridge: Cambridge University Press.

Klagge, James (ed.) 2001 *Wittgenstein: Biography and Philosophy.* Cambridge: Cambridge University Press.

Kraus, Karl 1912 *Nestroy und die Nachwelt: Zum 50. Todestage.* Vienna: Jahoda & Siegel.

Kripke, Saul 1982 *Wittgenstein on Rules and Private Language.* Cambridge, MA: Harvard University Press.

Lackey, Douglas 1999 'What Are the Modern Classics? The Baruch Poll of Great Philosophy in the Twentieth Century'. *Philosophical Forum* 30 (4): 329–46.

Lichtenberg, Georg Christoph 2000 *The Waste Books,* trans. R. J. Hollingdale. New York: New York Review Books. Originally published as *Aphorisms.* New York: Penguin, 1990.

Malcolm, Norman 1984 *Ludwig Wittgenstein: A Memoir.* Revised 2nd edn, with Wittgenstein's letters to Malcolm. Oxford: Oxford University Press. 1st edn 1958.

1986 *Nothing is Hidden: Wittgenstein's Criticism of his Early Thought.* Oxford: Blackwell.

McCarthy, Timothy G. and Sean C. Stidd 2001 *Wittgenstein in America.* Oxford: Oxford University Press.

McDowell, John 1981 'Non-Cognitivism and Rule-Following'. In S. H. Holtzmann and C. M. Leich (eds.) *Wittgenstein: To Follow a Rule,*

141–62. London: Routledge & Kegan Paul, 1981. Reprinted in Crary and Read 2000.

1992 'Meaning and Intentionality in Wittgenstein's Later Philosophy'. In P. A. French, T. E. Uehling, Jr., and H. Wettstein (eds.) *Midwest Studies in Philosophy*, 17: *The Wittgenstein Legacy*, 40–52. Notre Dame, IN: Notre Dame University Press.

1994 *Mind and World*. Cambridge, MA: Harvard University Press.

McGinn, Colin 1984 *Wittgenstein on Meaning*. Oxford: Blackwell.

McGinn, Marie 1997 *Wittgenstein and the 'Philosophical Investigations'*. London: Routledge.

McGuinness, Brian (ed.) 1982 *Wittgenstein and His Times*. Oxford: Blackwell.

1988 *Wittgenstein: A Life. Young Ludwig (1889–1921)*. London: Duckworth.

McKenzie, John R. P. 1985 'Nestroy's Political Plays'. In W. E. Yates and R. P. McKenzie (eds.) *Viennese Popular Theatre: A Symposium*. Exeter: University of Exeter.

McManus, Denis 1995 'Philosophy in Question: *Philosophical Investigations* 133'. *Philosophical Investigations* 18: 348–61.

Monk, Ray 1990 *Ludwig Wittgenstein: The Duty of Genius*. New York: The Free Press.

Mulhall, Stephen 2001 *Inheritance and Originality: Wittgenstein, Heidegger, Kierkegaard*. Oxford: Clarendon Press.

Nestroy, Johann Nepomuk 2000 *Stücke 24/II: Der Schützling*, ed. John R. P. McKenzie. Vienna: Deuticke.

Nyíri, J. C. 1976 'Wittgenstein's New Traditionalism'. In *Essays on Wittgenstein in Honour of G. H. von Wright. Acta Philosophica Fennica* 28: 1–3.

1982 'Wittgenstein's Later Work in Relation to Conservatism'. In McGuinness 1982, 44–68.

Ostrow, Matthew B. 2002 *Wittgenstein's 'Tractatus'*. Cambridge: Cambridge University Press.

Pears, David 1986 *Ludwig Wittgenstein*. 2nd edn with a new preface by the author. Cambridge, MA: Harvard University Press. 1st edn 1969.

1987 *The False Prison*, vol. I. Oxford: Clarendon Press.

1988 *The False Prison*, vol. II. Oxford: Clarendon Press.

Pichler, Alois 1997 *Wittgensteins 'Philosophische Untersuchungen': Zur Textgenese von PU §§1–4. [Wittgenstein's 'Philosophical Investigations': On the Genesis of the Text of PI §§1–4.]* Working Papers from the Wittgenstein Archives at the University of Bergen 14.

2004 *Wittgensteins 'Philosophische Untersuchungen': Vom Buch zum Album. [Wittgenstein's 'Philosophical Investigations': From Book to Album.]* Studien zur österreichischen Philosophie, 36. Amsterdam: Rodopi.

Pitcher, George 1964 *The Philosophy of Wittgenstein*. Englewood Cliffs, NJ: Prentice-Hall.

(ed.) 1966 *Wittgenstein: The 'Philosophical Investigations'*. Garden City, NY: Doubleday.

1967 'Wittgenstein, Nonsense and Lewis Carroll'. In Fann 1967, 315–35. First published in *Massachusetts Review* 6 (3) (1965).

Plato 1997 *Complete Works*, ed. John Cooper. Indianapolis, IN: Hackett. The translation of the *Theaetetus* is by M. J. Levett, revised by Myles F. Burnyeat.

Read, Rupert 1995 '"The *Real* Philosophical Discovery": A Reply to Jolley's "*Philosophical Investigations* 133: Wittgenstein and the End of Philosophy?"' *Philosophical Investigations* 18: 362–9.

Rhees, R. (ed.) 1984 *Recollections of Wittgenstein*. Revised edn. New York: Oxford University Press. Originally published as *Ludwig Wittgenstein: Personal Recollections*. Oxford: Blackwell, 1981.

Rorty, Richard 1982 *Consequences of Pragmatism*. Minneapolis: Minnesota University Press.

Savickey, Beth 1999 *Wittgenstein's Art of Investigation*. London: Routledge.

Schulte, Joachim 1983 'Wittgenstein and Conservatism'. *Ratio* 25: 69–80.

2002 'Wittgenstein's Quietism'. Unpublished typescript, University of Bielefeld.

Sluga, Hans 2004 'Wittgenstein and Pyrrhonism'. In Walter Sinnott-Armstrong (ed.) *Pyrrhonian Skepticism*. New York: Oxford University Press.

Sluga, Hans and David Stern (eds.) 1996 *The Cambridge Companion to Wittgenstein*. Cambridge: Cambridge University Press.

Spiegelberg, Herbert 1978 'The Significance of Mottoes in Wittgenstein's Major Works'. In E. Leinfellner et al. (eds.) *Wittgenstein and his Impact on Contemporary Thought*, 54–7. Vienna: Hölder-Pichler-Tempsky.

Staten, Henry 1984 *Wittgenstein and Derrida*. Lincoln: University of Nebraska Press.

Stern, David G. 1991 'Heraclitus' and Wittgenstein's River Images: Stepping Twice into the Same River'. *Monist* 74: 579–604.

1995 *Wittgenstein on Mind and Language*. Oxford: Oxford University Press.

1996a 'The Availability of Wittgenstein's Philosophy'. In Sluga and Stern 1996, 442–76.

1996b 'Towards a Critical Edition of the *Philosophical Investigations*'. In K. S. Johannessen and T. Nordenstam (eds.) *Wittgenstein and the Philosophy of Culture*, 298–309. Vienna: Hölder-Pichler-Tempsky.

2002 'Sociology of Science, Rule Following and Forms of Life'. In Michael Heidelberger and Friedrich Stadler (eds.) *History of Philosophy of Science: New Trends and Perspectives*, 347–67. Vienna Circle Institute Yearbook, 9. Dordrecht: Kluwer.

2003 'The Practical Turn'. In Stephen P. Turner and Paul Roth (eds.) *Blackwell Guidebook to the Philosophy of the Social Sciences*, 185–206. Oxford: Blackwell.

2004 'Weininger and Wittgenstein on "Animal Psychology"'. In Stern and Szabados 2004.

forthcoming a Critical Review of Wittgenstein 2000. *European Journal of Philosophy*.

forthcoming b Critical Review of Ostrow 2002. *Inquiry*.

Stern, David G. and Béla Szabados (eds.) 2004 *Wittgenstein Reads Weininger: A Reassessment*. Cambridge: Cambridge University Press.

Stern, J. P. 1959 *Lichtenberg: A Doctrine of Scattered Occasions*. Bloomington: Indiana University Press.

Stroud, Barry 2000 *Meaning, Understanding, and Practice*. Oxford: Oxford University Press.

Tilghman, B. R. 1987 'The Moral Dimension of the *Philosophical Investigations*'. *Philosophical Investigations* 10: 99–117.

Tugendhat, Ernst 1989 *Self-Consciousness and Self-Determination*. Translated from the German. Cambridge, MA: MIT Press.

Von Savigny, Eike 1991 'No Chapter "On Philosophy" in the *Philosophical Investigations*'. *Metaphilosophy* 22:307–19.

1994–6 *Wittgenstein's 'Philosophische Untersuchungen': Ein Kommentar für Leser [Wittgenstein's 'Philosophical Investigations': A Commentary for Readers]*. 2nd edn, 2 vols. Frankfurt am Main: Klostermann.

Von Wright, Georg Henrik 1982 'Wittgenstein in Relation to his Times'. In Brian McGuinness (ed.) *Wittgenstein and his Times*, 108–20. Oxford: Blackwell.

1982 *Wittgenstein*. Oxford: Blackwell.

Williams, Bernard 1992 'Left-wing Wittgenstein, Right-wing Marx'. *Common Knowledge* 1: 33–42.

Wilson, Brendan 1998 *Wittgenstein's 'Philosophical Investigations': A Guide*. Edinburgh: Edinburgh University Press.

Wilson, Bryan (ed.) 1970 *Rationality*. Oxford: Blackwell.

Winch, Peter 1964 'Understanding a Primitive Society'. *American Philosophical Quarterly* 1: 307–24.

1987 'Language, Thought and World in Wittgenstein's *Tractatus*'. In *Trying to Make Sense*, 3–17. Oxford: Blackwell.

1990 *The Idea of a Social Science and its Relation to Philosophy*. Revised 2nd edn. London: Routledge & Kegan Paul. 1st edn 1958.

1992 'Persuasion'. In P. A. French, T. E. Uehling, Jr, and H. Wettstein (eds.) *Midwest Studies in Philosophy*, 17: *The Wittgenstein Legacy*, 123–37. Notre Dame, IN: University of Notre Dame Press.

Wittgenstein, Ludwig 1922 *Tractatus Logico-Philosophicus*, trans. on facing pages by C. K. Ogden. London: Routledge & Kegan Paul. 2nd edn 1933.

1953 *Philosophical Investigations*, ed. G. E. M. Anscombe and R. Rhees, trans. on facing pages by G. E. M. Anscombe. Oxford: Blackwell. 2nd edn 1958; revised edn 2001.

1958 *The Blue and Brown Books: Preliminary Studies for the 'Philosophical Investigations'*. 2nd edn 1969. Oxford: Blackwell. References are to the *Blue Book* or *Brown Book*.

1961a *Notebooks 1914–1916*, ed. G. H. von Wright and G. E. M. Anscombe, trans. on facing pages by G. E. M. Anscombe. 2nd edn 1979.

1961b *Tractatus Logico-Philosophicus*, trans. D. F. Pears and B. F. McGuinness. London: Routledge & Kegan Paul.

1964 *Philosophical Remarks (Philosophische Bemerkungen)*, German text only, ed. R. Rhees. Oxford: Blackwell. 2nd edn 1975, trans. R. Hargraves and R. White. Oxford: Blackwell.

1967 *Zettel*, ed. G. E. M. Anscombe and G. H. von Wright, trans. on facing pages by G. E. M. Anscombe. Oxford: Blackwell. 2nd edn 1981.

1969a *Philosophical Grammar (Philosophische Grammatik)*, German text only, ed. R. Rhees. Oxford: Blackwell. English trans. by A. Kenny, Oxford: Blackwell, 1974.

1969b *On Certainty*, ed. G. E. M. Anscombe and G. H. von Wright, trans. G. E. M. Anscombe and D. Paul. Oxford: Blackwell.

1980a/1998 *Culture and Value*, 2nd edn. Oxford: Blackwell, 1980. Revised 3rd edn, with revised translation on facing pages by P. Winch, Blackwell, 1998; not yet available in the USA. First published 1977 as *Vermischte Bemerkungen*, German text only, ed. G. H. von Wright. References provide pagination for both the 1980 and 1998 editions; translations are from the 1998 edition.

1980b *Remarks on the Philosophy of Psychology*, vol. II, ed. G. H. von Wright and H. Nyman, trans. C. G. Luckhardt and M. A. E. Aue. Chicago: University of Chicago Press.

1993a *Philosophical Occasions, 1912–1951*, ed. James Klagge and Alfred Nordmann. Indianapolis, IN: Hackett.

1993b *Wiener Ausgabe [Vienna Edition]*, ed. Michael Nedo. Vienna: Springer.

1994a *A Wittgenstein Reader*, ed. Anthony Kenny. Oxford: Blackwell.

1994b *Wiener Ausgabe*, vol. I: *Philosophische Bemerkungen*, ed. Michael Nedo. Vienna: Springer.

1995 *Cambridge Letters: Correspondence with Russell, Keynes, Moore, Ramsey, and Sraffa*, ed. Brian McGuinness and G. H. von Wright. Oxford: Blackwell.

2000 *Wittgenstein's Nachlass: The Bergen Electronic Edition.* Oxford: Oxford University Press.

2001 *Philosophische Untersuchungen: Kritisch-genetische Edition* [*Philosophical Investigations: Critical-Genetic Edition*], ed. Joachim Schulte. Frankfurt am Main: Suhrkamp.

2004 *The Big Typescript: TS 213*, trans. Grant Luckhardt and Maximilian Aue, in an en-face English-German edn. Oxford: Blackwell.

Wright, Crispin 1980 *Wittgenstein on the Foundations of Mathematics.* Cambridge, MA: Harvard University Press.

Yates, W. E. 1994 *Nestroy and the Critics.* Columbia, SC: Camden House.

Index